T0073190

LOW-POWER WIRELESS COMMUNICATION CIRCUITS AND SYSTEMS

LOW-POWER WIRELESS COMMUNICATION CIRCUITS AND SYSTEMS

60 GHz and Beyond

edited by
Kaixue Ma | Kiat Seng Yeo

PAN STANFORD PUBLISHING

Published by

Pan Stanford Publishing Pte. Ltd.
Penthouse Level, Suntec Tower 3
8 Temasek Boulevard
Singapore 038988

Email: editorial@panstanford.com
Web: www.panstanford.com

British Library Cataloguing-in-Publication Data
A catalogue record for this book is available from the British Library.

**Low-Power Wireless Communication Circuits and Systems:
60 GHz and Beyond**
Copyright © 2018 Pan Stanford Publishing Pte. Ltd.

ISBN 978-981-4745-96-3 (Hardcover)
ISBN 978-1-315-15653-8 (eBook)

Contents

Preface   xiii
Acknowledgments   xv

1. Introduction   **3**

Kaixue Ma and Kiat Seng Yeo

   1.1   Background and Motivation   3
   1.2   Contributions   9
   1.3   Scope and Organization   12

2. Fundamentals of Circuit Networks   **21**

Wei Xu, Kaixue Ma, and Kiat Seng Yeo

   2.1   Introduction   21
   2.2   Two-Port Scattering Matrix   22
   2.3   Two-Port Z Matrix   23
   2.4   Two-Port Y Matrix   24
   2.5   Two-Port ABCD Matrix   24
   2.6   Network Connections   26
   2.7   Network Conversions   28
   2.8   Resonant Network   29
   2.9   Even-Odd Mode Analysis   33
   2.10 Multi-Port Network   34

3. Active Devices   **39**

Bharatha Kumar Thangarasu, Kaixue Ma, and Kiat Seng Yeo

   3.1   Diode   40
   3.2   Transistor   41
         3.2.1 Transistor Design Consideration for RF
                and Millimeter-Wave Frequency Applications   43
   3.3   BJT versus MOS Transistors and Hybrid Use   44

4. Passive Elements   **49**

Yongqiang Wang, Kaixue Ma, and Kiat Seng Yeo

4.1   Introduction   50
4.2   Resistor   50
4.3   Capacitor   52
     4.3.1   MIM Capacitors   52
     4.3.2   Interdigital Capacitors   52
4.4   Inductor   54
4.5   Transformer   55
4.6   Interconnects   57
4.7   Transmission Lines   58

5. Variable Gain Amplifier   **63**

Bharatha Kumar Thangarasu, Kaixue Ma, and Kiat Seng Yeo

5.1   Introduction   64
5.2   VGA Design Analysis   64
     5.2.1   dB-Linearity   66
     5.2.2   DC Offset Cancellation   67
5.3   Variable Gain Amplifier Examples   68
     5.3.1   VGA1: Based on 0.18 µm SiGe BiCMOS Programmable Gain Amplifier Design   68
     5.3.2   VGA2: Based on 65 nm CMOS Variable Gain Amplifier Design   73

6. Power Amplifier   **83**

Bharatha Kumar Thangarasu, Kaixue Ma, and Kiat Seng Yeo

6.1   Introduction   84
6.2   PA Design Analysis   85
     6.2.1   Amplifier Linearity versus Power Added Efficiency   86
6.3   Power Amplifier Examples   87
     6.3.1   PA1: Differential Drive Amplifier Based on Variable Gain Control and Frequency-Tunable Load   87

6.3.1.1 Variable gain amplifier stage
analysis   87

6.3.1.2 Frequency-tunable amplifier
stage analysis   88

6.3.1.3 Frequency-tunable load design   91

6.3.1.4 Q-factor enhancement   91

6.3.2 PA2: Single-Ended Transformer-Based
Power Amplifier   94

7. Low-Noise Amplifier   **101**

Bharatha Kumar Thangarasu, Kaixue Ma, and Kiat Seng Yeo

7.1 Introduction   102

7.2 LNA Design Analysis   103

7.2.1 Noise Figure   104

7.2.2 Linearity   104

7.2.3 Variable Gain LNA as a Trade-Off between
Low Noise and Good Linearity Performance   105

7.3 Low-Noise Amplifier Examples   106

7.3.1 LNA1: Based on 65 nm CMOS with
Custom-Built Inductor   106

7.3.1.1 Marginally stable criteria and
gain boosting   108

7.3.1.2 Unstable criteria causing
oscillations   108

7.3.1.3 Unconditionally stable criteria   108

7.3.2 LNA2: Based on 0.18 μm SiGe BiCMOS
with Distributive Transmission Line
Inductor and Interconnect Design   113

8. Bi-Directional Low-Noise Amplifier   **121**

Bharatha Kumar Thangarasu, Kaixue Ma, and Kiat Seng Yeo

8.1 Introduction   122

8.2 BDA Design Analysis   124

8.2.1 Signal Flow Direction Switch Control   125

8.2.2 Interconnect Network Design   126

8.3   Bi-Directional Low-Noise Amplifier Examples   127

    8.3.1   BDA1—Based on 65 nm CMOS with
        Custom-Built Inductor and Micro-Strip
        Line Three-Port Interconnect Network   127

    8.3.2   BDA2—Based on 0.18 μm SiGe BiCMOS
        with Distributive Transmission Line
        Inductor and Interconnect Network Design   130

9. Millimeter-Wave Mixer   **137**

Shouxian Mou, Kaixue Ma, and Kiat Seng Yeo

9.1   Mixer Fundamentals   137

    9.1.1   Basic Mixer Operation   137

    9.1.2   Controlled Transconductance Mixer   139

    9.1.3   Transconductor Implementation   142

    9.1.4   The Issue of Balance in Mixers   144

9.2   Fundamental Mixers   148

    9.2.1   FET Resistive Mixer   148

    9.2.2   Gilbert Cell   151

    9.2.3   Gilbert Cell–Based Mixer   153

    9.2.4   Some Techniques Used in Gilbert
        Cell–Based Mixers   154

9.3   Sub-Harmonic Mixers   158

    9.3.1   LO Self-Mixing   158

    9.3.2   Anti-Parallel Diode Pair   159

    9.3.3   Techniques Used in Sub-Harmonic
        APDP Mixer   161

    9.3.4   Topology of Transistor-Based
        Sub-Harmonic Mixer   165

    9.3.5   Operation Mechanism of the
        Transistor-Based 2× HM   167

    9.3.6   A 60 GHz Transistor–Based 2×
        Sub-Harmonic Modulator   169

    9.3.7   Some Techniques Used in Sub-harmonic
        Mixer Designs   174

    9.3.8   The 4× Sub-Harmonic Mixer   176

9.4   Summary   177

10. Voltage-Controlled Oscillator   **183**

Zou Qiong, Kaixue Ma, and Kiat Seng Yeo

10.1 VCO Basics   184

    10.1.1 Overview of VCO Architectures   184

    10.1.2 Oscillator Theory   185

    10.1.3 Performance Parameter   186

10.2 LC-Tank   190

    10.2.1 Quality Factor   191

    10.2.2 Tank Components   193

10.3 LC-VCO Topologies for Millimeter-Wave
Frequency   195

    10.3.1 Cross-Coupled LC-VCO   195

    10.3.2 Colpitts VCO   198

10.4 Summary   201

11. Microwave and Millimeter-Wave Switches   **207**

Fanyi Meng, Kaixue Ma, and Kiat Seng Yeo

11.1 CMOS FET Transistor   208

11.2 SPDT Switches Based on $\lambda_g/4$ T-line Topology   212

11.3 SPDT Switches Based on Magnetically Switchable
Artificial Resonator Topology   213

11.4 Main Coupled Lines   213

11.5 Auxiliary Coupled Lines   218

11.6 State-of-the-Art Switches   221

12. Millimeter-Wave Beam Forming   **225**

Fanyi Meng, Kaixue Ma, and Kiat Seng Yeo

12.1 Current Tread   227

12.2 Recent Implementations   227

12.3 Variable Phase Shifters   228

12.4 Reflective-Type Phase Shifter   231

12.5 Switched-Type Phase Shifter   233

12.6 Vector-Modulation Phase Shifter   236

12.7 Loaded-Line Phase Shifter   237

12.8 Comparison   239

13. Frequency Synthesizer **245**

Nagarajan Mahalingam, Kaixue Ma, and Kiat Seng Yeo

13.1 Introduction to Concept of Frequency Synthesis 246
13.2 Phase-Locked Loop Frequency Synthesizer 247
   13.2.1 Performance Parameters 247
      13.2.1.1 Frequency tuning range 248
      13.2.1.2 Phase noise 248
      13.2.1.3 Spurious signals 249
      13.2.1.4 Frequency resolution and settling time 250
      13.2.1.5 Loop bandwidth 251
      13.2.1.6 Power consumption and output power 251
   13.2.2 Phase-Lock Loop Modeling 252
      13.2.2.1 Linearized PLL analysis 252
      13.2.2.2 PLL noise analysis 256
   13.2.3 Phase-Lock Loop Frequency Synthesizer Architectures 258
      13.2.3.1 Integer-*N* frequency synthesizer 258
      13.2.3.2 Fractional-*N* frequency synthesizer 260
13.3 Frequency Synthesizer Building Blocks 261
   13.3.1 Voltage-Controlled Oscillator 261
      13.3.1.1 Ring oscillator 261
      13.3.1.2 LC oscillator 262
      13.3.1.3 Phase noise in oscillators 262
      13.3.1.4 Circuit implementation of LC oscillators 264
   13.3.2 High-Frequency Divider 264
      13.3.2.1 Static frequency divider 265
      13.3.2.2 Injection locked frequency divider 266
      13.3.2.3 Circuit implementation of ILFD 267
      13.3.2.4 ILFD design example 268

13.3.3	Low-Frequency Divider	272
13.3.4	Phase Frequency Detector	273
13.3.5	Charge Pump	275
	13.3.5.1 Current mismatch	276
	13.3.5.2 Leakage current	276
	13.3.5.3 Clock feedthrough	277
	13.3.5.4 Charge sharing	277
	13.3.5.5 Charge injection	278

14. Digital IC Design for Transceiver SOC
283

Wang Yisheng, Kaixue Ma, and Kiat Seng Yeo

14.1	Digital Design Flow	284
14.2	Standard Library Introduction	284
14.2.1	Technology File	286
14.2.2	Standard Cell	286
14.2.3	RAM, ROM IP Compiler	287
14.2.4	IP from Third-Party Vendor	287
14.2.5	Power Management Kits	288
14.2.6	Library Files	289
	14.2.6.1 Timing and power library	289
	14.2.6.2 Physical definition	289
	14.2.6.3 Current source model	290
	14.2.6.4 Verilog and spice module	291
	14.2.6.5 Layout vs. schematic netlist	291
14.3	Digital Frontend Design Flow	291
14.3.1	System-Level Design	292
14.3.2	HDL Coding, Simulation, and Verification	294
	14.3.2.1 SystemVerilog-based verification	295
	14.3.2.2 DesignWare IP	295
	14.3.2.3 Hardware-based verification	297
14.3.3	Synthesis Based on Design Constraints	297
14.3.4	Static Timing Analysis	298
14.3.5	Formal Equivalence Checking	298
14.3.6	Design for Testability	299

14.4 Digital Backend Design Flow — 300
   14.4.1 Floorplanning — 300
      14.4.1.1 Pad ring — 301
      14.4.1.2 Macro IP placement — 302
      14.4.1.3 Power network — 302
   14.4.2 Placement — 303
   14.4.3 Clock Tree Synthesis — 303
   14.4.4 Routing — 304
   14.4.5 RC Extraction — 305
   14.4.6 Multi-Mode, Multi-Corner Analysis and Optimization — 306
   14.4.7 Signoff Static Timing Analysis — 306
   14.4.8 Formal Verification — 307
   14.4.9 DRC/LVS — 307
14.5 Low-Power IC Design Methodology — 308
   14.5.1 Power Consumption Source — 308
      14.5.1.1 Static power — 308
      14.5.1.2 Dynamic power — 310
   14.5.2 Low-Power Technologies — 311
      14.5.2.1 Clock gating — 311
      14.5.2.2 Logic-level power reduction — 312
      14.5.2.3 Multiple-V_T design — 313
      14.5.2.4 Multiple-voltage design — 313
      14.5.2.5 Power gating technology — 314
      14.5.2.6 Unified power format — 314

15. 60 GHz Transceiver SOC — 319

Kaixue Ma and Kiat Seng Yeo

15.1 60 GHz RF Transceiver SOC Architecture — 321
15.2 Synthesizer and the LO Feed Network — 323
15.3 Interface and Spurious Control — 325

Index — 333

Preface

The increasing demand for extremely high-data-rate communications has urged researchers to develop new communication systems. Currently, wireless transmission with more than 1 gigabit per second (Gbps) data rates is becoming essential due to increased connectivity between different portable and smart devices. To realize Gbps data rates, millimeter-wave (MMW) bands around 60 GHz are attractive due to the availability of a large bandwidth of 9 GHz.

The recent research work on Gbps date rates around the 60 GHz band has focused on short-range indoor applications, such as uncompressed video transfer, high-speed file transfer between electronic devices, and communication to and from kiosk. Many of these applications are limited to 10 m or less, because of the huge free space path loss and oxygen absorption for the 60 GHz band MMW signal.

This book introduces new knowledge and novel circuit techniques to design low-power MMW circuits and systems. It also focuses on unlocking the potential applications of the 60 GHz band for high-speed outdoor applications. The innovative design application significantly improves and enables high-data-rate low-cost communication links between two access points seamlessly. The 60 GHz transceiver system-on-chip provides an alternative solution to upgrade existing networks without introducing any building renovation or external network laying works.

In conclusion, this book addresses in depth technical issues, limitations, considerations, and challenges facing integrated circuit and system designers in designing high-speed wireless communication systems from the silicon perspectives. The information presented will be extremely beneficial and valuable for advanced undergraduate- and graduate-level students as well as faculty and researchers in electrical and electronic engineering, wireless communication, integrated circuit design, and circuits and systems. This book can be used as an excellent reference for RF/MMW IC designers, engineers, consultants, engineering managers and directors, instructors and scientists working in the foundry, fabless semiconductor companies, original equipment manufacturers, and integrated device manufacturers.

Acknowledgments

We are indebted to those who helped us in bringing this book through the process of idea to reality. Kaixue Ma and Kiat Seng Yeo are thankful to their families. Their constant support, warm companionship, and encouragement were instrumental in the successful completion of this book.

We are very grateful to Stanford Chong and Jenny Rompas, both Director and Publisher, and their team for their endless efforts to get this book into timely production.

We also wish to express our appreciation to the University of Electronic Science and Technology of China and Singapore University of Technology and Design for creating an environment in which one cannot help but to persevere.

Finally, the success of this book would not have been possible without the kind assistance provided by our research staff and graduate students: Wei Xu, Tao Liu, Yongqiang Wang, Bharatha Kumar Thangarasu, Shouxian Mou, Zou Qiong, Fanyi Meng, Nagarajan Mahalingam, and Wang Yisheng.

If you are small, think big. If you are big, act fast.

—Kiat Seng Yeo and Kaixue Ma

Chapter 1

Introduction

Kaixue Ma[a] and Kiat Seng Yeo[b]

[a]School of Physical Electronics,
University of Electronic Science and Technology of China,
#4 Section II, Jianshe North Road, Chengdu, 610054, P. R. China
[b]Engineering Product Development, Singapore University of Technology and Design,
8 Somapah Road, Singapore 487372

makaixue@uestc.edu.cn, kiatseng_yeo@sutd.edu.sg

1.1 Background and Motivation

The increasing worldwide demands for a variety of information and communication services required by different types of wireless communication, wireless sensor network, Internet of things and future fifth-generation wireless communication, etc., greatly prompt the development of contemporary wireless communication systems. The wireless communication, undergoing a revolution during the twentieth century [1–10], becomes one of the most promising areas of growth in the 21st century [3]. The demands for ubiquitous communications have led to the development of various mobile/wireless systems, including GSM (global system of mobile communication), PCS (personal

Low-Power Wireless Communication Circuits and Systems: 60 GHz and Beyond
Edited by Kaixue Ma and Kiat Seng Yeo
Copyright © 2018 Pan Stanford Publishing Pte. Ltd.
ISBN 978-981-4745-96-3 (Hardcover), 978-1-315-15653-8 (eBook)
www.panstanford.com

communication system), W-LAN (wireless local area network), Bluetooth, etc., which are evolving toward the convergence of disparate networks and standards, including all-IP (Internet Protocol) network, interoperable networks, and even satellite networks. The technology advancement and new frequency allocation for the new communication systems such as the third-generation and the fourth-generation wireless systems and future fifth-generation wireless communication are creating numerous business and technique opportunities. Generally speaking, mobile/wireless communications are in many ways penetrating and changing daily lives and work methods of the people all over the world.

However, tremendous growth in wireless communications has greatly crowded the frequency spectrum, which may transfer into a higher likelihood of user interference with one another. Moreover, according to IMT2020, the speed of the future 5G wireless communication was planned to be more than 1000 times of that for 4G. Thus, more and more effort has been put on the development of the wireless technique in the millimeter wave and sub-millimeter wave, where much more spectrum resource can be found as shown in Fig. 1.1. For example, 28 GHz, 39 GHz and 60 GHz are arranged for 5G applications to support different communication distances and data rates. Moreover, millimeter wave and THz have also the advantage of operation under all weather. The brief applications of the millimeter-wave frequency bands are arranged for vehicular radar, military and communication applications like point-to-point wireless links and radar systems. More and more research and development efforts have been put on the millimeter wave and designed toward 1 THz gradually. However, for the commercial wireless applications using millimeter wave, it is limited by the expensive chip cost based on the III–V semiconductor process, especially for the system on chip (SOC). In recent years, with progress of the fabrication process and downscaling of silicon-based integrated processes such as CMOS, SOI CMOS, and SiGe BiCMOS, the cutoff frequencies of these processes have increased toward several hundred GHz, which makes it possible to support the circuit designs and implementation in the millimeter-wave frequency band and beyond. The advantages of silicon-based processes are the low cost and high integration density for mass production due to the big wafer size and the ease to integrate with digital, analog and RF as SOC for applications.

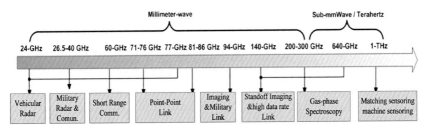

Figure 1.1 Spectrum allocation for millimeter wave and sub-millimeter wave.

Among the millimeter-wave and sub-millimeter-wave frequency bands, 60 GHz is most popular frequency band for short-range wireless applications and is supported by the IEEE802.11ad standard. The 9 GHz bandwidth worldwide is assigned as four channels with bandwidth of 2.16 GHz each, as shown in Fig. 1.2. The protection bands are required for the reliability of information transmission. Different from military millimeter-wave applications, where performance and security are usually the main factors, low cost, compact size, and low power consumption with satisfactory performance are required for commercial millimeter-wave applications. In addition, the cost of the transceivers has to be affordable for end users. As a result, the electric components for the transceiver systems become extremely difficult to design with ever-increasing stringent requirements [7]. In addition, millimeter-wave communication systems with fast services, low cost, and compact size are necessary for commercial applications. The typical targeted commercial applications are shown in Fig. 1.3. These targeted applications include wireless docking stations, mobile distributed computing, wireless gigabit Ethernet, fast bulky file transfer, wireless gaming, radio over fiber to home end, WPAN in an in-building environment; wireless HDMI interface, and other applications such as military and satellite. All of these applications must fully consider the characteristics of 60 GHz frequency bands, where the oxygen loss is large with the attenuation of about 15 dB/km and the wavelength is short; thus the dominant application is targeted for short-range wireless communication in the indoor environment.

Channel Number	Low Freq. (GHz)	Center Freq. (GHz)	High Freq. (GHz)	3 dB BW (MHz)	Roll-Off Factor
1	57.240	58.320	59.400	1728	0.25
2	59.400	60.480	61.560	1728	0.25
3	61.560	62.640	63.720	1728	0.25
4	63.720	64.800	65.880	1728	0.25

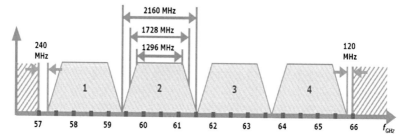

Figure 1.2 Spectrum allocation for 60 GHz based on IEEE802.11ad Standard.

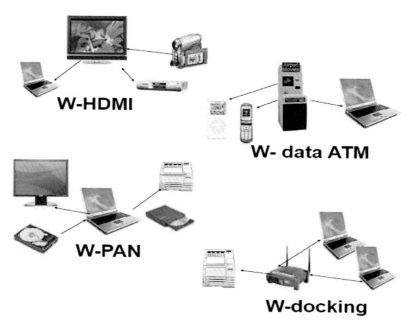

Figure 1.3 Targeted applications for the 60 GHz wireless.

Since 60 GHz millimeter-wave has 9 GHz of unlicensed bandwidth and is characterized as low probability of detect/ low probability of intercept, it is suitable for high-security, high-speed, point-to-point, and time-critical security applications. It is also aimed to be adopted to complement and compensate the limitations of the existing wireless communication applications as shown in Fig. 1.4. It can support wireless high-definition media interface (HDMI) for video streaming from laptops, cameras and video compact disc (VCD) players to the high-definition TV. It can also be used to form a wireless data download station or wireless-data automatic teller machine (W-data ATM) applications. The other applications include wireless docking station to support high-data-rate communication from the docking station to the laptop, printer, projector, etc. People also talk about applications of wireless personal area network (W-PAN) to support high-data-rate personal network.

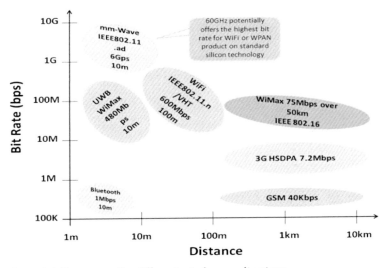

Figure 1.4 Data range for different wireless applications.

Some people believed that the 60 GHz band would replace some existing wireless communications. This is not true because the application of the 60 GHz millimeter wave is to compensate the shortcoming of the existing wireless standards as shown in Fig. 1.4. It can be seen clearly that the 60 GHz standard, i.e., IEEE802.11ad, is meant to cover the communication distance within 10 m while supporting data rates up to 10 Gbps, which cannot supported by the existing standards. The adoption of 60 GHz is actually value addition to the existing wireless communication. Actually, IEEE802.11ad is mainly targeted toward the next generation WiFi standard, which can exist in combination with or facilitate value addition to the current 2.4 and 5 GHz WiFi for short-range and high-speed wireless applications.

What's the research value or development value for 60 GHz Radio? We should think about the application needs from the end users' point of view as shown in Fig. 1.5. The market need for high-speed wireless communication from consumer electronics forms the main driver for the millimeter-wave wireless market. On the other hand, it also defines the design constraints for the technologies since the end users, especially portable end users, require 60 GHz radio to be low cost, low power, and compact size while supporting a wide bandwidth and very high data rate. Even for the same 60 GHz technologies, it will have different application scenario, which may cause the design to be different according to scenarios. To match the design to the different application scenarios, the system link design is necessary for the budget calculation of the wireless link while trade-off among the power consumption, size and cost, etc. This large and complex system-level integration has to take into account the interaction and trade-off between digital, analog, and millimeter-wave building blocks. The core of this development is in the SOC design, which involves digital, analog, and millimeter-wave design with full consideration of circuit, electromagnetic, and material characteristics. Of course, the proper process should be chosen according to cost as well as performance considerations. For low-cost and commercial applications, silicon-based IC technologies such as CMOS or BiCMOS have become the excellent choice with the process downscaling, which makes the cutoff frequency increase to hundreds of GHz, while the cost of the silicon-based process is much cheaper than that of the conventional III–V group semiconductor technologies. However, the commercial silicon-based process faces challenges, especially high substrate loss and metal loss for millimeter-wave IC design and implementation. Moreover, the transistor characteristics are poorer than that of the III–V group for the same process size. Additional challenges are faced actually from commercial end users, who require the SOC to be low cost, compact size, and less power consuming. As shown in Fig. 1.5, besides the SOC itself, the packaging for the millimeter-wave SOC has to be considered carefully, as the cost of packaging can be higher than the SOC itself in the millimeter-wave frequency range due to the parasitic issues related to the packaging.

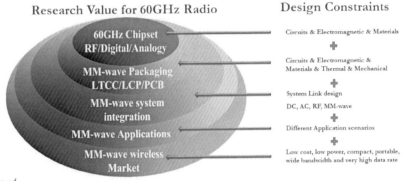

Figure 1.5 Design constraint and research value for millimeter-wave IC.

1.2 Contributions

This book covers silicon-based millimeter-wave IC in great depth and from the practical perspectives. It is becoming increasingly important due to the following four reasons: (1) the progress of the wireless communication requires much more information bandwidth and the speed to meet users' needs; (2) process downscaling makes silicon a possible choice for millimeter-wave SOC applications; (3) there are much more spectrum resources in millimeter-wave either license-free or re-usable in terms of space re-use; (4) stringent performance requirements such as size, cost, and power consumption require a mature process to support the commercial electronic applications. The earlier work on 60 GHz silicon-based transceiver circuits, which verified the possibility, was recorded by IBM Thomas J. Watson Research Center in 2005. Later extensive work was carried on to build millimeter-wave circuits using silicon-based technologies such as SiGe BiCMOS and CMOS technologies, which are expected to be low cost when they go to mass production for commercial applications. Several standards, including IEEE802.15.3C, WirelessHD™ Consortium, and ECMA-387, are targeted for 60 GHz applications. On January 4, 2013, the WiGiG alliance was taken over by the WiFi alliance to form the new IEEE802.11ad standard. The new standard aims to promote a fast wireless LAN technology that operates at millimeter-wave frequencies.

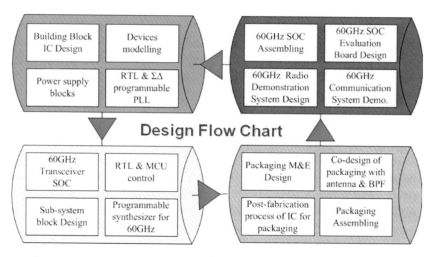

Figure 1.6 Project design flow for millimeter-wave SOC and demo.

Sponsored by the Mega project from ETPL Singapore, more than three years' efforts were devoted to the research and development of the 60 GHz solution, including baseband and 60 GHz RF transceiver as well as a demonstration system. When the project started in December 2009, the IEEE802.11ad standard had not formed then and the WiGiG alliance was just formed on May 7, 2009. During the development, we adapted to the WiGiG alliance standard, which became IEEE802.11ad standard after four years.

On the other hand, when the project started, the design kits for silicon-based technologies just started to approach millimeter wave. Most of the foundry support process design kits just close to 30 GHz or below. However, the project is targeted to design the complete 60 GHz high-speed communication system, which needs to be in standard compliance and include both 60 GHz transceiver and baseband chipset operated as a high-speed demonstration system. The project development was based on a top-down approach, i.e., from system design to the building blocks, while being practically based on the building block specifications used for the silicon process, which is not fully verified at the millimeter-wave frequency range. A high-speed baseband chipset includes the media access layer, i.e., MAC; physical layer, i.e., PHI, and high-speed interfaces, all of which have to be implemented based on the commercial CMOS process through FPGA until the ASIC design including mixed signal, digital and analog IC design. This book focuses on the 60 GHz transceiver SOC portion of the project. The design flow for the 60 GHz RF SOC is presented in Fig. 1.6. There are four portions or procedures for the development: (1) transistor- and circuit-level design portion, (2) function subsystem and SOC, (3) packaging-related portion, and (4) demonstration system–related portion. The four portions are correlated and multiple iteration design efforts are needed to make sure the in-time delivery of the project. The key efforts are put in the above-mentioned four aspects as follows:

(1) Transistor- and circuit-level design portion including device modeling, building blocks and power supply blocks, and RTL design as well as programmable PLL design are the fundamental design portions for the SOC. For the millimeter-wave IC design, the circuit model is crucial as the parasitic effects become non-negligible and even become dominant. With the design kits, we can design the building blocks such as the amplifier, mixer, power supply, RTL, and PLL circuit, which are all needed to build the 60 GHz transceiver.

(2) Function subsystem and SOC are targeted to form the 60 GHz transceiver SOC, which includes transmitter, receiver, and programmable synthesizer for 60 GHz. The subsystem has been fully considered the overall system success according to the application requirement.

(3) Packaging-related portion includes mechanic and electronic (M&E) package design, co-design of the packaging with antenna and bandpass filter as well as post-fabrication

process of IC for packaging and package assembling. For millimeter-wave IC with package design, it is crucial to co-design with the IC with the packaging because the wiring interconnects and package housing can affect the IC performance. Therefore, for practical applications, M&E characteristics of the package have to be fully considered during the design stage under the constraints of the power, temperature, and thermal effect. For low cost and small size requirements, it is necessary to co-design the packaging and antenna in the same platform. Of course, the post-fabrication process of IC for packaging has to be addressed as well to select the right flip-chip packaging, wire-bonding packaging, or even chip-scale-packaging (CSP). The last step is about the assembling technique for the IC with the packaging, which may also have significant effects on the performance, reliability, and yield for mass production.

(4) The demonstration system–related portion is targeted to form the 60 GHz transceiver SOC, which includes transmitter, receiver and programmable synthesizer, together with the printed circuits board for board-level integration and video streaming by using 60 GHz board and baseband demonstration board.

These four portions, which are closely related to each other, have to be investigated in the earlier research and development stages. The iteration design and simulation may be required to give a better compromise among the four crucial aspects as given in Fig. 1.6.

1.3 Scope and Organization

This book focuses on the silicon-based IC design for the application of millimeter wave and beyond. As mentioned earlier, the book is supported by the successful development of the 60 GHz transceiver, while the scope of this book is not limited to 60 GHz project development. We systematically cover the fundamental concepts, approaches, theories, and design techniques. Successful designs of related circuits are used as the study and verification cases for the readers to better understand the related techniques. The design approaches or methodologies are not limited to the designs demonstrated in this book; they can be applicable for the millimeter-wave design even toward design in the THz domain.

The organization of this book flows from the basic concepts and building blocks to the subsystem as well as the system. The arrangement of each chapter is given as follows:

The fundamental circuit networks, including the scattering matrix, Z-matrix, Y-matrix, ABCD matrix, and connections and conversion of these matrixes, which are crucial to understanding and deriving the theoretical analysis in the following chapter, are presented in Chapter 2. The resonant network, even–odd mode analysis, and multiple-port network are also discussed briefly as the basis for the following chapters.

In Chapter 3, the basic active device concept and design or selection of the active devices such as a diode and a transistor, which is very important for RF IC especially for millimeter-wave IC design and implementation, are presented. Based on our hands-on experience with different IC processes, including CMOS, BiCMOS, GaAs, and SiGe BiCMOS, the characteristics of the diode and transistor are also investigated and compared accordingly.

The investigation and the realization of passive circuits, including the resistor, capacitor, inductor, transformer, interconnects, and transmission lines, which are the foundation for accurate circuits and system design and implementation at RF especially millimeter-wave frequency range, are presented in Chapter 4.

Chapter 5 discusses a variable gain amplifier (VGA), which is one of key RF front-end building blocks that supports reliable mobile communication of wireless transceivers. The range of the VGA gain control also determines the receiver input dynamic range that provides a stable regulated power to the baseband chipset. More challenges will be brought in when the VGA is required to be used in high-data-rate or broadband communication systems. The chapter focuses on the design of the dB-linear VGA from the normal operation to embedded DC offset-canceling techniques as well as the temperature compensation technique.

Chapter 6 presents a power amplifier (PA) as one of the most vital and power hungry building blocks in the transmitter chain of the radio frequency (RF) transceiver. The ways to improve the linearity performance even at a large power level condition and a trade-off with the PA power efficiency are investigated in this chapter. It covers the fundamental specification definition, basic theory, and advanced design techniques such as transformer-based loaded tank for high efficiency and wide tuning ability.

In Chapter 7, a low-noise amplifier (LNA), a prerequisite building block in the receiver chain of the RF transceiver, is presented. This chapter starts from the basic parameters of the LNA and then presents the updated design by using two different topologies based on the SiGe BiCMOS process to showcase the LNA design.

In Chapter 8, bi-directional amplifier with switchable directional control capability is introduced. The operation mechanism and topologies for the bi-directional amplifier are presented, starting from the basic operation, analysis, and simulation to the silicon-based implementation and measurement verification. Both micro-strip-type inductor-based bi-directional amplifier and conductor-backed coplanar waveguide-type bi-directional amplifier are demonstrated with on-wafer measurement.

Chapter 9 discusses the mixer, a critical component used in the demodulator and modulator designs that translates the RF signals to and from baseband or IF (intermediate frequency) signals. In this chapter, we introduce the fundamentals of the mixers, including operation, transconductance operation, and balance issues of the mixer. Then the different types of the basic mixers such as an FET resistor-type mixer, Gilbert cell mixer, and other types of the mixers are introduced. Then we introduce different types of harmonic mixers, including anti-parallel diode pair (ADPD) mixer, transistor-based sub-harmonic mixers, and fourth-harmonic mixers. Examples of 60 and 79 GHz mixers are demonstrated in this chapter.

In Chapter 10 presents the voltage-controlled oscillator (VCO), one of the key building blocks that significantly influences the performance of the synthesizer and also the transceiver. In this Chapter, the VCO basics, including theory, basic topologies, specification parameters, and figure of merit, are discussed first, and then the LC-VCO and the properties of LC-tank and tank components are introduced. Finally, some typical topologies of LC-VCO and their advantages and disadvantages applicable to millimeter-wave frequency are introduced.

In Chapter 11, the design of the silicon-based RF and millimeter-wave switch, which is widely used in the RF front-end, is presented. The analysis of CMOS FET transistors that are essential for switching functions in RF/mmW ICs is carried out. Then, the analysis and design of the widely adopted SPDT switch topology is introduced. Next, a proposed switch topology called magnetic switchable artificial resonator is introduced. Finally, a comparison between state-of-the-art SPDTs is presented.

Chapter 12 focuses on a beamforming system, a crucial technique especially for millimeter-wave communication such as 60 GHz and radar system to provide an excellent trade-off of antenna gain and beam coverage. This chapter presents the fundamental concept of beamforming techniques and recent progress in the publication domain. The key building blocks of phase shifters are introduced in detail and different types of phase shifters are introduced and compared accordingly for a good trade-off in the beamforming system.

In Chapter 13, the frequency synthesizer, which is an indispensable subsystem in almost any RF communication system, especially in transceiver, is presented. The basic function of the frequency synthesizer is to generate a stable, clean, and programmable local oscillator (LO) signal for frequency conversion in the transmitter and the receiver in the transceiver. This chapter provides an introduction to the design of high-performance frequency synthesizers with system architecture techniques and building block techniques. The chapter covers the fundamental concept, performance parameters, and different synthesizer types. Then the key building blocks for the synthesizer, such as VCO, frequency divider, phase frequency detector, and different charging-pumping technique are also presented.

Chapter 14 asserts that the digital design is very important for the re-configurable SOC, which has one SOC to support multiple functions with re-configuration capability. This chapter introduces the essential design steps needed in the digital hardware design flow for low-power SOC design with detailed information for each step, from the algorithm design to physical implementation. The goal of this chapter is to give the readers a basic understanding of the digital design flow. The standard design methodology and background knowledge will be presented based on the tools from Synopsys. The chapter begins with a standard library introduction, following by a detailed explanation of design flow, from functional design to physical implementation. The new technologies involved in low-power design methodology for deep sub-micron CMOS are also introduced.

Chapter 15 focuses on the hardware design portion of the 60 GHz transceiver SOC, which is controlled by SPI interfaces as introduced in Chapter 14 on digital design. It presents the basic development based on the fundamental building blocks introduced in the previous chapters to form the fully functional SOC under the constraints of the system specifications and the architecture. As a demonstration, a 60 GHz re-configurable full transceiver SOC with Serial Peripheral Interface (SPI) in a commercial 0.18 μm BiCMOS technology is developed as the demonstration case. The 60 GHz transceiver SOC has the re-configurable capabilities for both gain and operation frequency bands covering 9 GHz bandwidth in total. The demonstration system based on the SOC and the control board is fully integrated. The test following the standard is carried out for data rate and performance evaluation.

References

1. S. Reynolds, et al., 60 GHz transceiver circuits in SiGe bipolar technology, *ISSCC Dig. Tech. Papers*, pp. 442–443, February 2004.

2. B. Floyd, et al., A silicon 60 GHz receiver and transmitter chipset for broadband communications, *ISSCC Dig. Tech. Papers*, pp. 218–219, February 2006.

3. C.-H. Wang, et al. A 60 GHz transmitter with integrated antenna in 0.18 μm SiGe BiCMOS Technology, *ISSCC Dig. Tech. Papers*, pp. 659–668, February 2006.

4. K. Okada et al., A full 4-channel 6.3 Gb/s 60 GHz direct-conversion transceiver with low-power analog and digital baseband circuitry, *ISSCC Dig. Tech. Papers*, pp. 218–219, February 2012.

5. K. Ma, et al. An integrated 60 GHz low power two chip wireless system based on IEEE802.11ad standard, *IEEE MTT-S International Microwave Symposium (IMS)*, *2014.*

6. M. Boers et al., A 16TX/16RX 60 GHz 802.11ad chipset with single coaxial interface and polarization diversity, *IEEE J. Solid-State Circuits*, vol. 49, no. 12, pp. 3031–3045, December 2014.

7. K. Sengupta, D. Seo, L. Yang, and A. Hajimiri, Silicon integrated 280 GHz imaging chipset with 4 × 4 SiGe receiver array and CMOS source, *IEEE Trans. Terahertz Sci. Technol.*, vol. 5, no. 3, pp. 427–437, May 2015.

8. D.-J. van den Broek, E. Klumperink, and B. Nauta, A self-interference cancelling front-end for in-band full-duplex wireless and its phase noise performance, in *Proc. IEEE Radio Freq. Integr. Circuits*, pp. 75–78, May 2015.

9. S. Zihir, O. D. Gurbuz, A. Karroy, S. Raman, and G. M. Rebeiz, A 60 GHz 64-element wafer-scale phased-array with full-reticle design, in *IEEE MTT-S Int. Microw. Symp. Dig. Tech. Papers*, pp. 1–3, May 2015.

10. Ericsson: E. Dahlman, et al., 5G Radio Access, *Ericsson Review*, June 2014.

Entrepreneurs, Leaders, Innovators, Thinkers and Experts: The "ELITE" workforce for the 21st century.

—Kiat Seng Yeo and Kaixue Ma

Chapter 2

Fundamentals of Circuit Networks

Wei Xu,[a] Kaixue Ma,[a] and Kiat Seng Yeo[b]

[a]School of Physical Electronics,
University of Electronic Science and Technology of China,
#4 Section II, Jianshe North Road, Chengdu 610054, P. R. China
[b]Engineering Product Development, Singapore University of Technology and Design,
8 Somapah Road, Singapore 487372

makaixue@uestc.edu.cn

2.1 Introduction

Circuit networks are essential elements in circuit studies. Although the physical realization of a circuit at RF frequencies may vary, the circuit network topology is common to all. In order to work out the desirable circuit components better and economically and analyze their working characteristics conveniently, good command of network theory is necessary.

This chapter describes various network concepts, including Scattering matrix, short-circuit admittance matrix, open-circuit impedance matrix, and transfer matrix and their properties. Some useful equations are provided for circuit analysis [1–13].

Low-Power Wireless Communication Circuits and Systems: 60 GHz and Beyond
Edited by Kaixue Ma and Kiat Seng Yeo
Copyright © 2018 Pan Stanford Publishing Pte. Ltd.
ISBN 978-981-4745-96-3 (Hardcover), 978-1-315-15653-8 (eBook)
www.panstanford.com

2.2 Two-Port Scattering Matrix

Most circuits can be presented by a two-port network, as shown in Fig. 2.1, where V_1, V_2 and I_1, I_2 are the voltage and current variables at ports 1 and 2, respectively.

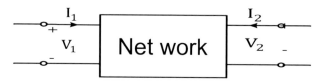

Figure 2.1 Two-port network showing network variables.

The scattering or S parameters are widely used in microwave circuit analysis, since using the concepts of incident and reflected wave is considerably better than voltage and current. The two-port S parameters are defined in terms of the voltage wave as

$$\begin{bmatrix} V_1^- \\ V_2^- \end{bmatrix} = \begin{bmatrix} S_{11} & S_{12} \\ S_{21} & S_{22} \end{bmatrix} \begin{bmatrix} V_1^+ \\ V_2^+ \end{bmatrix} \tag{2.1}$$

or

$$[V^-] = [S][V^+], \tag{2.2}$$

where V_n^+ indicates the amplitude of voltage wave which is incident on the n-port, and V_n^- is the amplitude of voltage wave which is reflected from the n-port. A specific element of the scattering matrix can be determined as

$$S_{ij} = \frac{V_i^-}{V_j^+} \bigg|_{V_k^+ = 0, \, k \neq j, \, k = 1,2} \quad (i, j = 1,2), \tag{2.3}$$

where $V_k^+ = 0$ implies a perfect impedance match (no reflection from terminal impedance) at port k.

The parameters S_{11} and S_{22} are also called the reflection coefficients, whereas S_{12} and S_{21} are the transmission coefficients. These are the parameters directly measureable at RF/microwave frequencies.

The S parameters have several properties that are useful for network analysis. For a reciprocal network (not containing any active devices or nonreciprocal media, such as ferrites or plasmas), the S matrix is symmetrical such that $S_{12} = S_{21}$. If the network is symmetrical, an addition property, $S_{11} = S_{22}$, holds. Therefore, the symmetrical is also a reciprocal. For a lossless passive network, the transmitting power and the reflected power must be equal to the total incident power. The S matrix is a unitary matrix. The conservation could be written as

$$|S_{21}|^2 + |S_{11}|^2 = 1$$

$$|S_{12}|^2 + |S_{22}|^2 = 1'$$

(2.4)

where the asterisk denotes a conjugate quantity.

2.3   Two-Port Z Matrix

If the voltage and current of a circuit network at various points are defined, we can use the impedance matrix of circuit theory to relate these port quantities to each other and thus to essentially arrive at a matrix description of the network. The study of the Z matrix is quite useful for design of passive components such as couplers and filters.

As shown in Fig. 2.1, the two-port Z matrix is defined as

$$\begin{bmatrix} V_1 \\ V_2 \end{bmatrix} = \begin{bmatrix} Z_{11} & Z_{12} \\ Z_{21} & Z_{22} \end{bmatrix} \begin{bmatrix} I_1 \\ I_2 \end{bmatrix}$$

(2.5)

or

$$[V] = [Z][I].$$

(2.6)

From Eq. (2.5), we see that the elements of Z matrix can be found as

$$Z_{ij} = \frac{V_i}{I_j} \bigg|_{I_k = 0, \, k \neq j, \, k = 1,2} \quad (i, j = 1, 2),$$

(2.7)

where $I_k = 0$ implies a perfect open-circuited at port k. Z_{ii} is the input impedance seen looking into port i when the other port is open-circuited, and Z_{ij} is the transfer impedance between ports i and j when the other port is open circuited.

Hence, the Z matrix is known as the open-circuited impedance. For reciprocal networks, we have $Z_{12} = Z_{21}$. If networks are symmetrical, then $Z_{12} = Z_{21}$ and $Z_{11} = Z_{22}$. For a lossless network, the Z parameters are all purely imaginary.

2.4 Two-Port Y Matrix

The Y matrix and the Z matrix are the inverse of each other. Both the Z and the Y matrix relate the total port voltages and currents. Take the two-port network as an example, as shown in Fig. 2.1. The Y matrix is defined as

$$\begin{bmatrix} I_1 \\ I_2 \end{bmatrix} = \begin{bmatrix} Y_{11} & Y_{12} \\ Y_{21} & Y_{22} \end{bmatrix} \begin{bmatrix} V_1 \\ V_2 \end{bmatrix} \tag{2.8}$$

or

$$[I] = [Y][V]. \tag{2.9}$$

From Eq. (2.8), the element of Y matrix can be determined as

$$Y_{ij} = \left. \frac{I_i}{V_j} \right|_{V_k = 0,\, k \neq j,\, k = 1,2} \quad (i, j = 1,2), \tag{2.10}$$

where $V_k = 0$ implies a perfect short circuit at port k. For reciprocal networks, $Y_{12} = Y_{21}$. In addition to this, if networks are symmetrical, then $Y_{11} = Y_{22}$. For a lossless network, the Y parameters are all purely imaginary.

2.5 Two-Port ABCD Matrix

The S, Z, and Y parameters can be used to characterize a network with an arbitrary number of ports, but in practice many networks consist of a cascade connection of two or more two-port networks. In this case, as shown in Fig. 2.1, it will be very useful to define a two-port transmission, or $ABCD$ matrix as

$$\begin{bmatrix} V_1 \\ I_1 \end{bmatrix} = \begin{bmatrix} A & B \\ C & D \end{bmatrix} \begin{bmatrix} V_2 \\ I_2 \end{bmatrix}. \tag{2.11}$$

The *ABCD* parameters are given by

$$A = \frac{V_1}{V_2}\bigg|_{I_2=0} \qquad B = \frac{V_1}{-I_2}\bigg|_{V_2=0}$$

$$C = \frac{I_1}{V_2}\bigg|_{I_2=0} \qquad D = \frac{I_1}{-I_2}\bigg|_{V_2=0} \qquad\qquad (2.12)$$

If the network shown in Fig. 2.1 is tuned around, then the transmission matrix defined in Eq. (2.11) becomes

$$\begin{bmatrix} A_m & B_m \\ C_m & D_m \end{bmatrix} = \begin{bmatrix} D & B \\ C & A \end{bmatrix}, \qquad\qquad (2.13)$$

where the parameters with m subscripts are for the network after being turned around, and the parameters without subscripts are for the network before being turned around.

The *ABCD* matrix makes sense only for a two-port network which is different from the matrix referred to above. If the network is symmetrical, then, $A = D$. For a reciprocal network, $AD - BC = 1$. If the network is lossless, then A and D will be purely real and B and C will be purely imaginary.

The usefulness of the *ABCD* matrix representation lies in the fact that a library of *ABCD* matrix for elementary two-port networks can be built up, and applied in a building-block fashion to more complicated microwave networks that consist of cascades of these simpler two-ports. Table 2.1 lists a number of useful two-port networks and their *ABCD* matrices.

Table 2.1 Some useful two-port networks and their ABCD parameters

	ABCD parameters
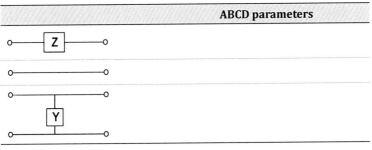	

(*Continued*)

Table 2.1 (*Continued*)

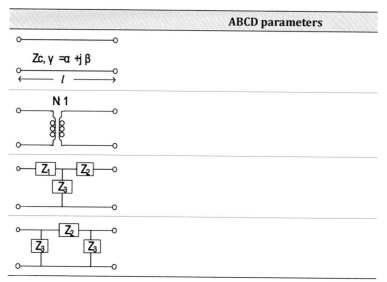

	ABCD parameters

2.6 Network Connections

Often in the analysis of a complex network, it is fairly convenient to divide it into some individual subnetworks and then to get the ultimate parameters via matrix calculation according to a certain rule. There are three basic types of connection which are usually encountered: series, parallel, and cascade.

Series: Suppose there networks N_a and N_b are connected in series as shown in Fig. 2.2a. It would be much easier to use the Z matrix. Since

$$\begin{bmatrix} I_1 \\ I_2 \end{bmatrix} = \begin{bmatrix} I_{1a} \\ I_{2a} \end{bmatrix} = \begin{bmatrix} I_{1b} \\ I_{2b} \end{bmatrix} \text{ and } \begin{bmatrix} V_1 \\ V_2 \end{bmatrix} = \begin{bmatrix} V_{1a} \\ V_{2a} \end{bmatrix} + \begin{bmatrix} V_{1b} \\ V_{2b} \end{bmatrix}, \tag{2.14}$$

Hence

$$\begin{bmatrix} V_1 \\ V_2 \end{bmatrix} = \left(\begin{bmatrix} z_{11a} & z_{12a} \\ z_{21a} & z_{22a} \end{bmatrix} + \begin{bmatrix} z_{11b} & z_{12b} \\ z_{21b} & z_{22b} \end{bmatrix} \right) \cdot \begin{bmatrix} I_1 \\ I_2 \end{bmatrix} \tag{2.15}$$

or the Z matrix of the combined Z matrix is

$$[Z] = [Z_a] + [Z_b]. \tag{2.16}$$

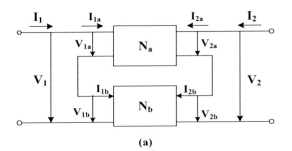

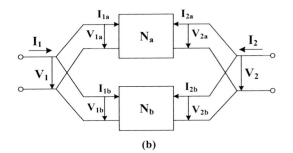

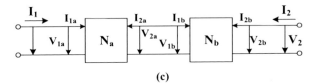

(c)

Figure 2.2 Basic types of network connection: (a) series, (b) parallel, and (c) cascade.

Similarly, more than two two-port networks are to be connected, the Z matrix of the composite network is equal to the sum of all the two-port subnetworks' Z matrix.

In the same manner, if two two-port networks are parallel as shown in Fig. 2.2b, it is easy to get

$$\begin{bmatrix} I_1 \\ I_2 \end{bmatrix} = \begin{bmatrix} I_{1a} \\ I_{2a} \end{bmatrix} + \begin{bmatrix} I_{1b} \\ I_{2b} \end{bmatrix} \text{ and } \begin{bmatrix} V_1 \\ V_2 \end{bmatrix} = \begin{bmatrix} V_{1a} \\ V_{2a} \end{bmatrix} = \begin{bmatrix} V_{1b} \\ V_{2b} \end{bmatrix}, \tag{2.17}$$

Therefore,

$$\begin{bmatrix} I_1 \\ I_2 \end{bmatrix} = \left(\begin{bmatrix} Y_{11a} & Y_{12a} \\ Y_{21a} & Y_{22a} \end{bmatrix} + \begin{bmatrix} Y_{11b} & Y_{12b} \\ Y_{21b} & Y_{22b} \end{bmatrix} \right) \cdot \begin{bmatrix} V_1 \\ V_2 \end{bmatrix}. \tag{2.18}$$

Thus, the ultimate Y matrix of the combined network is

$$[Y] = [Y_a] + [Y_b]. \tag{2.19}$$

Likewise, if there are more than two two-port networks that are parallel, the Y matrix of the composite network is equal to the sum of all the individual Y matrixes.

The cascade connection of a two-port network is fairly common in network analysis, since a complicated circuit system often consists of many components. This time, it is supposed to turn to the *ABCD* matrix. As shown in Fig. 2.2c, the relationships between voltages and currents are obvious:

$$\begin{bmatrix} V_1 \\ I_1 \end{bmatrix} = \begin{bmatrix} V_{1a} \\ I_{1a} \end{bmatrix} \text{ and } \begin{bmatrix} V_2 \\ I_2 \end{bmatrix} = \begin{bmatrix} V_{2a} \\ I_{2b} \end{bmatrix}. \tag{2.20}$$

It is evident that the outputs of the first network, N_a, are the inputs of the followed network N_b, namely

$$\begin{bmatrix} V_{2a} \\ -I_{2a} \end{bmatrix} = \begin{bmatrix} V_{1b} \\ I_{1b} \end{bmatrix}. \tag{2.21}$$

This gives

$$\begin{bmatrix} V_1 \\ I_1 \end{bmatrix} = \left(\begin{bmatrix} A_a & B_a \\ C_a & D_a \end{bmatrix} \cdot \begin{bmatrix} A_b & B_b \\ C_b & D_b \end{bmatrix} \right) \cdot \begin{bmatrix} V_2 \\ -I_2 \end{bmatrix} = \begin{bmatrix} A & B \\ C & D \end{bmatrix} \cdot \begin{bmatrix} V_2 \\ -I_2 \end{bmatrix}. \tag{2.22}$$

In this way, the transfer matrix is easy to get via the multiplication of the transfer matrices of the cascaded subnetworks. This argument is valid for any number of two-port networks in cascade connection.

2.7 Network Conversions

From what we discussed above, it is obvious that a matrix has its advantages in a specific situation. However, it is often required to obtain different parameters in network analysis. Hence, converting one type of parameter to another is rather important in circuit studies.

The easiest conversion is between the Y and Z matrixes since they are the inverse of each other. In principle, the relations between any two types of parameters can be determined by the relationships of terminal variables. The impedance parameters of a network can be easily converted to *ABCD* parameters. Suppose that there is a two-port Z matrix and apparently

$$V_1 = I_1 Z_{11} = I_2 Z_{12}$$
$$V_2 = I_2 Z_{21} = I_2 Z_{22}$$

(2.23)

Therefore,

$$A = \left. \frac{V_1}{V_2} \right|_{I_2=0} = \frac{I_1 Z_{11}}{I_1 Z_2} = \frac{Z_{11}}{Z_2}$$

$$B = \left. \frac{V_1}{I_2} \right|_{V_2=0} = \left. \frac{I_1 Z_{11} - I_2 Z_{12}}{I_2} \right|_{V_2=0} = \frac{Z_{11} Z_{12} - Z_{12} Z_{21}}{Z_{21}}.$$

(2.24)

$$C = \left. \frac{I_1}{V_2} \right|_{I_2=0} = \frac{I_1}{I_1 Z_{21}} = \frac{1}{Z_{21}}$$

$$D = \left. \frac{I_1}{I_2} \right|_{V_2=0} = \frac{I_2 Z_{22}/Z_{21}}{I_2} = \frac{Z_{22}}{Z_{21}}$$

The *ABCD* matrix is obtained obviously from the Z matrix. All the network conversions can be found in this way. For convenience, the conversions are listed in Table 2.2.

2.8 Resonant Network

When it comes to resonators, we will begin by simply reviewing the basic characteristics of series and parallel LC resonant circuits. These are the most basic resonance model.

Series resonant circuit. As shown in Fig. 2.3a, suppose there is a two-port network of series LC circuits. The input impedance is

$$Z_{in} = jwL + \frac{1}{jwC}.$$

(2.25)

Table 2.2 Conversions between two-port networks

	S	Z	Y	ABCD
S_{11}	S_{11}	$\dfrac{(Z_{11}-Z_0)(Z_{22}+Z_0)-Z_{12}Z_{21}}{(Z_{11}+Z_0)(Z_{22}+Z_0)-Z_{12}Z_{21}}$	$\dfrac{(Y_0-Y_{11})(Y_0+Y_{22})+Y_{12}Y_{21}}{(Y_0+Y_{11})(Y_0+Y_{22})-Y_{12}Y_{21}}$	$\dfrac{A+B/Z_0-CZ_0-D}{A+B/Z_0+CZ_0+D}$
S_{12}	S_{12}	$\dfrac{2Z_{12}Z_0}{(Z_{11}+Z_0)(Z_{22}+Z_0)-Z_{12}Z_{21}}$	$\dfrac{-2Y_{12}Y_0}{(Y_0+Y_{11})(Y_0+Y_{22})-Y_{12}Y_{21}}$	$\dfrac{2(AD-BC)}{A+B/Z_0+CZ_0+D}$
S_{21}	S_{21}	$\dfrac{2Z_{21}Z_0}{(Z_{11}+Z_0)(Z_{22}+Z_0)-Z_{12}Z_{21}}$	$\dfrac{-2Y_{21}Y_0}{(Y_0+Y_{11})(Y_0+Y_{22})-Y_{12}Y_{21}}$	$\dfrac{2}{A+B/Z_0+CZ_0+D}$
S_{22}	S_{22}	$\dfrac{(Z_{11}+Z_0)(Z_{22}-Z_0)-Z_{12}Z_{21}}{(Z_{11}+Z_0)(Z_{22}+Z_0)-Z_{12}Z_{21}}$	$\dfrac{(Y_0+Y_{11})(Y_0-Y_{22})+Y_{12}Y_{21}}{(Y_0+Y_{11})(Y_0+Y_{22})-Y_{12}Y_{21}}$	$\dfrac{-A+B/Z_0-CZ_0+D}{A+B/Z_0+CZ_0+D}$
Z_{11}	$Z_0\dfrac{(1+S_{11})(1-S_{22})+S_{12}S_{21}}{(1-S_{11})(1-S_{22})-S_{12}S_{21}}$	Z_{11}	$\dfrac{Y_{22}}{Y_{11}Y_{22}-Y_{12}Y_{21}}$	$\dfrac{A}{C}$
Z_{12}	$Z_0\dfrac{2S_{12}}{(1-S_{11})(1-S_{22})-S_{12}S_{21}}$	Z_{12}	$\dfrac{-Y_{12}}{Y_{11}Y_{22}-Y_{12}Y_{21}}$	$\dfrac{AD-BC}{C}$
Z_{21}	$Z_0\dfrac{2S_{21}}{(1-S_{11})(1-S_{22})-S_{12}S_{21}}$	Z_{21}	$\dfrac{-Y_{21}}{Y_{11}Y_{22}-Y_{12}Y_{21}}$	$\dfrac{-1}{B}$
Z_{22}	$Z_0\dfrac{(1-S_{11})(1+S_{22})+S_{12}S_{21}}{(1-S_{11})(1-S_{22})-S_{12}S_{21}}$	Z_{22}	$\dfrac{Y_{11}}{Y_{11}Y_{22}-Y_{12}Y_{21}}$	$\dfrac{A}{B}$

	S	Z	Y	ABCD
A	$\dfrac{(1+S_{11})(1-S_{22})+S_{12}S_{21}}{2S_{21}}$	$\dfrac{Z_{11}}{Z_{21}}$	$\dfrac{-Y_{22}}{Y_{21}}$	A
B	$Z_0\dfrac{(1+S_{11})(1+S_{22})-S_{12}S_{21}}{2S_{21}}$	$\dfrac{Z_{11}Z_{22}-Z_{12}Z_{21}}{Z_{21}}$	$\dfrac{-1}{Y_{21}}$	B
C	$\dfrac{1}{Z_0}\dfrac{(1-S_{11})(1-S_{22})-S_{12}S_{21}}{2S_{21}}$	$\dfrac{1}{Z_{21}}$	$\dfrac{-(Y_{11}Y_{12}-Y_{12}Y_{21})}{Y_{21}}$	C
D	$\dfrac{(1-S_{11})(1+S_{22})+S_{12}S_{21}}{2S_{21}}$	$\dfrac{Z_{22}}{Z_{21}}$	$\dfrac{-Y_{11}}{Y_{21}}$	D
Y_{11}	$Y_0\dfrac{(1-S_{11})(1+S_{22})+S_{12}S_{21}}{(1+S_{11})(1+S_{22})-S_{12}S_{21}}$	$\dfrac{Z_{22}}{Z_{11}Z_{22}-Z_{12}Z_{21}}$	Y_{11}	$\dfrac{A}{B}$
Y_{12}	$Y_0\dfrac{-2S_{12}}{(1+S_{11})(1+S_{22})-S_{12}S_{21}}$	$\dfrac{-Z_{12}}{Z_{11}Z_{22}-Z_{12}Z_{21}}$	Y_{12}	$\dfrac{-(AD-BC)}{C}$
Y_{21}	$Y_0\dfrac{-2S_{21}}{(1+S_{11})(1+S_{22})-S_{12}S_{21}}$	$\dfrac{-Z_{21}}{Z_{11}Z_{22}-Z_{12}Z_{21}}$	Y_{21}	$\dfrac{-1}{B}$
Y_{22}	$Y_0\dfrac{(1+S_{11})(1-S_{22})+S_{12}S_{21}}{(1+S_{11})(1+S_{22})-S_{12}S_{21}}$	$\dfrac{Z_{11}}{Z_{11}Z_{22}-Z_{12}Z_{21}}$	Y_{22}	$\dfrac{A}{B}$

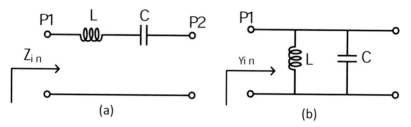

Figure 2.3 Two-port network of (a) series LC circuit and (b) parallel LC circuit.

And this circuit is resonant at

$$w = \frac{1}{\sqrt{LC}}.$$ (2.26)

We can easily get the impedance at resonance frequency

$$Z_{in} = j\sqrt{\frac{L}{C}} + \frac{1}{j}\sqrt{\frac{L}{C}} = 0$$ (2.27)

From Eq. (2.7), Z_{21} of the two ports, which equals Z_{in}, is 0. And Z_{11} is infinite.

Parallel resonant circuit. The two-port network with a parallel LC circuit is shown in Fig. 2.3b; the input impedance is

$$Z_{in} = \left(jwC + \frac{1}{jwL} \right)^{-1}.$$ (2.28)

Similarly, this circuit is resonant at $w = \frac{1}{\sqrt{LC}}$ as Eq. (2.26).

We can easily get the input admittance at resonance frequency:

$$Z_{in} = \left(j\sqrt{\frac{C}{L}} + \frac{1}{j}\sqrt{\frac{C}{L}} \right)^{-1} = \infty$$ (2.29)

From Eq. (2.7), Z_{11} of the two ports, which equals Z_{in}, is infinite, and Z_{21} is zero.

In actual cases, the network may have complex components; however, the mechanism of the resonance is the same. If we see the whole two-port network as a resonator, and the type of resonance is similar to the two kinds of fundamental resonator introduced above, at resonance frequency we are supposed to get $Z_{21} = 0$ and $Z_{11} = \infty$. In this situation, the resonator generates a transmission pole.

In a similar way, if we put the series LC circuit in parallel in network or put the parallel LC circuit in series, it is easy to find that $Z_{11} = 0$ and $Z_{21} = \infty$, at resonance frequency analogously.

2.9 Even-Odd Mode Analysis

If a network is symmetrical, then it is rather convenient to bisect the symmetrical network into two identical halves with respect to its symmetrical interface. As shown in Fig. 2.4, since any excitation to an asymmetrical two-port network can be obtained by a linear combination of even and odd excitations, separating the even and odd modes individually will greatly simplify the network analysis.

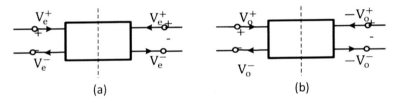

(a)   (b)

Figure 2.4 Symmetrical two-port networks under (a) even-mode excitation and (b) odd-mode excitation.

As shown in Fig. 2.4a, the even excitation is applied to the network, the two network halves become the two identical one-port even-mode networks with the other port open-circuited. Under an odd excitation, as shown in Fig. 2.4b, the symmetrical interface is short-circuited, and the two network halves become the two identical one-port with the other port short-circuited.

Figure 2.4 shows

$$V_1^+ = V_e^+ + V_o^+ \quad V_2^+ = V_e^+ - V_o^+$$
$$V_1^- = V_e^- + V_o^- \quad V_2^- = V_e^- - V_o^- \tag{2.30}$$

and

$$S_{11e} = V_e^-/V_e^+ \quad S_{11o} = V_o^-/V_o^+ , \tag{2.31}$$

where the subscripts e and o indicate the even-mode and odd-mode, respectively. From Eq. (2.3), the S parameters are

$$S_{11} = \left.\frac{V_1^-}{V_1^+}\right|_{V_2^+=0} = \frac{V_e^- + V_o^-}{2 \cdot V_o^-} = \frac{1}{2}(S_{11e} + S_{11o}) \tag{2.32}$$

$$S_{21} = \left.\frac{V_2^-}{V_1^+}\right|_{V_2^+=0} = \frac{V_e^- - V_o^+}{2 \cdot V_o^+} = \frac{1}{2}(S_{11e} - S_{11o})$$

and since the network is symmetrical, $S_{22} = S_{11}$, $S_{12} = S_{21}$.

Assume that Z_{ine} and Z_{ino} represent the input impedances of the one-port even- and odd-mode networks, respectively. By calculation [6], we can arrive at fairly useful equations:

$$S_{21} = S_{12} = \frac{Z_0 Z_{ine} - Z_0 Z_{ino}}{(Z_0 + Z_{ino})(Z_0 + Z_{ine})} \tag{2.33}$$

$$S_{11} = S_{22} = \frac{Z_{ino} Z_{ine} - Z_0^2}{(Z_0 + Z_{ino})(Z_0 + Z_{ine})}$$

2.10 Multi-Port Network

Until now, we have talked about two-port networks and their characteristics. However, networks with more than two ports, called multiport networks, are fairly common in circuit analysis. Except for the *ABCD* matrix, which only makes sense for two-port networks, the *S*, *Z*, and *Y* parameters for a multiport network are defined analogously to two-port network.

Take the *S* parameters as an example; from Eqs. (2.1), (2.2), and (2.3), an *M*-port network can be given as

$$\begin{bmatrix} V_1^- \\ V_2^- \\ \vdots \\ V_M^- \end{bmatrix} = \begin{bmatrix} S_{11} & S_{12} & \cdots S_{1M} \\ S_{21} & S_{22} & \cdots S_{1M} \\ \vdots & \vdots & \cdots \vdots \\ S_{M1} & S_{M2} & \cdots S_{MM} \end{bmatrix} \begin{bmatrix} V_1^+ \\ V_2^+ \\ \vdots \\ V_M^+ \end{bmatrix} \tag{2.34}$$

or

$$[V^-] = [S][V^+]. \tag{2.35}$$

A specific element of this $M \times M$ scattering matrix can be determined as

$$S_{ij} = \left. \frac{V_i^-}{V_j^+} \right|_{V_k^+ = 0, \, k \neq j, \, k = 1,2,\ldots,M} \qquad (i, j = 1,2,\ldots,M), \qquad (2.36)$$

For a reciprocal network, $S_{ij} = S_{ji}$ and $[S]$ is a symmetrical matrix such that

$$[S]^t = [S], \qquad (2.37)$$

where the superscript t denotes the transpose of matrix. For a lossless passive network, we have

$$[S]^t [S]^* = [U], \qquad (2.38)$$

where the superscript * denotes the conjugate of matrix, and [U] is a unity matrix.

References

1. E. A. Guillemin, *Introductory Circuit Theory*, John Wiley & Sons, New York, 1953.

2. R. E. Collin, *Foundations for Microwave Engineering*, McGraw-Hill, New York, 1992.

3. L. Weinberg, *Network Analysis and Synthesis*, McGraw-Hill, New York, 1962.

4. J. L. Stewart, *Circuit Theory and Design*, John Wiley & Sons, New York, 1956.

5. H. J. Carlin, The scattering matrix in network theory, *IRE Trans. Circuit Theory*, **CT-3**, 1956, 88–97.

6. J.-S. Hong, *Microstrip Filters for RF/Microwave Applications*, John Wiley & Sons, Inc., Hoboken, New Jersey, 2011.

7. D. M. Pozar, *Microwave Engineering*, John Wiley & Sons, Inc, 2012.

8. S. Haykin, *Communication Systems*, 3rd edition, John Wiley & Sons, New York, 1994.

9. C. G. Montagomery, R. H. Dicke, and E. M. Purcell, *Principles of Microwave Circuits*, McGraw-Hill, New York, 1948.

10. S. Ramo, T. R. Whinnery, and T. van Duzer, *Fields and Waves in Communication Electronics*, John Wiley & Sons, New York, 1965.

11. J. S. Wright, O. P. Jain, W. J. Chudobiak, and V. Makios, Equivalent Circuits of Microstrip Impedance Discontinuities and Launchers, *IEEE Transactions on Microwave Theory and Techniques*, vol. MTT-22, pp. 48–52, January 1974.

12. G. Matthaei, L. Young, and E. M. T. Jones, *Microwave Filters, Impedance-Matching Networks, and Coupling Structures*, Artech House, Dedham, Mass., 1980, Chapter 5.

13. J.-S. Hong, J.-M. Shi, and L. Sun, Exact computation of generalized scattering matrix of suspended microstrip step discontinuities, *Electron. Lett.*, **25**(5), 1989, 335–336.

New knowledge is created every day. But knowledge is limited to what we know, whereas imagination embraces everything we do not know. Those who can make imagination real are the ones who make a better world.

—Kiat Seng Yeo and Kaixue Ma

Chapter 3

Active Devices

Bharatha Kumar Thangarasu,[a] **Kaixue Ma,**[b] **and Kiat Seng Yeo**[a]

[a]*Engineering Product Development, Singapore University of Technology and Design,*
8 Somapah Road, Singapore 487372
[b]*School of Physical Electronics,*
University of Electronic Science and Technology of China,
#4 Section II, Jianshe North Road, Chengdu 610054, P. R. China

bharatha_kumar@sutd.edu.sg, makaixue@uestc.edu.cn

Active devices are used in the semiconductor circuit design to provide the most essential signal (current, voltage, or power) amplification in the analog domain as well as the ON/OFF switch functionality in the digital domain. Unlike passive devices, the characteristics of active devices are dependent not only on the physical dimensions but also on the electrical bias conditions. This chapter describes two most frequently used active devices in the RF integrated circuit design, namely the transistor and the PN junction diode.

Low-Power Wireless Communication Circuits and Systems: 60 GHz and Beyond
Edited by Kaixue Ma and Kiat Seng Yeo
Copyright © 2018 Pan Stanford Publishing Pte. Ltd.
ISBN 978-981-4745-96-3 (Hardcover), 978-1-315-15653-8 (eBook)
www.panstanford.com

3.1 Diode

A diode is a two-terminal semiconductor device and consists of a p-type and an n-type junction [1]. The diode is a unipolar device and conducts a negligible leakage current when reverse biased, i.e., when the cathode's (N-terminal) voltage is more than the anode voltage (P-terminal). On the contrary, when it is forward biased, i.e., when the anode voltage is more than the cathode voltage, the current (I_D) is exponentially related to the voltage across it (V_D) as shown in Fig. 3.1 and as given by [1] the following equation:

$$I_D = I_o \cdot e^{\left(\frac{V_D}{\eta \cdot V_T}\right)},$$ (3.1)

where, I_o is the reverse-biased saturation current, η is the ideality factor, which depends on the fabrication process and the semiconductor material property, and V_T is the thermal voltage $(k \cdot T/q)$, with k as the Boltzmann constant = 1.38×10^{-23} J/K, T as the absolute temperature in K, and q as the electronic charge in C.

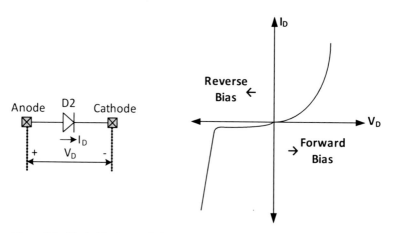

Figure 3.1 Diode biasing and characteristics.

Based on the diffusion layers on the silicon substrate (P-type), there are two possible diodes [1], namely P-substrate/N-well and P-diffusion/N-well, as shown in Fig. 3.2.

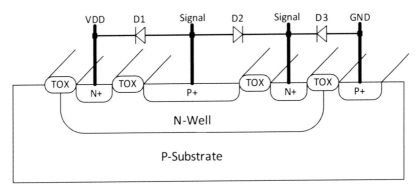

Figure 3.2 Diode PN junction cross section (three variants) on silicon substrate.

The former type of diode (D3) has the anode always connected to ground potential and the cathode with the signal node, which is mainly required for the electrostatic discharge (ESD) protection. The latter type has two variants: (1) D2, with the signal to the anode and the supply voltage (VDD) to the cathode also used for ESD protection and (2) D1, with signal nodes at both the anode and the cathode used for RF applications such as peak detectors, switches, and mixers.

Additionally, in a CMOS process, there are parasitic back-to-back connected diodes, which result in a latch-up condition and need to be reverse biased at all times.

3.2 Transistor

As we know, the transistor is a three-terminal device, with one common terminal, one control terminal, and an output terminal depending on the selected transistor configuration [1]. Over the past decades, transistors have evolved with many flavors, each with their own performance traits. The most predominant ones are the silicon bipolar junction transistor (BJT), silicon complementary metal oxide semiconductor (CMOS) transistor, silicon–germanium (SiGe) hetero-junction bipolar transistor (HBT), and III–V composite transistors such as gallium–arsenide (GaAs) and indium-phosphate (InP) [1–4]. The initial transistors were individually fabricated as monolithic packaged circuit components which are assembled on the printed circuit board (PCB), and later on, with the semiconductor technology downscaling more and more, transistors (recently about multi-million transistors) are incorporated within a single integrated circuit (IC) [5].

Transistors are mainly included in the radio frequency (RF) IC design for implementing the RF, analog, and digital functionalities. The market share of digital functionalities has been taken over by CMOS transistors as they offer low-power, high-speed, and high-density integration features unlike other transistor types. However, the other transistor types as mentioned above are prevalent in the semiconductor industry but are mainly used in analog and RF domains.

HBTs such as GaAs pseudomorphic high-electron-mobility transistors (pHEMT) have existed for many decades and are still a promising option [3, 4]. These devices can achieve high power handling capability and high power conversion efficiency even at high operating frequencies. However, due to their high manufacturing cost involving a complex fabrication process with multiple semiconductor layers and controlled doping to achieve a high device breakdown voltage (V_{beo}) as well as a high transition frequency (f_T). In addition, III–V devices come with their inability to be easily integrated with the silicon CMOS digital process, making them a less viable choice for mobile, low-cost, mass production applications [5].

An alternative to analog and RF designs is the CMOS transistor, which mitigates the fabrication cost and enables easy system integration [5–8]. To operate the CMOS transistor at frequencies toward millimeter-wave range and above, the device size should be smaller for reduced parasitics, higher f_T, and lower V_{beo}. However, CMOS transistors have limited power handling capability. An increased output power level can be achieved with an increase in the supply voltage of the output stage as discussed in [4, 9, 10]. To mitigate the device limitation of low V_{beo} and support a large supply voltage to increase the output power, a stacked transistor technique was proposed in [9]. However, this requires a large supply voltage and such a limitation of the CMOS transistors can be simplified by using several other design techniques.

The SiGe BiCMOS process is based on the silicon substrate with an epitaxial layer of germanium (Ge) grown to form the hetero-junction (SiGe) base region, improves the device performance, including gain, linearity, and noise characteristics, and provides an additional improvement for high-frequency designs, and easy integration with the CMOS process [3].

3.2.1 Transistor Design Consideration for RF and Millimeter-Wave Frequency Applications

To characterize the transistor behavior and verify its operation before fabrication, a model defined by equations or curve-fitting based on the device measurement data is provided by the foundries. The model is an interface between the foundry (actual hardware) and the circuit designer (electronic design automation software). The design success for a desired circuit performance depends on the accuracy of the model. At low frequencies, the model can still achieve an increased accuracy due to the reduced secondary effects and the availability of the supported measuring equipment at such low frequencies. However, the behavior of transistors at high frequencies is affected by the additional parasitics of interconnects to the external connection leads as well as due to the frequency limitation of the measuring equipment on the extracted data imposes a model approximation by frequency extrapolation [3–7].

For high frequencies, if the transistor is operated in the linear region such as for the amplifier design, one way to accurately model the transistor is to extract the S-parameters from the measurement data [4]. However, this results in a plenty of extracted S-parameter data files based on discrete transistor sizes as well as discrete bias conditions. This approach is not scalable and is modeled in discrete steps inhibiting the fine-tuning design optimization. Another approach is to use the low frequency model for the active device and extract S-parameters of the interconnects to the active device by full-wave EM simulation [10]. However, both these approaches based on S-parameters cannot be applied to large-signal nonlinear operating circuits such as voltage-controlled oscillators (VCOs) and mixers. Also, this approach does not give any perception to the designer about the device's physical properties on the secondary effects [4, 10].

After determining the transistor configuration, the transistor dimensions and its bias are selected on the basis of a few initial parameters such as f_{max}, f_T, and low noise or output power drive. To support the cascading of stages and interfacing to the external RF ports, the matching network needs to be designed to provide a better compromise between the gain, low noise, high power, and unconditional stability [4]. The input and output matching networks are designed on the basis of the S-parameter of the transistor [10] as shown in Fig. 3.3.

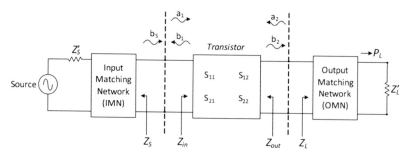

Figure 3.3 Block diagram of millimeter-wave transistor design using S-parameters.

3.3 BJT versus MOS Transistors and Hybrid Use

With the invention of semiconductor transistors, the IC industry evolved, and by device downscaling the level of integration increased over the past several decades from single transistor until system-on-chip (SoC) [5]. Transistors are the most critical design components used in RFIC and their characteristics determine functionality and performance. For utilizing them in high-frequency millimeter-wave wireless transceivers, they must be engineered to meet certain desirable characteristics, such as, providing device gain for a wide frequency range, low DC power consumption, handling wide signal levels and temperatures, and low noise. In the past, only the III–V (GaAs pHEMT) technology was used in designing such high-frequency amplifiers, as such devices were engineered to provide high performance by involving complex fabrication steps and eventually resulted in a higher fabrication cost [3]. Recently, the CMOS process has evolved as a contender for high-frequency amplifier designs although with limitations due to the device physics [5–7]. As a contemporary technology, the SiGe BiCMOS process consisting of both the devices, namely the SiGe HBT (to support high power) and MOS devices (for high-density digital integration), can meet the high-frequency performance requirements of micro-wave and millimeter-wave applications [3].

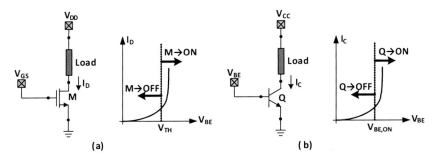

Figure 3.4 Transistor transfer characteristics: (a) MOS and (b) BJT.

MOS transistors [5–8] have performance advantages such as compact size, large dynamic range with low power consumption, and transconductance with square law characteristics [11] as shown in Fig. 3.4a and given by

$$g_{m,CMOS} = \frac{\delta I_D}{\delta V_{GS}} = \sqrt{2\beta I_D},$$ (3.2)

where I_D is the drain current, V_{GS} gate to source voltage, and β MOS transistor parameter.

Bipolar transistors have exponential transconductance characteristics based on the bias voltage (V_{BE}) and have linear transconductance characteristics based on the bias current (I_{CT}) [12], as shown in Fig. 3.4b and given by

$$g_{m,BJT} = \frac{\delta I_{CT}}{\delta V_{be}} = \frac{I_0 \cdot e^{\left(\frac{V_{be}}{\eta \cdot V_T}\right)}}{\eta \cdot V_T} = \frac{I_{CT}}{\eta \cdot V_T}.$$ (3.3)

The bias voltage in the BJT cannot be precisely controlled, but the bias current using current mirrors can be controlled precisely. BJTs are predominantly used for amplification and linearity and MOS devices are mainly used as current mirrors to precisely control the current.

One way to replace the bulky (large area occupying) passives in a small footprint as well as with a reconfigurable option is to implement them by using active devices [11, 12] such as a varistor (variable resistor), a varactor (variable capacitor), and an active inductor. However, this is accompanied by the trade-off of an increased noise and bias-dependent (linearity) performance.

References

1. Sze, S. M. (1998) *Physics of Semiconductor Devices*, 2nd ed. (John Wiley & Sons, Inc., USA).

2. Gray, P. R., Hurst, P. J., Lewis, S. H., and Meyer, R. G. (2009). *Analysis and Design of Analog Integrated Circuits*, 5th ed. (John Wiley & Sons, Inc., USA).

3. Cressler, J. D. (1998). SiGe HBT technology: A new contender for Si-based RF and microwave circuit applications, *IEEE Trans. Microw. Theory Tech., TMTT*, vol. 46, no. 5, pp. 572–589.

4. Gonzalez, G. (1997). *Microwave Transistor Amplifiers: Analysis and Design*, 2nd ed. (Prentice-Hall, USA).

5. http://www.itrs.net/.

6. Lee, T. H. (1998). *The Design of CMOS Radio Frequency Integrated Circuits*. (Cambridge Univ. Press, UK).

7. Razavi, B. (1998). *RF Microelectronics*, 1st ed. (Prentice-Hall, USA).

8. Baker, R. J. (2010). *CMOS Circuit Design, Layout, and Simulation*, 3rd ed. (IEEE Press Series on Microelectronic Systems and John Wiley & Sons, Inc., USA).

9. Chen, J.-H., Helmi, S. R., and Mohammadi, S. (2013). A fully-integrated Ka-band stacked power amplifier in 45 nm CMOS SOI technology, *Proc. IEEE Topical Meet. Silicon Monolithic Integr. Circuits RF Syst., SiRF*, pp. 75–77.

10. Pozar, D. M. (2012). *Microwave Engineering*, 4th ed. (John Wiley & Sons, Inc., USA).

11. Kumar, T. B., Ma, K., and Yeo, K. S. (2015). A 4 GHz 60 dB variable gain amplifier with tunable dc offset cancellation in 65 nm CMOS, *IEEE Microw. Wireless Compon. Lett., MWCL*, vol. 25, no. 1, pp. 37–39.

12. Kumar, T. B., Ma, K., Yeo, K. S., and Yang, W. (2014). A 35-mW 30-dB gain control range current mode linear-in-decibel programmable gain amplifier with bandwidth enhancement, *IEEE Trans. Microw. Theory Tech., TMTT*, vol. 62, no. 12, pp. 3465–3475.

The 21st century STEM education:
Skill, Training, Experience, and Mindset.

—Kiat Seng Yeo and Kaixue Ma

Chapter 4

Passive Elements

Yongqiang Wang,[a] **Kaixue Ma,**[a] **and Kiat Seng Yeo**[b]

[a]*School of Physical Electronics,*
University of Electronic Science and Technology of China,
#4 Section II, Jianshe North Road, Chengdu 610054, P. R. China
[b]*Engineering Product Development, Singapore University of Technology and Design,*
8 Somapah Road, Singapore 487372

makaixue@uestc.edu.cn; kiatseng_yeo@sutd.edu.sg

This chapter describes passive elements, including the resistor, capacitor, inductor, transformer, interconnects, and transmission lines, which are widely used in the integrated circuits especially used in the radio frequency integrated circuit (RFIC) and millimeter-wave integrated circuits. These passive elements, especially at higher frequency in RF and millimeter-wave range, are different from what we understand about the general elements. The reason is that at a higher frequency range, these passive elements have lots of the high-frequency parasitic effects and a simple typical model cannot describe the response behaviors at high frequency. Hence, this chapter will present these passive elements with consideration

Low-Power Wireless Communication Circuits and Systems: 60 GHz and Beyond
Edited by Kaixue Ma and Kiat Seng Yeo
Copyright © 2018 Pan Stanford Publishing Pte. Ltd.
ISBN 978-981-4745-96-3 (Hardcover), 978-1-315-15653-8 (eBook)
www.panstanford.com

of the high-frequency parasitic effects for RF and millimeter-wave applications.

4.1 Introduction

For the RF and millimeter-wave circuits design, it is crucial to design the circuit in full consideration of the circuit matching at the higher frequency range, as the active devices such as the diode and the transistor have the look-in impedance different from the system impedances, e.g., 50, 75, or 100 ohm under differential drive. Thus, the passive elements such as the resistor, capacitor, inductor, transformer, and transmission lines are required for the purpose of matching the active devices. Moreover, these passive elements are also required for the circuit bias and the spectrum filtering of the noise, etc. For example, if the wideband bias circuit, which covers a multiple-octave bandwidth, is needed, the circuit may leak the RF power at a higher frequency but block RF at a low–frequency range. To make good use of passive elements at the RF and millimeter-wave range, it is important to have a better understanding of the RF and millimeter-wave behaviors of these parts with full consideration of the frequency-dependent characteristics. We will illustrate these considerations according to different passive elements.

4.2 Resistor

The resistors in monolithic microwave integrated circuit (MMIC) and RFIC can be produced by using deposited thin metal films in doped regions of the semiconductor substrate, or multilayer polysilicon in silicon RF integrated circuit. The schematic of a generic resistor is shown in Fig. 4.1.

The resistance can be given by

$$R = R_M \frac{s}{W} + 2R_T,\tag{4.1}$$

where R_M is the sheet resistance of the metal film or doped semiconductor region, s is the separation between ohmic contacts,

W is the width of the resistor and R_T is the resistance of the contact at the end of the structure.

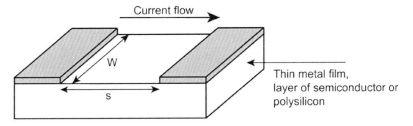

Figure 4.1 Schematic of a generic resistor.

Most poly is silicided specifically to reduce resistance. As the resistivity tends to be about 5 to 10 ohms per square, poly is mainly applicable for moderately small-valued resistors. Poly resistors have poor tolerance (e.g., 35%), low temperature coefficient (TC), low parasitic capacitance, and lowest voltage coefficient in a standard CMOS technology.

Resistors can also be made from source-drain diffusion. The resistivities and TC are typically within twice those of silicided polysilicon. It has a lower TC with heavier doping, but the parasitic capacitance and voltage coefficient are significant. Forward-biasing should be avoided at the either end of the resistor. Therefore, the diffused resistors are usually limited to use in noncritical circuits.

Wells can provide high resistance in the range of 1–10 kΩ. However, the large-area junction formed between the well and the substrate will lead to large parasitic parasitic capacitance, and the resistor has poor initial tolerance (±50–80%) and large TC and voltage coefficient.

Excellent resistors, such as those made of NiCr or SiCr, which have low TC and absolute accuracies better than 1%, are made by a few companies. However, the additional process steps increase the cost significantly. The resistor in an IC chip has the highest tolerance compared with the other parts. The tolerance can be lowered by replacing a resistor with a combination of resistors with higher resistance.

4.3 Capacitor

4.3.1 MIM Capacitors

Metal–insulator–metal (MIM) capacitors [1] are formed by two or more parallel plates, as shown in Fig. 4.2. The capacitance of the MIM capacitor can be given by

$$C \approx \varepsilon \frac{A}{d},$$

(4.2)

where A denotes the plate area and d the dielectric thickness. The formula above is accurate only on the condition that the plate dimensions are much larger than the plate separation d. Besides, in most cases, the parasitic capacitance generated by the bottom plate and any conductor beneath it cannot be negligible. This parasitic bottom plate capacitance is usually as large as 10–30% (or more) of the main capacitance and degrades the circuit performance. Generally, the capacitance value of an MIM capacitor is low. The total capacitance per unit area can be increased by using more than one pair of interconnect layers.

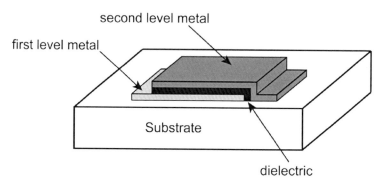

Figure 4.2 Schematic of an MIM capacitor.

4.3.2 Interdigital Capacitors

Now that the allowable space of adjacent metal traces is smaller than the spacing between layers, the capacitance generated by the adjacent traces on the same layer is substantial. Interdigital capacitors [2] comprise thin parallel conducting strips, as shown in Fig. 4.3. The value of the total capacitance can be further increased by arranging the segments of a different metal layer in a complementary pattern, as shown in Fig. 4.4. As shown in Fig. 4.4, this type of capacitor has much smaller parasitic bottom plate capacitance compared with MIM capacitors, since it occupies a smaller area for a desired total capacitance. Besides, the adjacent plates make the flux away from the substrates, and the parasitic capacitance becomes smaller.

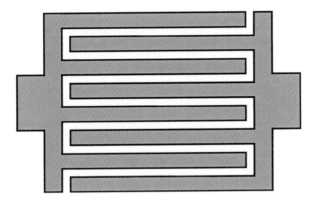

Figure 4.3 Configuration of a typical interdigital capacitor (top view).

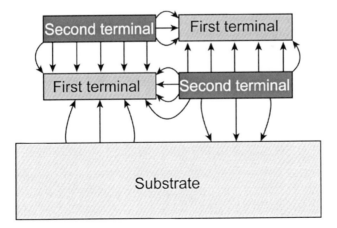

Figure 4.4 Development of the interdigital capacitor with complementary patterns.

4.4 Inductor

Inductors in an IC die are typically implemented in the spiral form, as shown in Fig. 4.5. Spirals have a higher inductance than a straight line because of the manual coupling between every two turns, especially between adjacent turns. Octagonal or circular spirals are moderately better than squares and they are preferred if the layout tools permit their use. A typical model [3] of the spiral inductor is given in Fig. 4.6. This model is accurate for a bandwidth of about ±20% around the center frequency.

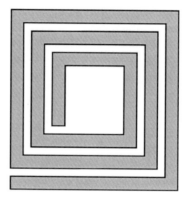

Figure 4.5 Configuration of a spiral inductor.

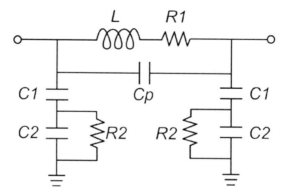

Figure 4.6 Model of the spiral inductor.

The spiral inductor is usually implemented on the top metal layer to reduce the series resistor and parasitic capacitance.

The value of the inductor can be increased by increasing the number of turns, decreasing spacing between adjunct turns, decreasing the width of the traces, and increasing the length of turns. Due to the skin effect, the current distribution is inhomogeneous at high frequencies. The reduction of the effective cross section will increase the series resistance. Additionally, when the substrate is close to the spiral inductors, the capacitance to the substrate will limit the resonant frequency. And the Q of the inductor is often degraded since the energy is coupled to the lossy substrate. There are trade-offs in the inductor design, especially those between quality factor and the capacitance, or between the inductance and the dimensions.

Usually, inductors occupy a large area, which leads to a large chip size and long interconnects traveling from one block to another. This issue can be resolved by using stacking spirals. Stacking spirals are implemented by placing two or more spirals vertically, thus obtaining a higher inductance not only due to the series connection but also as a result of strong mutual coupling. Differential inductors (driven by differential signals) have a higher Q and smaller size when compared with conventional spiral inductors, as shown in Fig. 4.7.

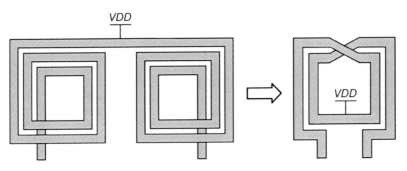

Figure 4.7 Use of a differential inductor in a differential circuit.

4.5 Transformer

An ideal transformer model is shown in Fig. 4.8. N is the secondary-to-primary turn ratio. The current and voltage transformations are related to the turn ratio by the following equation:

$$N = \frac{v_2}{v_1} = \frac{i_1}{i_2} = \sqrt{\frac{L_2}{L_1}},$$ (4.3)

where L_1 and L_2 are the self-inductance of the primary and secondary winding, respectively. The ideal transformer is based on the condition that the all of the magnetic flux produced by the primary couples to the secondary. However, not all the transformers are designed to be perfect coupling, and then, the coupling coefficient is introduced as

$$K = \frac{M}{\sqrt{L_1 L_2}},$$ (4.4)

where M is the mutual inductance that models the coupling degree between the primary and secondary. If the primary and secondary inductors are close enough, nearly all of the flux from one inductor will couple to the other, and M will be close to 1, which is the ideal case. If they are far from each other, M will be very small. For passive transformers, M is always smaller than 1. For transformers on chip, the available coupling coefficient can be as high as 0.9 [4].

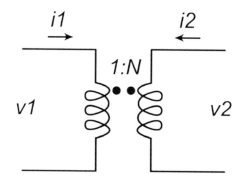

Figure 4.8 An ideal 1:N transformer.

Figure 4.9 shows some common configurations of monolithic transformers [5]. For the concentric spiral transformer in Fig. 4.9a, the mutual coupling between adjacent conductors contributes mainly to the self-inductance of the each winding and not to mutual inductance between the two windings. This type of transformer has higher self-inductance, less mutual inductance and smaller coupling coefficient than the configurations of Fig. 4.9b,c. The parallel conductor winding in Fig. 4.9b has inherent symmetry which ensures that the electrical characteristics of primary and secondary are identical. Stacked transformers shown in Fig. 4.9c have a relatively high coupling coefficient. Although the winding shown in the figure are identical, asymmetry still exists as the conductors are implemented on different metal layers. The parallel-plate capacitance between the winding on different layers is large, which may limit the frequency response. However, this can be reduced by offsetting the upper and lower metal layers by some distance.

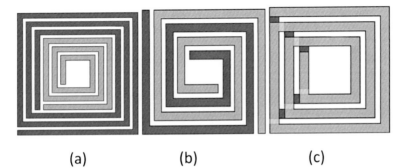

(a) (b) (c)

Figure 4.9 Configuration of monolithic transformers. (a) Concentric spiral winding. (b) Parallel conductor winding. (c) Stacked spiral winding.

4.6 Interconnects

In the IC design, we need interconnects to connect different blocks with each other, and the ideal interconnect should be a wire. However, the actual interconnect has specific width and length, which will introduce undesired parasitic capacitance and inductance. Besides, due to the lossy silicon substrate, the attenuation of the interconnect at high frequencies is inevitable. The modeling [6, 7] of interconnect lines, including crossovers and vias, has been reported for a better understanding of their properties.

4.7   Transmission Lines

In the IC fabrication technology, planar transmission lines, including microstrip lines and the coplanar waveguide (CPW), are usually utilized [8, 9]. Generally, compared with the conventional CPW, microstrip lines have a higher effective inductance per unit length and more flexibility in connection. Besides, the ground plane under the mircorstrip can shield the signal paths from the lossy substrate. However, in practice, an on-chip ground reference usually suffers some voltage variation because of parasitics from circuit and package interconnections. The CPW can help reduce the energy coupling into the troublesome substrate, thanks to the edge-coupled nature of the CPW. Moreover, floating shield can be introduced to implement a good approximation of an ideal ground on an MMIC. Additionally, slow-wave CPWs [10, 11] are reported to obtain a better performance of transmission lines on chip.

References

1. G. Bartolucci, F. Giannini, E. Limiti, and S. P. Marsh (1995). MIM capacitor modeling: a planar approach, *IEEE Trans. Microw. Theory Tech.*, vol. 43, no. 4, pp. 901–903.

2. G. D. Alley (1970). Interdigital capacitors and their application to lumped-element microwave integrated circuits, *IEEE Trans. Microw. Theory Tech.*, vol. 18, no. 12, pp. 1028–1033.

3. C. P. Yue and S. S. Wong (2000). Physical modeling of spiral inductors on silicon, *IEEE Trans. Electron Devices*, vol. 47, no. 3, pp. 560–568.

4. J. R. Long (2000). Monolithic transformers for silicon RF IC design, *IEEE J. Solid-State Circuits*, vol. 35, no. 9, pp. 1368–1382.

5. S. S. Mohan, C. P. Yue, M. del M. Hershenson, S. S. Wong, and T. H. Lee (1998). Modeling and characterization of on-chip transformers, *IEEE IEDM*, pp. 531–534.

6. S.-P. Sim, S. Krishnan, D. M. Petranovic, N. D. Arora, K. Lee, and C. Y. Yang (2003). A unified RLC model for high-speed on-chip interconnects, *IEEE Trans. Electron Devices*, vol. 50, no. 6, pp. 1501–1510.

7. H. H. M. Ghouz and E. B. El-Sharawy (1996). An accurate equivalent circuit model of flip chip and via interconnects, *IEEE Trans. Microw. Theory Tech.*, vol. 44, no. 12, pp. 2543–2554.

8. A. C. Reyes, S. M. El-Ghazaly, S. J. Dorn, M. Dydyk, D. K. Schroder, and H. Patterson, Coplanar waveguides and microwave inductors on silicon substrates, *IEEE Trans. Microw. Theory Tech.*, vol. 43, no. 9, pp. 2016–2022.

9. C. L. Ko, C. N. Kuo, and Y. Z. Juang (1995). on-chip transmission line modeling and applications to millimeter-wave circuit design in 0.13 um CMOS technology, in *International Symposium on VLSI-DAT*, pp. 1–4.

10. T. S. D. Cheung and J. R. Long (2006). Shielded passive devices for silicon-based monolithic microwave and millimeter-wave integrated circuits, *IEEE J. Solid-State Circuits*, vol. 41, no. 5, pp. 1183–1200.

11. I. C. H. Lai, Y. Kambayashi, and M. Fujishima (2006). 60-GHz CMOS down-conversion mixer with slow-wave matching transmission lines, *IEEE ASSCC*, pp. 195–198.

When you are determined to go further, there is no end to what you can do.

—Kiat Seng Yeo and Kaixue Ma

Chapter 5

Variable Gain Amplifier

Bharatha Kumar Thangarasu,[a] Kaixue Ma,[b] and Kiat Seng Yeo[a]

[a]*Engineering Product Development, Singapore University of Technology and Design,
8 Somapah Road, Singapore 487372*
[b]*School of Physical Electronics,
University of Electronic Science and Technology of China,
#4 Section II, Jianshe North Road, Chengdu 610054, P. R. China*

bharatha_kumar@sutd.edu.sg, makaixue@uestc.edu.cn

This chapter describes the variable gain amplifier (VGA) used in the radio frequency integrated circuit (RFIC) transceiver. The VGA is a key RF frontend building block that supports reliable mobile communication of wireless transceivers. The range of the VGA gain control also determines the receiver input dynamic range that provides a stable regulated power to the baseband chipset. The recent RFIC design focuses on high-data-rate communication in the gigabit per second (Gbps) range [1]. Hence, the VGA that interfaces with the baseband may need to support wide bandwidth. As the state of the art improves, the supported applications as

Low-Power Wireless Communication Circuits and Systems: 60 GHz and Beyond
Edited by Kaixue Ma and Kiat Seng Yeo
Copyright © 2018 Pan Stanford Publishing Pte. Ltd.
ISBN 978-981-4745-96-3 (Hardcover), 978-1-315-15653-8 (eBook)
www.panstanford.com

well as the design density for the system integration of the RF transceivers also gradually move toward system-on-chip (SoC) solutions.

5.1 Introduction

A VGA is an amplifier that provides variable gain based on the external control signal as shown in Fig. 5.1a. The typical frequency response of an amplifier is shown in Fig. 5.1b, which is characterized by its gain (A), bandwidth (BW), and center frequency (fc). For the VGA to be integrated in a compact transceiver system, it is desirable to have enhanced features which are independent of a stable gain control such as low dc power consumption, wide bandwidth, small die area, impedance matching at input and output ports, less sensitive to process-voltage-temperature (PVT) variations, high linearity performance for both RF signal input and gain control input, good gain-flatness across a wide frequency range, and easy interface to digital baseband.

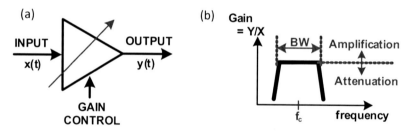

Figure 5.1 (a) VGA (b) frequency response.

5.2 VGA Design Analysis

The gain expression of a typical amplifier shown in Fig. 5.2 is given by

$$A_V = \frac{g_m \cdot R_{LOAD}}{(1 + g_m \cdot R_{DEGEN})},$$

$$(5.1)$$

where, g_m is the transconductance of the amplifying transistor determined by the bias condition and the transistor aspect ratio, R_{LOAD} is the load resistance, and R_{DEGEN} is the degeneration resistance.

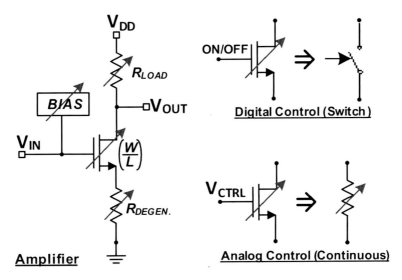

Figure 5.2 Typical amplifier topology to support variable gain.

The gain control can be achieved by either discrete steps (digital variable gain amplifier (DVGA) or programmable gain amplifier (PGA)) or by continuous gain variation (VGA). One or more of the amplifier design parameters can be changed using controllable switches that can select or fine tune either the load resistance, biasing voltage, biasing current, and degeneration resistance or the transistor size to reflect in gain variation. Additionally, this gain variation may also influence other amplifier performance parameters. Similarly, along with the amplification control, even variable attenuation control can be achieved in the same design. In an analog VGA, the digital baseband requires an additional digital-to-analog converter (DAC) to control the gain variation that eventually increases circuit complexity. In comparison, the DVGA can be directly interfaced with the digital baseband without the need for a DAC.

A DVGA can be implemented at circuit level by switching between fixed gain amplifier stages [2] or by using a binary weighted array of passive or active circuit components selected discretely using transistor switches [3–5]. The switching gain stage DVGA consumes a large die area due to circuit duplication, while the DVGA with switching circuit components is compact and also provides small gain control linearity errors.

5.2.1 dB-Linearity

Practically, gain is expressed in decibel (dB) scale, which has a logarithmic equation defined as

$$A_v\big|_{dB} = 20 \cdot \log_{10}(A_v) = 20 \cdot \log_{10}\left[\frac{g_m \cdot R_{LOAD}}{(1 + g_m \cdot R_{DEGEN})}\right]. \qquad (5.2)$$

By design, we can achieve $g_m \cdot R_{DEGEN} \ll 1$, R_{LOAD} as constant and g_m as an exponential function of a parameter such as "x." Then the gain in dB, $\log_{10}(g_m \cdot R_{LOAD})$ will become directly proportional to the exponential parameter (x). This property of gain control is called linear-in-decibel or dB-linearity.

Although the state-of-the-art VGA designed in the CMOS process [6–15] has a few advantages, such as large dynamic range with low power consumption, it also possesses the transconductance [12] with square law characteristics as

$$g_{m,CMOS} = \frac{\delta I_D}{\delta V_{GS}} = \sqrt{2\beta I_D}, \qquad (5.3)$$

where, I_D is the drain current and V_{GS} is gate to source voltage, with β as the MOS transistor parameter.

A CMOS-based VGA design demonstrating a linear gain control variation without dB-linearity, yet achieving a large gain control range and wide bandwidth performance is illustrated as example in this chapter [17]. To achieve dB-linear gain variation, the CMOS DVGA requires additional pseudo-exponential conversion circuits.

The DVGA implemented by using bipolar transistors have exponential transconductance characteristic based on the bias voltage (V_{BE}) and have a linear transconductance characteristic based on the bias current (I_{CT}) as

$$g_{m,BJT} = \frac{\delta I_{CT}}{\delta V_{be}} = \frac{I_0 \cdot e^{\left(\frac{V_{be}}{\eta \cdot V_T}\right)}}{\eta \cdot V_T} = \frac{I_{CT}}{\eta \cdot V_T}. \tag{5.4}$$

The bias voltage in BJT cannot be precisely controlled but the bias current using current mirrors can be controlled precisely. Hence, we need an exponential current conversion to achieve a precise dB-linear gain control design by varying the bias current using digital switches.

$$I_{CT} \propto e^{(I_{CTRL} \times K)} \tag{5.5}$$

Therefore, the BJT transconductance characteristic provides a dB-linear variation as

$$A_V\big|_{dB} \propto I_{CTRL} \cdot K. \tag{5.6}$$

5.2.2   DC Offset Cancellation

DC offsets are caused mainly by the mismatch in the differential pair and such DC offsets are amplified by the high-gain amplifiers that eventually saturate the baseband stages. This results in signal distortion and increases received data errors. To mitigate the effects of the DC offset, a DC offset cancellation (DCOC) circuit has to be incorporated in the VGA design. The two possible solutions of implementing DCOC are as follows:

(1) Filtering the DC component (feed-forward HPF) by placing a high pass filter with a cut-off frequency close to DC and a sharp roll-off to suppress the DC component as shown in Fig. 5.3.

(2) Cancel the DC component (feedback LPF) by extracting the DC offset using a low pass filter with a cut-off frequency close to DC and a sharp roll-off in the feedback path to subtract with the input signal will cancel the input DC component and contribute in the DCOC as shown in Fig. 5.4. However, such LPF DCOC has higher path loss due to large RC component values to provide small cut-off frequency and hence requires additional amplifiers to significantly cancel the DC offsets.

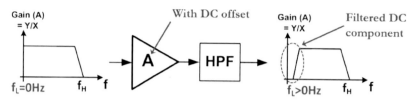

Figure 5.3 Feed-forward DCOC using HPF.

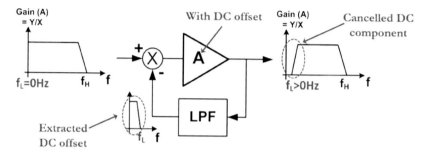

Figure 5.4 Feed-back DCOC using LPF.

5.3 Variable Gain Amplifier Examples

In this section, two VGA design examples are presented: (1) one using the bipolar SiGe HBT technology and (2) the other using a 65 nm CMOS process. The various techniques described in this chapter are incorporated in these designs to illustrate on the benefits and trade-offs.

5.3.1 VGA1: Based on 0.18 μm SiGe BiCMOS Programmable Gain Amplifier Design

The block diagram of the proposed PGA is shown in Fig. 5.5. The PGA consists of a fully differential three-stage cascaded topology consisting of two identical DVGA core stages, a post amplifier stage and RC interconnect networks with a symmetric RF signal path. Each of the DVGA core stage amplifier is a 6-bit dB-linear low-power digitally controlled –11 to +8 dB DVGA with on-chip HPF DCOC. The corresponding gain control bits B5~B0 in both the DVGA core stages are shorted in pairs to provide an overall 6-bit programmable gain control for the PGA. The post amplifier design is based on the similar topology as DVGA core and provides a +16 dB fixed gain with DCOC capability.

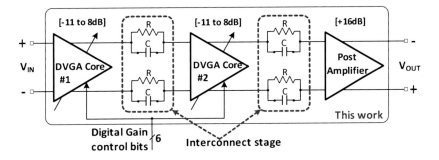

Figure 5.5 Block diagram of the proposed PGA [16], © IEEE 2014.

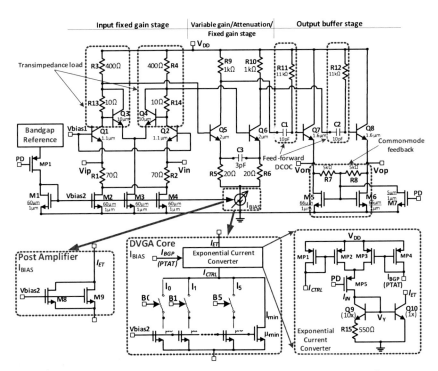

Figure 5.6 Circuit schematic of proposed PGA (DVGA core and post amplifier) [16], © IEEE 2014.

The detailed circuit schematic of the VGA1 along with the circuit for the DVGA core and post amplifier is shown in Fig. 5.6. The amplifier stages are biased by using current mirrors from a bandgap reference. The input stage is a common-base topology with the transimpedance load used as the linearizer and the buffer stage has a feed-forward HPF DCOC located between the main amplifier and the output buffer. The exponential current converter block generates exponential gain control current from the linear binary current converter. The post amplifier has the same topology as the DVGA core with the exception of the fixed current bias of VGA core.

The die microphotographs of the PGA building blocks are shown in the Fig. 5.7. The measurement plots of the overall PGA are shown in Figs. 5.8–5.10. The performance parameters for each of the DVGA core and the post amplifier stages against the estimated and the actual PGA are tabulated in Table 5.1. The main advantage of this design is the improved gain bandwidth product which is shown in the enhanced bandwidth with almost same gain as the estimated result.

Table 5.1 Measured performance of PGA, DVGA core and post amplifier, [16] © IEEE 2014

Parameter	DVGA core	Post amplifier	PGA (Actual)	PGA (Estimated)
Gain range (dB)	−10 to 7.8	+16	−1.4 to 30.2	−4 to 31.6
3-dB Bandwidth (Hz)	2M to 1.9G	2M to 2.4G	3M to 1.7G	2M to 0.97G*
DC power (mW)	12.2	9.9	35.3	34.3
Input P_{1dB} (dBm)	−12.5 to −11	−22	−9 to −36	−8.5 to −38.5
Output P_{1dB} (dBm)	−22.4 to −5.8	−7.1	−10 to −7.5	−7.5
Gain control	6-bit	Fixed	6-bit	12-bit
Power down (μA)	310	308	915	926
Core die area (mm²)	0.048	0.03	0.25**	0.126

*$\omega_T = \omega_0 \cdot \sqrt{2^{1/n} - 1} = 1.9 \times 10^9 \cdot \sqrt{2^{1/3} - 1} = 0.97$ GHz.

**Area increased due to parallel RC interstage network.

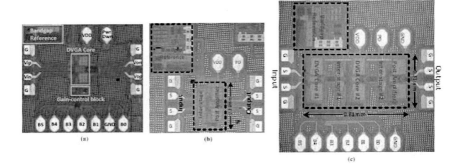

Figure 5.7 Die microphotograph of (a) DVGA core, (b) post amplifier, and (c) PGA [16], © IEEE 2014.

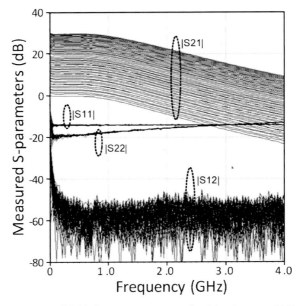

Figure 5.8 Measured PGA *S*-parameters over the 64 gain steps [16], © IEEE 2014.

The estimated values of the PGA in Table 5.1 are determined as follows:

- PGA gain = DVGA core gain × 2 + Post amplifier gain
  For minimum gain condition, PGA gain = −10 × 2 + 16 = −4 dB
  For maximum gain condition, PGA gain = +7.8 × 2 + 16 = 31.6 dB

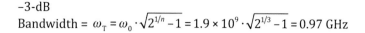

$$\text{Bandwidth} = \omega_T = \omega_0 \cdot \sqrt{2^{1/n} - 1} = 1.9 \times 10^9 \cdot \sqrt{2^{1/3} - 1} = 0.97 \text{ GHz}$$

with the -3-dB label preceding it.

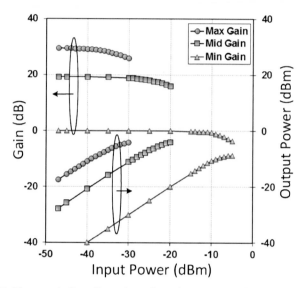

Figure 5.9 Measured P_{1dB} linearity plots for max, mid and min PGA gain at 1 GHz [16], © IEEE 2014.

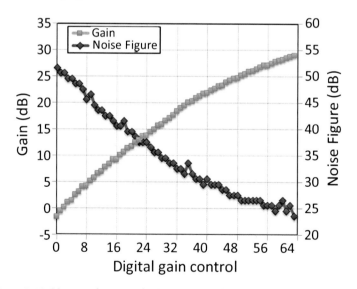

Figure 5.10 Measured gain and NF at 1 GHz of proposed PGA [16], © IEEE 2014.

- DC power consumption = 12.2 × 2 + 9.86 = 34.26 mW
- Input P_{1dB} (IP_{1dB}) = Output P_{1dB} – PGA gain
  For minimum gain condition, IP_{1dB} = –12.5 – (–4) = –8.5 dBm
  (due to saturation of both DVGA core + post amplifier)
  For maximum gain condition, IP_{1dB} = –7.1 – (31.6) = –38.7
  dBm (due to saturation of only post amplifier)
- Output P_{1dB} = Output P_{1dB} (post amplifier)
- Gain control = DVGA core × 2 = 6 × 2 = 12 bits
- Power down current = 310 × 2 + 308 = 928 μA
- Core die area = 0.048 × 2 + 0.03 = 0.126 mm^2

5.3.2 VGA2: Based on 65 nm CMOS Variable Gain Amplifier Design

The second VGA example is based on a 65 nm CMOS process as shown in Fig. 5.11. The corresponding circuit implementation of the four sub-blocks, namely, input buffer, four-stage VGA core, output buffer, and programmable DCOC, is shown in Fig. 5.12.

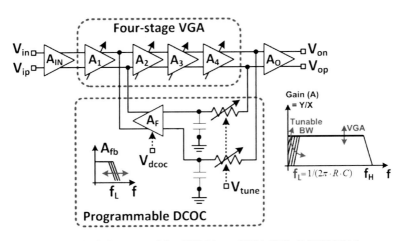

Figure 5.11 Block diagram of the CMOS based VGA [17], © IEEE 2015.

The proposed VGA has a tunable DCOC to lower the cutoff frequency based on varying the resistance of the feedback LPF implemented by using PMOS transistor operating in triode region. The triode operating PMOS transistor's channel resistance is given as

$$R_{ch} \cong \left[\mu_p \cdot C_{ox} \cdot \left(\frac{W}{L}\right)_P \cdot \left(V_{DD} - V_{tune} - |V_{THP}|\right) \right]^{-1},$$ (5.7)

where μ_p, C_{ox}, $(W/L)_p$, and V_{THP} are the electron mobility, gate oxide capacitance per unit area, aspect ratio, and threshold voltage of the LPF PMOS transistors.

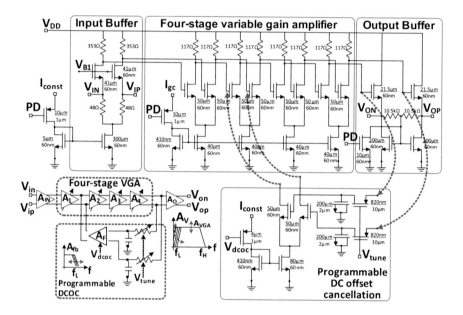

Figure 5.12 Circuit schematic of the CMOS based VGA [17], © IEEE 2015.

To maintain or achieve a low DC power consumption, the design is biased using NMOS current sinks mirrored from the stable current sources (Iconst and Igc) that limits the rail-to-rail DC current of the overall design. The input stage is a common-gate topology to provide fixed gain biased by Iconst (≈ 50 μA) and a wideband input impedance matching which are independent of the VGA gain. The VGA core comprises a four-stage common-source topology with a resistive load to provide a wideband gain flatness. The output buffer is a common-drain topology with common mode feedback circuit providing a stable output common mode voltage and a good output impedance matching.

The VGA2 is fabricated in a GLOBALFOUNDRIES 65 nm CMOS process, and the die microphotograph is shown in Fig. 5.13. The VGA has a compact die area of 75 µm × 80 µm (excluding the measurement pads).

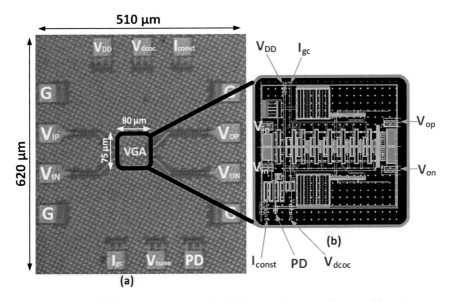

Figure 5.13 (a) Die microphotograph (b) Layout of core CMOS variable gain amplifier [17], © IEEE 2015.

The measured data of VGA2 is obtained by on-wafer probing with the Agilent E8364B network analyzer (PNA) and HP 8970B noise figure (NF) meter by using differential calibration until the RF probe tips. The measured S-parameters are shown in Figs. 5.14 and 5.15 by varying I_{gc} from 3 to 150 µA. The gain control as shown in Fig. 5.14 is not dB-linear. The tunable DCOC in the design example is achieved by controlling the VGA's lower cutoff frequency using the V_{tune} voltage from 0 to 1.2 V as shown in Fig. 5.16. The monotonous not-dB-linear trend of the measured gain and NF against I_{gc} is shown in Fig. 5.17.

Table 5.2 Measured performance of the CMOS VGA [16] ©IEEE 2015

Parameter	Units	This work [16]
Technology	—	65 nm CMOS
Gain range	(dB)	–39.4 to 20.2
–3dB Bandwidth	(Hz)	(0~0.2M) to 4G
Noise Figure	(dB)	10 to 27
Input P_{1dB}	(dBm)	–17 to –30
Core area	(μm^2)	75 × 80
DC power consumption	(mW)	26
On-chip DCOC	—	Yes
Tunable DCOC	(Hz)	Yes (0 to 0.2M)
Gain control mode	—	Analog current

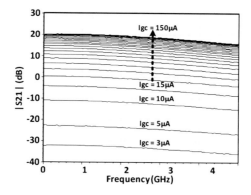

Figure 5.14 Measured VGA gain (I_{gc} = 3 to 150 μA, step = 5 μA) [17], © IEEE 2015.

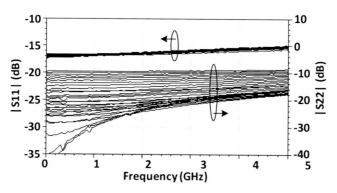

Figure 5.15 Measured VGA input/output return loss (I_{gc} = 3 μA to 150 μA, step = 5 μA) [17], © IEEE 2015.

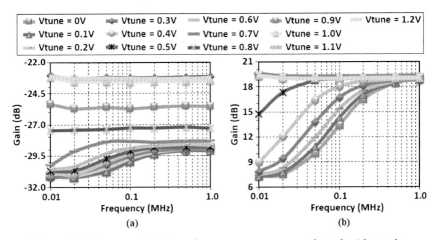

Figure 5.16 Measured VGA low frequency response with and without the DCOC (V_{dcc} = 0 V and V_{tune} = 0 to 1.2 V, step = 0.1 V). (a) Minimum gain with I_{gc} = 3 µA and (b) maximum gain with I_{gc} = 150 µA [17], © IEEE 2015.

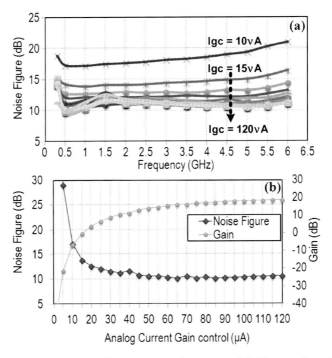

Figure 5.17 (a) Measured NF against frequency (b) Measured variable gain and NF at 1 GHz for I_{gc} = 5 µA to 120 µA, step = 5 µA [17], © IEEE 2015.

The measured results of the VGA2 are summarized in Table 5.2. The proposed CMOS VGA has a better bandwidth, compact die area, and tunable DCOC while simultaneously achieving comparable gain range and DC power consumption.

Acknowledgments

The authors would like to thank Tower Jazz Semiconductors for providing the fabrication service of the design in 0.18 μm SiGe BiCMOS and GLOBALFOUNDRIES in the 65 nm CMOS process. The authors would also like to thank W. Yang of Nanyang Technological University (NTU), Singapore, for assisting in the on-wafer measurement of the proposed design.

References

1. Ma, K., Mou, S., Mahalingam, N., Wang, Y., Kumar, T. B., Yan, J., et. al. (2014). An integrated 60 GHz low power two-chip wireless system based on IEEE 802.11ad standard, *IEEE MTT-S Int. Microwav. Symp. Dig., IMS*, FL, pp. 1–4.

2. Otaka, S., Tanimoto, H., Watanabe, S., and Maeda, T. (2002). A 1.9–GHz Si–bipolar variable attenuator for PHS transmitter, *IEEE J. Solid-State Circuits, JSSC*, vol. 32, no. 9, pp. 1424–1429.

3. Teo, T. H., and Yeoh, W. G. (2007). Low-power digitally controlled CMOS source follower variable attenuator, *IEEE Int. Symp. Circuits Syst., ISCS*, New Orleans, LA, pp. 229–232.

4. Meghdadi, M., Bakhtiar, M. S., and Medi, A. (2009). A UHF variable gain amplifier for direct-conversion DVB-H receivers, *IEEE Radio Frequency Integrated Circuits Symp., RFIC*, Boston, pp. 551–554.

5. Im, D., Kim, H.-T., and Lee, K. (2009). A CMOS resistive feedback differential low-noise amplifier with enhanced loop gain for digital TV tuner applications, *IEEE Trans. Microw. Theory Tech., TMTT*, vol. 57, no. 11, pp. 2633–2642.

6. Wang, I. H., and Liu, S. I. (2008). A 0.18-μm CMOS 1.25-Gbps automatic gain-control amplifier, *IEEE Trans. Circuits Syst. II, Exp. Briefs, TCAS-II*, vol. 55, no. 2, pp. 136–140.

7. Tadjpour, S., Behbahani, F., and Abidi, A. A. (2002). A CMOS variable gain amplifier for a wideband wireless receiver, *VLSI Circuits Symp. Tech. Dig., VLSI*, Honolulu, HI, pp. 86–89.

8. Wu, C.-H., Liu, C.-S., and Liu, S.-I. (2004). A 2 GHz CMOS variable-gain amplifier with 50 dB linear-in-magnitude controlled gain range for 10 Gbase-LX4 ethernet, *IEEE Int. Solid-State Circuits Conf. Tech. Dig., ISSCC*, pp. 484–541.

9. Byrne, N., Murphy, P. J., McCarthy, K. G., and Foley, B. (2005). A SiGe HBT variable gain amplifier with 80 dB control range for applications up to 3 GHz, *7th Eur. Wireless Technol. Conf., EWTC*, Amsterdam, Netherlands, pp. 193–196.

10. Wang, Y., Afshar, B., Ye, L., Gaudet, V. C., and Niknejad, A. M. (2012). Design of a low power, inductorless wideband variable-gain amplifier for high speed receiver systems, *IEEE Trans. Circuits Syst. I, Reg. Papers, TCAS-I*, vol. 59, no. 4, pp. 696–707.

11. Duong, Q.-H., Le, Q., Kim, C.-W., and Lee, S.-G. (2006). A 95-dB linear low power variable gain amplifier, *IEEE Trans. Circuits Syst. I, Reg. Papers, TCAS-I*, vol. 53, no. 8, pp. 1648–1657.

12. Lee, H. D., Lee, K. A., and Hong, S. (2007). A wideband CMOS variable gain amplifier with an exponential gain control, *IEEE Trans. Microw. Theory Tech., TMTT*, vol. 55, no. 6, pp. 1363–1373.

13. Huang, Y.-Y., Woo, W., Jeon, H., Lee, C.-H., and Kenney, J. S. (2012). Compact wideband linear CMOS variable gain amplifier for analog-predistortion power amplifiers, *IEEE Trans. Microw. Theory Tech., TMTT*, vol. 60, no. 1, pp. 68–76.

14. Li, Z., Guo, F., Chen, D., Li, H., and Wang, Z. (2007). A wideband CMOS variable gain amplifier with a novel linear-in-decibel gain control structure, *IEEE Int. RFIT Workshop*, RFIT, Sentosa, Singapore, pp. 337–340.

15. Teo, T. H., and Yeoh, W. G. (2007). Low-power digitally controlled CMOS source follower variable attenuator, *IEEE Int. Circuits Syst. Symp., ICSS*, New Orleans, LA, pp. 229–232.

16. Kumar, T. B., Ma, K., Yeo, K. S., and Yang, W. (2014). A 35-mW 30-dB gain control range current mode linear-in-decibel programmable gain amplifier with bandwidth enhancement, *IEEE Trans. Microw. Theory Tech., TMTT*, vol. 62, no. 12, pp. 3465–3475.

17. Kumar, T. B., Ma, K., and Yeo, K. S. (2015). A 4 GHz 60 dB variable gain amplifier with tunable dc offset cancellation in 65 nm CMOS, *IEEE Microw. Wireless Compon. Lett., MWCL*, vol. 25, no. 1, pp. 37–39.

When you don't know, ask "Why?" But when you know, say "Why not?"

—Kiat Seng Yeo and Kaixue Ma

Chapter 6

Power Amplifier

Bharatha Kumar Thangarasu,[a] Kaixue Ma,[b] and Kiat Seng Yeo[a]

[a]*Engineering Product Development, Singapore University of Technology and Design,
8 Somapah Road, Singapore 487372*
[b]*School of Physical Electronics,
University of Electronic Science and Technology of China,
#4 Section II, Jianshe North Road, Chengdu 610054, P. R. China*

bharatha_kumar@sutd.edu.sg, makaixue@uestc.edu.cn

A power amplifier (PA) is the most vital building block in the transmitter chain of the radio frequency (RF) transceiver. This chapter illustrates the PA integrated circuit (IC) design. The PA is used to boost the transmitted output power level and along with the transmitting antenna's gain, the maximum communication distance that can be achieved is determined. The PA is the most power-hungry building block in the whole RF transceiver. To improve the linearity performance even at a large power level in a low-power transceiver enforces a trade-off with the PA power efficiency. At 60 GHz, the PA also needs to support a wide bandwidth for high-data-rate communication in gigabit per second (Gbps) range.

Low-Power Wireless Communication Circuits and Systems: 60 GHz and Beyond
Edited by Kaixue Ma and Kiat Seng Yeo
Copyright © 2018 Pan Stanford Publishing Pte. Ltd.
ISBN 978-981-4745-96-3 (Hardcover), 978-1-315-15653-8 (eBook)
www.panstanford.com

6.1 Introduction

The benefit offered by the 60 GHz millimeter-wave frequency range is the 9 GHz wide unlicensed industry-science-medical (ISM) frequency band as allocated by the Federal Communications Commission (FCC) in the range from 57 to 66 GHz. This supports large-data-rate communication in the multi-Gbps range and is governed by many standards such as the IEEE 802.11ad.

For the past several decades, power amplifiers operating at the millimeter-wave frequencies have been designed using composite III–V semiconductors such as GaAs and GaN. Such process fabrications are expensive and the designs cannot be integrated with the high-density silicon CMOS digital process. Hence, such PAs are included as a chipset or die which are separate from the CMOS chipset, resulting in a complex IC packaging, increased assembly cost, and increased system form-factor. Such composite semiconductor transistors provide good linearity performance and power handling capability [1–6]. However, they require higher supply voltage than the low-voltage CMOS process. Hence, the research effort to implement the PA that can be integrated with the standard silicon process has been of great interest in the recent years. A few possible process technologies to support integrating the PA design on the silicon substrate are the silicon-germanium (SiGe) BiCMOS, standard CMOS, silicon SOI, etc.

The main considerations for the transistors used in PA designs are the unity power gain frequency f_{max} and the device breakdown-voltage limit, which are complementary and cannot be achieved together unlike complex III–V devices.

Another major consideration of the front-end amplifiers is the loss contributed by the on-chip passive components at such high frequencies dominated by the skin effect. However, despite these limitations, there are a few favorable factors at such high frequencies. As the process technology has been continuously downscaling in recent years, the f_{max} requirement has improved to support the millimeter-wave frequency range. However, the device breakdown-voltage to support such high f_{max} has decreased affecting the device reliability. For the same feature size, SiGe HBT has improved f_{max} as well as breakdown voltage compared with the standard CMOS process. To mitigate this concern about reliability, many new implementation techniques, such as parallel combining PA and distributed PA, have been proposed in the recent works [3, 6–8].

In addition to the active devices considerations, the passive components consuming most of the area, mainly inductors, have IC implementation implications. At such high frequencies, the size of the passive devices, either lumped or distributive transmission line, is small due to the smaller wavelength in the silicon process.

The integrated PA is an RF transmitter's front-end amplifier, and the PA design has certain challenges when operating around the 60 GHz frequency range. First, the amplifying transistor's $f_{\max}$ is closer to its operating frequency at 60 GHz. Therefore, a single transistor's power gain and linearity performance are limited and the need for cascaded amplifier stages becomes inevitable. Second, to mitigate the high insertion loss due to the interconnect traces and the passive devices, the quality (Q) factor for the load and the matching networks becomes critical. Also, there is a high possibility for the RF signals at such high frequency to be leaked through parasitic feedback paths resulting in oscillation condition. Third, at the 60 GHz range, it is desirable for the PA to provide high linear output power, high power gain, improved power added efficiency (PAE), wide bandwidth, unconditional stability, and compact design size.

In this chapter, typical PA design considerations at the 60 GHz range are illustrated with two design examples implemented in the 0.18 μm SiGe HBT.

6.2 PA Design Analysis

The PA design challenge involves the proper device selection for both the transistor and passive components. The main trade-offs for the transistor choice are the power gain, stability, and breakdown voltage. The transistor's (BJT or MOS) aspect ratio or dimensions, number of fingers, layout parastics, etc., determine the suitable performance trade-off and need to be properly optimized to achieve enhanced performance. We also mitigate the limitations on the performance trade-off by various design techniques such as cascode topology, switch-mode techniques, etc.

6.2.1 Amplifier Linearity versus Power Added Efficiency

The PA design often involves a trade-off between the efficiency and linearity. Over the years, this limitation has been mitigated by using several design techniques such as the stacked transistor amplifier design proposed in [7], which supports a large voltage swing to increase the output power by assisting the high-frequency device's low V_{beo} at the cost of a large supply voltage. An alternative design approach is the switched mode PA, in which the circuit operation (bias condition) adapts dynamically based on the instantaneous characteristics (amplitude, phase, frequency) of the input signal such as the class E discussedin [8] and class F^{-1}/F in [9] that minimizes power dissipation in the amplifying transistors by avoiding overlap between the current and voltage waveform profiles using the digital ON/OFF switches. However, such designs introduce nonlinearities at the output by the higher harmonics of switching distorted waveforms and hence require some special linearization techniques to reduce such effects. Alternatively, to mitigate the output non-linearities of the PA implemented based on the continuous real-time power control such as the adaptive biasing technique [10] and using load impedance modulation technique of the Doherty PA [11]. However, these PA design techniques involve complex circuitry with a large dynamic range that consumes additional dc power. An implementation technique to enhance the PA efficiency as well as linearity is by reducing the passive component losses and interconnect losses by using distributed structure equivalents in a physical layout such as Wilkinson couplers [12], thin-film micro-strip lines (MSL) [13] as the power splitter/combiner between multiple parallel PA stages, the substrate-shielded coplanar waveguide (CPW) structure [14], the transmission line transformer (TLT) [3], and the substrate-shielded MSL [6, 15]. However, the trade-off with such low-loss distributed structures is that they occupy a large die area. The power efficiency of the amplifier can be enhanced by using some current-reuse topologies [16] such as capacitive-coupling [17], interstage LC series resonance, and transformer-coupling. The transformer-based LC tank is already available in the design of various types of transceiver building such as the voltage-controlled oscillator (VCO) [17], low noise amplifier (LNA) [18], and Class-F PA [19].

6.3 Power Amplifier Examples

Following are the two examples of the millimeter-wave PA based on the 0.18 µm SiGe BiCMOS technology: One is a 30 GHz differential drive amplifier with frequency-tunable load (PA1) and the second design is a 60 GHz transformer-based power amplifier (PA2). The examples illustrate the design analysis, implementation, trade-offs, and achieved performance.

6.3.1 PA1: Differential Drive Amplifier Based on Variable Gain Control and Frequency-Tunable Load

The proposed PA1 is a fully differential two-stage dc stacked and ac cascade amplifier using the SiGe HBT process as shown in Fig. 6.1a. The first stage is a variable gain amplifier with a 4-bit $(B_3 \sim B_0)$ digital gain control and the second-stage amplifier has a frequency-tunable load tank circuit. The frequency-tunable load is the tank circuit that consists of an integrated two-coil spiral transformer and the varactor (MOS-based variable capacitor) bank. To significantly improve the die area utilization, the inductors and the transformer used in the proposed differential circuit are chosen with a center tap/differential configuration. The symmetric circuit schematic in Fig. 6.1a can be folded along the axis of symmetry as shown in Fig. 6.1b.

6.3.1.1 Variable gain amplifier stage analysis (A_{v1})

The linear output power of the proposed tunable amplifier can be controlled by varying the gain of the first-stage amplifier using the four digital bits $(B_3 \sim B_0)$. The first-stage amplifier gain is given as follows:

$$A_{v1}(s) = g_{m1} \cdot \frac{V_{A1}}{\left[\left(\dfrac{\beta_f}{\lambda_0} \right) \cdot \left(\displaystyle\sum_{n=0}^{3} B_n \cdot I_n \cdot 2^n + I_{min} \right) \right]}, \tag{6.1}$$

where, g_{m1} is transconductance, V_{A1} is early voltage, β_f $(=I_{C1}/I_{B1})$ is common-emitter forward current gain, and the output resistance's ($r_{o1} \approx V_{A1}/I_{C1}$) degradation factor due to transistor saturation λ_0 with ($0 < \lambda_0 \leq 1$) that are indicated for the transistor pair $Q1/Q2$, I_n ($n = 0$ to 3) are the constant coefficients of the estimated linear gain function, B_n ($n = 0$ to 3) are the digital gain control bits as received from the digital controller or the digital baseband, and I_{min} which is the DC current corresponding to the amplifier minimum gain when all the digital control bits $B_n = 0$ V.

The gain control based on the base bias current variation of the first-stage amplifier in the stacked structure mainly affects the output resistance r_{o1} and does not significantly alter the transconductance (g_{m1}) of the HBT pair $Q1/Q2$.

6.3.1.2 Frequency-tunable amplifier stage analysis (A_{v2}):

The second-stage amplifier gain from Fig. 6.1 is based on the fixed biasing transconductance (g_{m3}) of the $Q3/Q4$ transistor pair [20] and frequency-dependent load impedance $Z_L(s)$ as

$$A_{v2}(s) = g_{m3} \cdot \left[r_{o3} \, || \, Z_L(s) \right].　\tag{6.2}$$

As shown in Fig. 6.2a, the load impedance of the second-stage amplifier is determined by a high Q-factor transformer with the magnetically coupled LC tank circuit built by using the transformer secondary coil (L_s) and the MOS varactor bank (C_{vT}). The two-coil transformer can be represented as a T-network with the varactor bank modeled as a series combination [20] of the capacitor C_{vT} and varactor loss r_{vT} as shown in Fig. 6.3b.

Tunable load tank circuit Q-factor

For the tunable load impedance, we can deduce that

$$\omega_n^2 = \frac{1}{L_s \cdot C_{vT}}　\tag{6.3}$$

$$\omega_n \cdot Q_{tank} = \frac{1}{(r_s + r_{vT}) \cdot C_{vT}},　\tag{6.4}$$

where, ω_n is angular resonant frequency and Q_{tank} is overall tank Q-factor.

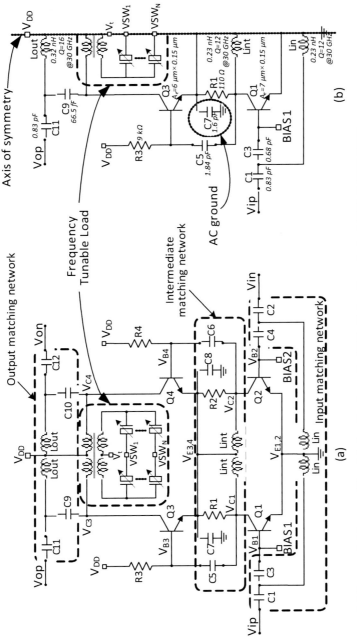

Figure 6.1 Proposed drive amplifier (a) circuit schematic, (b) half circuit equivalent [20], © IEEE 2015.

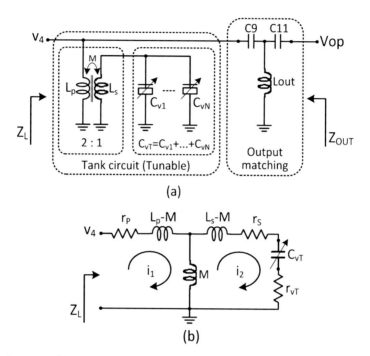

Figure 6.2 (a) Tunable load with output matching network. (b) T-section model of transformer with MOS-varactor [20], © IEEE 2015.

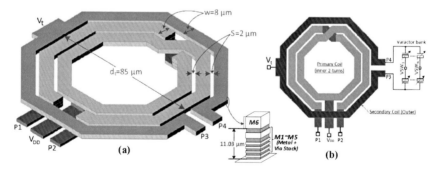

Figure 6.3 Transformer layout: (a) 3D view. (b) Top view with interface to the varactor bank [20], © IEEE 2015.

By re-arranging Eq. (6.4), the overall tank Q-factor is given as

$$Q_{tank} = \frac{1}{(r_S + r_{vT})} \cdot \sqrt{\frac{L_S}{C_{vT}}}. \tag{6.5}$$

Furthermore, the Q-factor of second-stage amplifier response in Eq. (6.2) is mainly determined by Q_{tank}. Hence, the second-stage amplifier load Q-factor is obtained by considering the mutual magnetic coupling due to the in-phase currents of the transformer primary coil and the magnetically induced current from the secondary coil shunted with the varactor bank. This facilitates the overall amplifier frequency response to be tunable in frequency with a controlled voltage (VSW1 = VSW2 = VSW).

6.3.1.3 Frequency-tunable load design

The frequency-tunable load in this design consists of a transformer with a two-coil center tap and a capacitor band with MOS varactors connected to the secondary coil as shown in Fig. 6.3. The transformer is designed and optimized using the Agilent ADS Momentum 2.5D EM simulator. The turn ratio of the transformer is 2:1, as evident in Fig. 6.3.

Due to the increased effective coil inductance by the magnetic coupling, the coil length can be decreased to provide the same inductance value as a standalone inductor within the interested frequency range. This reduces the series resistive loss associated with the transformer coil dependent on its length and eventually enhances the overall Q-factor compared with the standalone load inductor.

6.3.1.4 Q-factor enhancement

There are two instances in which the load tank Q-factor (Q_{tank}) is enhanced, as evident from the simulation plot in Fig. 6.4.

(i) Loaded tank Q-enhancement from Q_{t2} to Q_{t1}

The loaded tank Q-factor curves from Q_{t2} to Q_{t1} in Fig. 6.4 are obtained by reducing the transformer size of the primary outer coil (d_t) from 94 μm to 85 μm as well as by concurrently decreasing the MOS varactor-bank's channel length (l_v) from 650 to 500 μm. From Fig. 6.5, the Q_{tank} curves from Q_{t2} to Q_{t1} are upshifted along both the frequency and the peak value. This can be illustrated by the simultaneous reduction of the tank circuit component dimensions (d_t and l_v) from Q_{t2} to Q_{t1}, which results in a frequency upshift due to the decreased $(L_s \cdot C_{vT})$ product according to Eq. (6.3) as well as an increased Q_{tank} peak value by the resulting decreased resistive losses r_S and r_{vT}, as discussed in Eq. (6.5).

(ii) Load tank Q-enhancement by band-select VSW from "00" to "11"

From Fig. 6.4, we also observe that for either of the curves Q_{t1} and Q_{t2}, the frequency upshifts for the band-select input VSW configuration switching from "00" to "11" as well as the peak Q_{tank} value is enhanced. This can be analytically justified by considering the intrinsic tank frequency (ω_n) characteristics for an increase in the VSW voltage from 0 to 1.8 V.

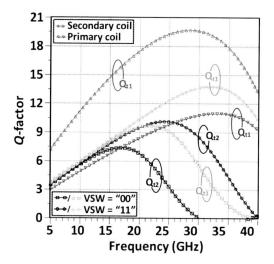

Figure 6.4 Simulated open circuit (self-inductance) and varactor bank loaded tank Q-factor for two versions of the tank with transformer size (d_t) and varactor length (l_v) as Q_{t1} $(d_t = 85$ μm, $l_v = 500$ μm) and Q_{t2} $(d_t = 94$ μm, $l_v = 650$ μm) [20], © IEEE 2015.

Both these Q-factor enhancements simultaneously improve the proposed PA's PAE, linearity, and peak gain performance by reduced tank circuit losses, which are evident from the on-wafer measurement results.

The die microphotograph of the proposed differential PA fabricated in a 0.18 μm SiGe BiCMOS process from Tower

Jazz Semiconductors is shown in Fig. 6.5. The total die area is 0.89 mm × 0.81 mm, including IO pads. The proposed design performance is experimentally verified by using on-wafer probing with the Agilent E8364B PNA network analyzer that supports a four-port calibration and mixed-mode scattering parameter measurement by avoiding the use of any balun.

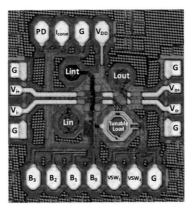

Figure 6.5 Microphotograph of proposed tunable load PA1 [20], © IEEE 2015.

Figure 6.6 shows the 16-step variable gain control using the four gain control bits $B_3 \sim B_0$ and the frequency band switching of the proposed amplifier as verified by the measured S-parameters.

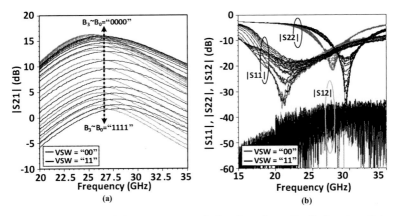

Figure 6.6 Measured S-parameter variation based on $B_3 \sim B_0$ band switch based on VSW (a) gain (b) return loss and isolation [20], © IEEE 2015.

Table 6.1 consolidates the measured performance of the proposed frequency-tunable PA1. By using dc current reuse topology along with a high-Q frequency-tunable transformer-coupled load and a variable gain control option, PAE and the overall amplifier performance are improved. Although the proposed PA1 design has enhanced PAE, the high linearity performance becomes a hard limit and a major concern in PA specifications.

Table 6.1 Measured performance of the PA1 [20], © IEEE 2015

Parameter	Units	Band#1	Band#2
Technology	—	0.18 µm SiGe BiCMOS	
Peak gain	(dB)	1.7 to 16.3	1.8 to 16.0
−3dB Bandwidth	(Hz)	24.3 G to 32.4 G	25.8 G to 35 G
Output P_{1dB}	(dBm)	+8.3	+9.6
Peak PAE	(%)	35.3	55.9
Core area	(mm^2)	0.89 × 0.81	
DC power consumption	(mW)	22.5	
Supply voltage	(V)	1.8	
Topology	—	Current-reuse + tunable load	

6.3.2 PA2: Single-Ended Transformer-Based Power Amplifier

The proposed PA2 is a three-stage amplifier using the SiGe HBT transistors with the input single-ended cascode stage followed by two differential amplifier stages terminated by a transformer-based balun to provide a single-ended output as shown in Fig. 6.7. The interstages are magnetically coupled using differential transformers. The transformers are built and modeled by the EM simulation using Agilent ADS Momentum v2011. As it is very compact, the design has the risk of possible oscillations. Hence, care must be taken during the layout to mitigate the formation of any undesired regenerative feedback paths. Additionally, neutralization capacitors are included across the two differential stages as shown in Fig. 6.7.

The PA2 is fabricated in a 0.18 µm SiGe BiCMOS process from Tower Jazz Semiconductor with die area of 0.43 mm × 0.18 mm as shown in Fig. 6.8. The measured S-parameter gain and output return loss for V_b = 0.9 V and V_{cc} = 1.8 V is shown in Figs. 6.9 and 6.10, respectively.

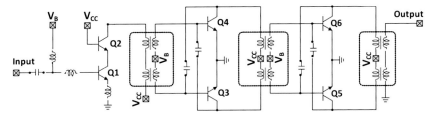

Figure 6.7 Proposed broadband PA2 circuit schematic.

Figure 6.8 PA2 die microphotograph.

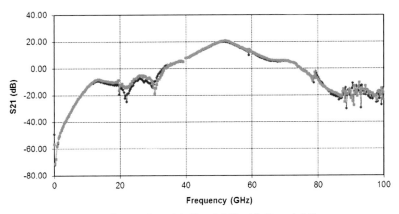

Figure 6.9 Measured gain plot with V_b = 0.9 V with V_{cc} = 1.8 V.

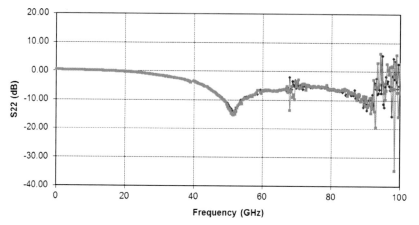

Figure 6.10 Measured output return loss plot with V_b = 0.9 V with V_{cc} = 1.8 V.

Acknowledgments

The authors would like to thank Tower Jazz Semiconductors for providing the fabrication service of the design in the 0.18 μm SiGe BiCMOS and GLOBALFOUNDRIES in the 65 nm CMOS process. The authors would also like to thank W. Yang of Nanyang Technological University (NTU), Singapore, for assisting in the on-wafer measurement of the proposed design.

References

1. Tokumitsu, T. (2001). K-band and millimeter-wave MMICs for emerging commercial wireless applications, *IEEE Trans. Microw. Theory Tech.*, *TMTT*, vol. 49, no. 11, pp. 2066–2072.

2. Gresham, I., et. al. (2004). Ultra-wideband radar sensors for short-range vehicular applications, *IEEE Trans. Microw. Theory Tech.*, *TMTT*, vol. 52, no. 9, pp. 2105–2122.

3. Kuo, C.-W., Chiou, H.-K., and Chung, H.-Y. (2013). An 18 to 33 GHz fully-integrated Darlington power amplifier with Guanella-type transmission-line transformers in 0.18 μm CMOS technology, *IEEE Microw. Wireless Compon. Lett.*, *MWCL*, vol. 23, no. 12, pp. 668–670.

4. Siddiqui, M. K., Sharma, A. K., Callejo, L. G., and Lai, R. (1998). A high power and high efficiency monolithic power amplifier for LMDS

applications, *IEEE Trans. Microw. Theory Tech., TMTT,* vol. 46, no. 12, pp. 2226–2232.

5. ET Docket 98–153. (2002). First report and order, revision of part 15 of the commission's rules regarding ultra wideband transmission systems, FCC. Washington, DC, 2002.

6. Lee, J.-W., and Heo, S.-M. (2008). A 27 GHz, +14 dBm CMOS power amplifier using 0.18 μm common-source MOSFETs, *IEEE Microw. Wireless Compon. Lett., MWCL,* vol. 18, no. 11, pp. 755–757.

7. Chen, J.-H., Helmi, S. R., and Mohammadi, S. (2013). A fully-integrated Ka-band stacked power amplifier in 45 nm CMOS SOI technology, *IEEE Topical Meeting Silicon Monolithic Integrated Circuits RF Systems, SIRF,* pp. 75–77.

8. Cao, C., Xu, H., Su, Y., and O, K. K. (2005). An 18-GHz, 10.9-dBm fully-integrated power amplifier with 23.5% PAE in 130-nm CMOS, *Proc. 31st Eur. Solid-State Circuits Conf., ESSCC,* pp. 137–140.

9. Mortazavi, S. Y., and Koh, K.-J. (2014). A Class F-1/F 24-to-31 GHz power amplifier with 40.7% peak PAE, 15 dBm OP1dB, and 50 mW Psat in 0.13 μm SiGe BiCMOS, *Int. Solid-State Circuits Conf. Tech. Dig., ISSCC,* San Francisco, CA, pp. 254–255.

10. Kuo, N.-C., Kao, J.-C., Kuo, C.-C., and Wang, H. (2011). K-band CMOS power amplifier with adaptive bias for enhancement in back-off efficiency, *IEEE MTT-S Int. Microw. Symp. Dig., IMS,* Baltimore, MD, pp. 1–4.

11. Kaymaksut, E., and Reynaert, P. (2012). Transformer-based uneven Doherty power amplifier in 90 nm CMOS for WLAN applications, *IEEE J. Solid-State Circuits, JSSC,* vol. 47, no. 7, pp. 1659–1671.

12. Kim, K., and Nguyen, C. (2014). A 16.5–28 GHz 0.18-μm BiCMOS power amplifier with flat 19.4 ± 1.2 dBm output power, *IEEE Microw. Wireless Compon. Lett., MWCL,* vol. 24, no. 2, pp. 108–110.

13. Huang, P.-C., Kuo, J.-L., Tsai, Z.-M., Lin, K.-Y., and Wang, H. (2010). A 22-dBm 24-GHz power amplifier using 0.18-μm CMOS technology, *IEEE MTT-S Int. Microw. Symp. Dig., IMS,* Anaheim, CA, pp. 248–251.

14. Komijani, A., Natarajan, A., and Hajimiri, A. (2005). A 24-GHz, +14.5-dBm fully integrated power amplifier in 0.18-μm CMOS, *IEEE J. Solid-State Circuits, JSSC,* vol. 40, no. 9, pp. 1901–1908.

15. Riemer, P. J., Humble, J. S., Prairie, J. F., Coker, J. D., Randall, B. A., Gilbert, B. K., and Daniel, E. S. (2007). Ka-band SiGe HBT power amplifier for single chip T/R module applications, *IEEE MTT-S Int. Microw. Symp. Dig., IMS,* pp. 1071–1074.

16. Giammello, V., Ragonese, E., and Palmisano, G. (2012). A transformer-coupling current-reuse SiGe HBT power amplifier for 77-GHz automotive radar, *IEEE Trans. Microw. Theory Tech., TMTT*, vol. 60, no. 6, pp. 1676–1683.

17. Krishnaswamy, H., and Hashemi, H. (2006). Inductor- and transformer-based integrated RF oscillators: A comparative study, *IEEE Proc. Custom Integrated Circuits Design Conf., CICC*, San Jose, CA.

18. Xiaohua, Y., and Neihart, N. M. (2013). Analysis and design of a reconfigurable multimode low-noise amplifier utilizing a multitap transformer, *IEEE Trans. Microw. Theory Tech., TMTT*, vol. 61, no. 3, pp. 1236–1246.

19. Sessou, K. K., and Neihart, N. M. (2015). An integrated 700–1200-MHz class-F PA with tunable harmonic terminations in 0.13-μm CMOS, *IEEE Trans. Microw. Theory Tech., TMTT*, vol. 63, no. 4, pp. 1315–1323.

20. Kumar, T. B., Ma, K., and Yeo, K. S. (2015). A low power programmable gain high PAE K-/Ka-band stacked amplifier in 0.18 μm SiGe BiCMOS technology, *IEEE MTT-S Int. Microwave Symp. Dig., IMS*, Phoenix, AZ, USA, pp. 1–4.

In order to succeed in this new global economy, you must be able to transform what you know into significant and impactful returns. You have to innovate and not imitate and to think and act like revolutionaries

—Kiat Seng Yeo and Kaixue Ma

Chapter 7

Low-Noise Amplifier

Bharatha Kumar Thangarasu,[a] Kaixue Ma,[b] and Kiat Seng Yeo[a]

[a]*Engineering Product Development, Singapore University of Technology and Design, 8 Somapah Road, Singapore 487372*
[b]*School of Physical Electronics,*
University of Electronic Science and Technology of China,
#4 Section II, Jianshe North Road, Chengdu 610054, P. R. China

bharatha_kumar@sutd.edu.sg, makaixue@uestc.edu.cn

A low-noise amplifier (LNA) is a prerequisite—as a building block—for the receiver chain of the radio frequency (RF) transceiver and is presented in this chapter. The LNA is used to extract the useful information signal in the midst of the noisy channel in order to improve the fidelity of the received signal. The low noise and high gain of the LNA design are mainly used to improve the signal-to-noise ratio in the receiver chain. To support a high-data-rate communication in the gigabit per second (Gbps) range, the operating frequency range becomes crucial.

Low-Power Wireless Communication Circuits and Systems: 60 GHz and Beyond
Edited by Kaixue Ma and Kiat Seng Yeo
Copyright © 2018 Pan Stanford Publishing Pte. Ltd.
ISBN 978-981-4745-96-3 (Hardcover), 978-1-315-15653-8 (eBook)
www.panstanford.com

7.1 Introduction

Many standards for the 60 GHz wireless personal area network (WPAN) have been recently introduced and have gradually gained popularity, such as the WiGig (from the Wireless Gigabit Alliance of several industry partners—Intel, Broadcom, NEC, Apple, Dell, Microsoft, Panasonic, Toshiba, Wilocity, etc.), ECMA TC48, Wireless HD, etc. Additionally, a few standards have been formulated by the IEEE at the 60 GHz range, of which the IEEE 802.15.3c was the forerunner, but it did not sustain for long and then the most promising standard 802.11ad was framed, which is still prevalent. Most of the recent transceiver designs operating at 60 GHz aim to meet the certification from the IEEE 802.11ad.

At 60 GHz, there are several advantages such as a 9 GHz wide industry-science-medical (ISM) unlicensed frequency band allocated by the Federal Communications Commission (FCC) in the range from 57 to 66 GHz. This wide bandwidth according to Shannon's formula supports large Gbps data rate communication. The multi-Gbps data rate allows uncompressed high-definition media transfers, quick transfer of large data files, real-time monitoring, processing systems, etc. [1–8].

At such high millimeter-wave frequencies, the passive circuit components can be realized in a compact size as on-chip due to smaller wavelength enabling a potential large market in portable mobile communication devices.

The low noise and high gain in the LNA are mainly used to suppress the noise contribution from the subsequent building blocks in the receiver chain to improve the overall signal-to-noise ratio in the receiver chain as [9]

$$F = \frac{(S/N)_{\text{IN}}}{(S/N)_{\text{OUT}}} = F_{\text{LNA}} + \frac{F_{\text{mixer}} - 1}{G_{\text{LNA}}} + \frac{F_{\text{VGA}} - 1}{G_{\text{LNA}} \cdot G_{\text{mixer}}} + \cdots, \tag{7.1}$$

where, F_X and G_X are the noise factor and gain, respectively, of the receiver building blocks (X).

An LNA is a RF transceiver's front-end amplifier, and there are certain design challenges when operating around the 60 GHz frequency range. First, the amplifying transistor's transition frequency (f_T), which is its unity gain bandwidth product, is closer to its operating frequency and hence limits the transistor's gain and noise performance. Second, the interconnect traces and the passive devices have high insertion loss together with low resistivity substrate, which reduces the quality (Q) factor for the load and the matching networks. Third, it is difficult to characterize both the passive and active devices at such high frequencies. The signals at such a high frequency can be leaked through parasitic feedback paths resulting in possible instability condition. Last, the designer must take care of improving the gain flatness over a wide bandwidth with low power consumption and compact size. The desirable performance criteria of the LNA circuit in general are low noise figure (NF), high power gain, low DC power consumption, good linearity, wide bandwidth, unconditional stability, process-temperature-voltage (PVT) insensitive performance, and compact design.

The wavelength at 60 GHz approaches the dimension of the passive components and interconnect metal traces. Additionally, the parasitics, which are frequency dependent, result in a PVT-sensitive design. Hence, the layout implementation of the designs at 60 GHz becomes a crucial factor in determining the LNA's integrated circuit performance. In the following section, the typical design considerations of the 60 GHz LNA are studied and two example designs are provided.

7.2 LNA Design Analysis

The RF LNA design must provide a better compromise between the available power gain and the NF based on the transistor S-parameters. By definition the NF is a measure of the signal-to-noise ratio (SNR) degradation at output compared with the input SNR. The total noise power at the output is increased by the thermal noise from the input noise resistance termination. The NF can be derived [9] as

$$F = F_{min} + \frac{4 \cdot r_n \cdot |\Gamma_s - \Gamma_{opt}|^2}{(1 - |\Gamma_s|^2) \cdot |1 + \Gamma_{opt}|^2}, \qquad (7.2)$$

where, F_{min} is the device minimum NF dependent on the frequency and bias condition, r_n is the normalized noise resistance, and Γ_s and Γ_{opt} are source reflection co-efficient and optimum source reflection co-efficient at minimum NF, respectively.

7.2.1   Noise Figure

Depending on the *S*-parameters of the transistor, often the maximum gain and the minimum NF point will not coincide as shown in Fig. 7.1. Hence, the source matching network is optimized to achieve a better trade-off between high gain and low NF. Additionally, to ensure the unconditional stability condition, the optimum value chosen should be placed well within the stability region. The minimum NF and the maximum gain conditions are determined over the entire interested frequency range with DC bias consuming low power.

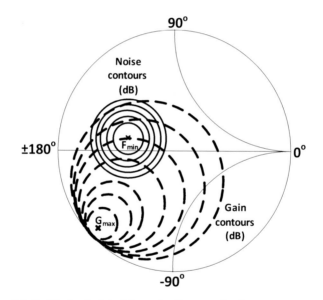

Figure 7.1 Smith chart plot of the noise figure and gain contours.

7.2.2   Linearity

In addition to the low NF performance, the LNA design must also have improved input linearity performance to achieve good overall receiver chain linearity. In this way, the subsequent amplifier stages and the receiver chain building blocks do not saturate for large input signal power levels. But the trade-off is with the DC power consumption.

7.2.3 Variable Gain LNA as a Trade-Off between Low Noise and Good Linearity Performance

The LNA design must provide low NF, high power gain, good linearity, and low DC power consumption. One encouraging fact which can be observed with the LNA design is that the desired requirements are mutually exclusive and are dependent on the input power level. For a low or weak input signal, in order to improve the SNR, the input signal must be amplified above the noise floor by using the amplifier's high gain and low NF, which becomes crucial unlike the linearity. Meanwhile, for the large or strong input power levels, to prevent saturation of the receiver chain, the amplifier's linearity and low gain become predominant factors over the low NF. Hence, by introducing a variable gain LNA design, we can achieve both these contrasting front-end amplifier's requirements to improve the overall receiver dynamic range. The LNA gain can be controlled based on the detected input power level using the received signal strength indicator (RSSI) by a RF front-end power detector or from the baseband chipset. The variable gain control can also introduced for the subsequent amplifiers and building blocks in the overall receiver chain. Hence, providing a regulated power level to the baseband chipset that eventually reduces the dynamic range requirement of the circuitry in the baseband section. The RSSI can be either the feedback or the feed-forward implementation and becomes a part of the automatic gain control technique to enhance the overall receiver performance.

The designer must ensure that the LNA's input and output impedance matching are not affected in the process of variable gain control. One of the LNA examples in the following section illustrates a variable gain control LNA by using the base bias voltage that does not significantly affect the LNA's impedance-matching condition (*S*-parameter return loss) over the variable gain control.

7.3 Low-Noise Amplifier Examples

This section presents two LNA design examples: one using the 65 nm CMOS process (LNA1) and the other using the bipolar SiGe HBT technology (LNA2). The two possibilities of implementing the passive structures, namely the lumped spiral inductor and the distributed transmission line–based coplanar waveguide design, are described in this chapter to illustrate the LNA design trade-offs and performance.

7.3.1 LNA1: Based on 65 nm CMOS with Custom-Built Inductor

The proposed LNA1 is a three-stage cascode single-ended amplifier using the NMOS transistors (MN1~MN6) and the circuit schematic is shown in Fig. 7.2. The design has impedance-matching T-networks consisting of two series capacitors and a shunt inductor. The power supply filter capacitors $C3$ are included in the design to bypass the supply-related high frequency noise fluctuations. The bottom NMOS common source (CS) transistors MNx [x: 1~3] are externally biased from VB_X through a high resistance RB_X, while the top common gate (CG) NMOS transistors MNy [y: 4~6] are biased by VDD. The input and output nodes (reference planes) are impedance matched to 50 Ω. The octagonal spiral-shaped inductors Lx [x: 1~3] are custom-built and modeled by the EM simulation using Ansoft HFSS v15.0 as shown in Fig. 7.3. Both the inductors $L1$ and $L3$ are identical with the outer dimension (diameter) of 63 µm and the trace width of 6 µm, while the smaller $L2$ inductor has the outer dimension of 52 µm and the width of 6 µm. The inductance and Q-factor as obtained from the EM simulation have less variation around the interested frequency range from 40 to 70 GHz as shown in Fig. 7.3a.

The impedance looking upward at the source terminal of the CG cascode transistors MNy [y: 4~6] as shown in Fig. 7.4a has a real part [1],

$$\mathrm{Re}\left\{Z_{\mathrm{int}}\right\} = \frac{(1 - \omega^2 L_{\mathrm{int}} C_{\mathrm{gsy}}) \times g_{\mathrm{my}}}{g_{\mathrm{my}}^2 + \omega^2 C_{\mathrm{gsy}}^2}, \qquad (7.3)$$

where, C_{gsy} is the gate capacitance and g_{my} is the transconductance of the cascode transistors *MNy* [where *y*: 4~6].

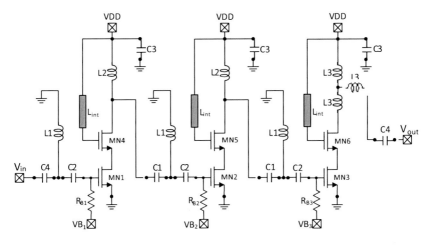

Figure 7.2 Proposed broadband LNA circuit schematic [10], © IEEE 2015.

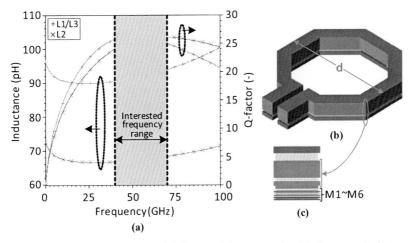

Figure 7.3 (a) Inductance and *Q*-factor of the customized inductors –*L1/L3* (*d* = 63 μm, *w* = 6 μm) and *L2* (*d* = 52 μm, *w* = 6 μm). (b) The 3D view. (c) The metal-stack supported by process technology [10], © IEEE 2015.

The voltage gain of the cascode configuration is given as [1]

$$A_v = \frac{g_{mx} \times \text{Re}\left\{Z_{int}\right\}}{1 + g_{mx} \times \text{Re}\left\{Z_{int}\right\}},$$

$$(7.4)$$

where g_{mx} in Eq. (7.3) is the transconductance of the CS NMOS transistors *MNx* [where *x*: 1~3].

Upon further analysis [1], we can obtain the following three scenarios based on different values of Re$\{Z_{int}\}$ as follows:

7.3.1.1 Marginally stable criteria and gain boosting

From Eq. (7.3), an undesirable negative resistance is obtained for $L_{int} \neq 0$ that also depends on the values of C_{gsy} and g_{my}. This negative resistance is taken into advantage in [2] to achieve gain boosting by pushing the dominant pole toward the higher frequency and eventually improving the overall bandwidth of the LNA. If the negative resistance value exceeds the resistive losses of the inductor load, then gain peaking will be severe, which results in a narrow bandwidth [1].

7.3.1.2 Unstable criteria causing oscillations

An extreme scenario of the increased undesirable negative resistance will result in oscillations caused by the instability shown in this work (LNA1 version 1). It can be theoretically shown by the denominator of Eq. (7.3) approaching zero when $g_{mx} \times \text{Re}\{Z_{int}\} = -1$, which is further discussed in the following section.

7.3.1.3 Unconditionally stable criteria

From Eq. (7.3), a positive resistance is obtained for $L_{int} = 0$, which then only depends on the values of C_{gsy} and g_{my} as given by

$$\text{Re}\left\{Z_{int}\right\} = \frac{g_{my}}{g_{my}^2 + \omega^2 C_{gsy}^2}. \tag{7.5}$$

The gate inductance effect can be minimized ($L_{int} = 0$) by physically placing bypass capacitors close to the cascode transistor gate as proposed in [3]. Equation (7.5) can also be achieved by an alternate layout technique as discussed in LNA1 version 2 implementation in the following section.

Last, the output stage has the compensation inductance *L3* looking along Z_{d6} that resonates with the parasitic capacitance of the cascode transistor looking via Z_{d6} as shown in Fig. 7.4b and improves the 3 dB bandwidth upper cut-off frequency.

Both the LNA1 versions 1 and 2 are fabricated in the 65 nm CMOS from GLOBALFOUNDRIES process with the same die area (0.6 × 0.4 mm^2) as shown in Figs. 7.5a and 7.6a, respectively.

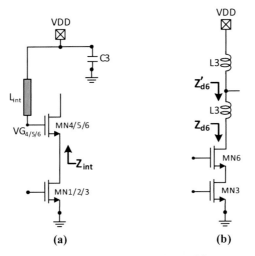

Figure 7.4 (a) Stability control technique with L_{int} (b) Output stage [10], © IEEE 2015.

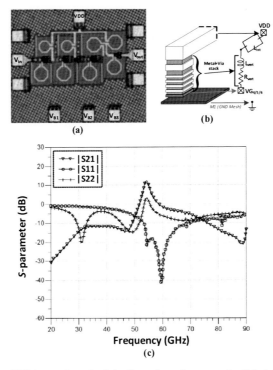

Figure 7.5 LNA1 version 1: (a) die microphotograph, (b) interconnect circuit equivalent, and (c) measured *S*-parameters showing instability [10], © IEEE 2015.

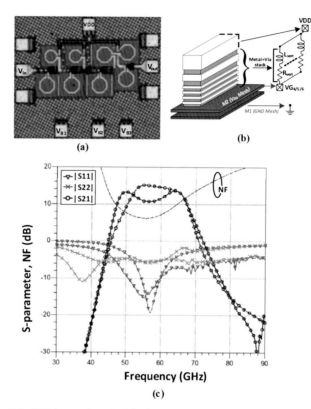

Figure 7.6 LNA1 version 2 (a) die microphotograph (b) interconnect circuit equivalent (c) measured (solid line), simulated (dotted line) *S*-parameters and simulated NF with unconditional stability [10], © IEEE 2015.

A. LNA1 version 1 with undesirable instability

The interconnect traces from the VDD pad to the CG transistors' gate $(VG_{4/5/6})$ of the LNA1 version 1 are shown in Fig. 7.5b, which consists of a top-metal series trace inductance L_{int} and a series combination of vertical inductance (L_{vert}) of the vias connected vertically along the metal-stack with resistance (R_{vert}). The measured *S*-parameters present instability, and Fig. 7.5c verifies the analysis done in the previous section.

B. LNA1 version 2 with unconditional stability

The extension of the metal stack using vias along the entire interconnect trace length from VDD pad to the bottom metal-

2 VDD mesh as shown in Fig. 7.6b results in the parallel distributed low-resistance equivalent network. This arrangement significantly reduces the voltage drop as well as the parasitic series trace inductance (Lint) from VDD pad to the VG4/5/6 nodes. This minimizes Lint by mitigating the formation of the negative resistance and hence results in an unconditional stability as illustrated in the previous section.

It can be observed that the measured *S*-parameter plots agrees very well with the simulation as shown in Fig. 7.6c and hence also verifies the stability condition. The simulated NF specifies a minimum value of 6.2 dB. The stability factors obtained from the extracted measured *S*-parameters, shown in Fig. 7.7, highlight the unconditional stability achieved by the LNA1 version 2 implementation.

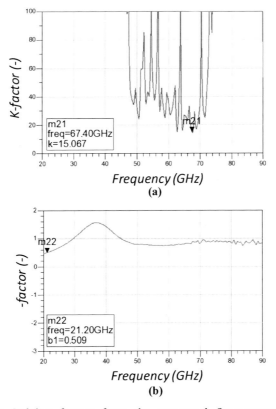

Figure 7.7 Stability factors from the measured *S*-parameters of the proposed LNA1 version 2: (a) *K*-factor; (b) *β*-factor [10], ©IEEE 2015.

From the linearity plot shown in Fig. 7.8, we observe that output 1 dB compression point (OP1dB) is +1 dBm, output saturation power (Psat) is +5.8 dBm, and the peak PAE is 10.3% with a 1.2 V supply voltage at 58 GHz frequency. Furthermore, for an increased 2.1 V supply voltage, the $OP_{1\ dB}$, the P_{sat}, and the peak PAE measured at 58 GHz frequency are +6.3 dBm, +9.6 dBm, and 16%, respectively, but at an increased DC power consumption.

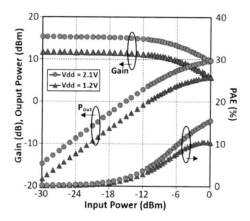

Figure 7.8 Measured linearity performance of the proposed LNA1 version 2 implementation [10], © IEEE 2015.

The measured performance of the proposed broadband LNA is summarized and compared with the state-of-the-art works in Table 7.1.

Table 7.1 Measured performance of the CMOS LNA1 version 2 [10], © IEEE 2015

Parameter	Units	This work [10]
Technology	—	65 nm CMOS
Peak gain	(dB)	13.7
−3dB Bandwidth	(Hz)	47.6 G to 67.1 G
Noise Figure	(dB)	6.2* (min.)
Output P_{1dB}	(dBm)	+1.0
Core area	(mm^2)	0.24
DC power consumption	(mW)	27.6
Supply voltage	(V)	1.2
Topology	—	Single-ended

*Simulation result.

7.3.2 LNA2: Based on 0.18 μm SiGe BiCMOS with Distributive Transmission Line Inductor and Interconnect Design

The proposed LNA2 is a four-stage cascode single-ended amplifier using the SiGe HBT transistors ($Q1{\sim}Q6$) and the circuit schematic is shown in Fig. 7.9. The design has impedance-matching networks, interconnects and load inductance implemented as coplanar waveguide (CPW) transmission lines with the cross sectional structure as shown in Fig. 7.10 with characteristic impedance around 60 GHz of 50 Ω. The structures are built and modeled by the EM simulation using Agilent ADS Momentum v2011.

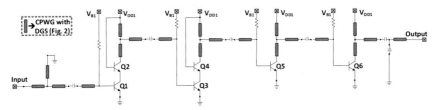

Figure 7.9 Proposed broadband LNA2 circuit schematic.

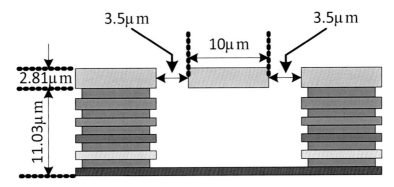

Figure 7.10 Cross-sectional view of CPW used in LNA2.

The LNA2 is fabricated in the 0.18 μm SiGe BiCMOS process from Tower Jazz Semiconductor with the die area (0.9×0.4 mm^2) as shown in Fig. 7.11.

A variable wideband gain control is achieved by the tuning bias voltage (V_b) of the LNA2 design as shown in the measured plot in Fig. 7.12.

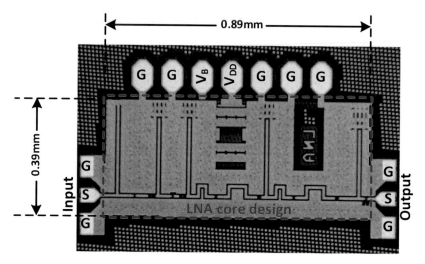

Figure 7.11 LNA2 die microphotograph [1], © IEEE 2015.

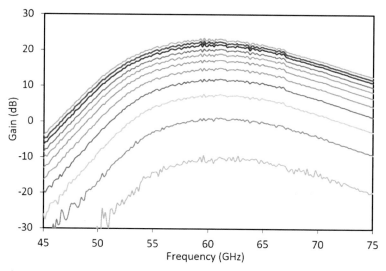

Figure 7.12 Measured gain plot with V_b = 1.0 to 2.0 V (step = 0.1 V) with V_{cc} = 1.8 V.

The *S*-parameters at the maximum gain condition with V_b = 1.8 V and minimum gain condition with V_b = 1.1 V suggest an improved gain flatness and good return loss performance over the entire interested frequency range as shown in Figs. 7.13 and Fig. 7.14, respectively. The NF is plotted by using the Y-factor method using Noisecom NC5115 source as shown in Fig. 7.15 for the three different gain condition using V_b voltage. The measured results are consolidated in Table 7.2.

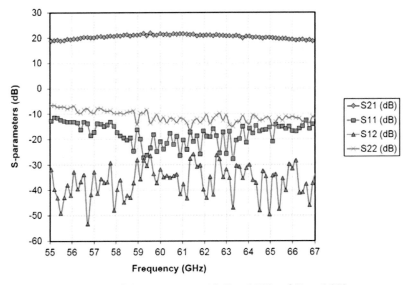

Figure 7.13 Measured *S*-parameters with V_b = 1.8 V and V_{cc} = 1.8 V.

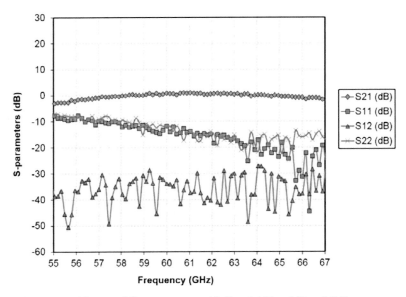

Figure 7.14 Measured *S*-parameters with V_b = 1.1 V and V_{cc} = 1.8 V.

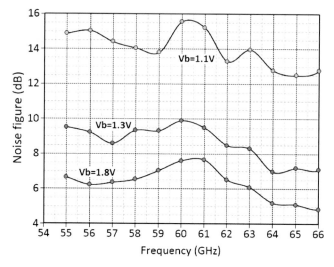

Figure 7.15 Measured NF at three different gain conditions.

Table 7.2 Measured performance of the SiGe LNA2

Parameter	Units	This work
Technology	—	0.18 μm SiGe BiCMOS
Peak gain	(dB)	21.9
–3dB Bandwidth	(Hz)	55 G to 66.6 G
Noise Figure	(dB)	5.1 to 7.6
Output P_{1dB}	(dBm)	+0.0
Core area	(mm^2)	0.34
DC power consumption	(mW)	19.3
Supply voltage	(V)	1.8
Topology	—	Single-ended

Acknowledgments

The authors would like to thank Tower Jazz Semiconductors for providing the fabrication service of the design in the 0.18 μm SiGe BiCMOS and GLOBALFOUNDRIES in the 65 nm CMOS process. The authors would also like to thank W. Yang of Nanyang Technological University (NTU), Singapore, for assisting in the on-wafer measurement of the proposed design.

References

1. Asgaran, S., and Deen, M. J. (2004). A novel gain boosting technique for design of low power narrow-band RF CMOS LNAs, *Proc. 2nd Annu. IEEE Northeast Circuits Syst. Workshop, NCSW*, pp. 293–296.

2. Jen, Y.-N., Tsai, J.-H., Huang, T.-W., and Wang, H. (2009). Design and analysis of a 55–71-GHz compact and broadband distributed active transformer power amplifier in 90-nm CMOS process, *IEEE Trans. Microw. Theory Tech., TMTT*, vol. 57, no. 7, pp. 1637–1646.

3. Ku, B.-H., Baek, S.-H., and Hong, S. (2011). A wideband transformer-coupled CMOS power amplifier for X-band multifunction chips, *IEEE Trans. Microw. Theory Tech., TMTT*, vol. 59, no. 6, pp. 1599–1609.

4. Hsieh, H.-H., Wu, P.-Y., Jou, C.-P., Hsueh, F.-L., and Huang, G.-W. (2011). 60 GHz high-gain low-noise amplifiers with a common-gate inductive feedback in 65 nm CMOS, *Proc. IEEE Radio Freq. Integr. Circuits Symp., RFIC*, Baltimore, MD, pp. 1–4.

5. Chang, P.-Y., Su, S.-H., Hsu, S. S. H., Cho, W.-H., and Jin, J.-D. (2012). An ultra-low-power transformer-feedback 60 GHz low-noise amplifier in 90 nm CMOS, *IEEE Microw. Wireless Compon. Lett., MWCL*, vol. 22, no. 4, pp. 197–199.

6. Chang, J. N., and Lin, Y. S. (2012). 60 GHz CMOS power amplifier with Psat of 11.4 dBm and PAE of 15.8%, *IET Electron. Lett.*, vol. 48, no. 17, pp. 1038–1039.

7. Hsieh, C.-A., Lin, Y.-H., Hsiao, Y.-H., and Wang, H. (2013). A 60 GHz low noise amplifier with built-in linearizer, *IEEE MTT-S Int. Microwav. Symp. Dig., IMS*, Seattle, WA, pp. 1–3.

8. Liu, G., and Schumacher, H. (2013). Broadband millimeter-wave LNAs (47–77 GHz and 70–140 GHz) using a T-type matching topology, *IEEE J. Solid-State Circuits, JSSC*, vol. 48, no. 9, pp. 2022–2029.

9. Lee, T. H. (1998). *The Design of CMOS Radio Frequency Integrated Circuits*. (Cambridge Univ. Press, UK).

10. Kumar, T. B., Ma, K., and Yeo, K. S. (2015). A compact 60 GHz LNA design with enhanced stability by layout optimization technique in a 65 nm CMOS technology, *IEEE Int. SoC Design Conf., ISOCC*.

To be a successful person, you have to be able to do ordinary things extraordinarily well with the right person, in the right way, and at the right time.

—Kiat Seng Yeo and Kaixue Ma

Chapter 8

Bi-Directional Low-Noise Amplifier

Bharatha Kumar Thangarasu,[a] Kaixue Ma,[b] and Kiat Seng Yeo[a]

[a]Engineering Product Development, Singapore University of Technology and Design, 8 Somapah Road, Singapore 487372
[b]School of Physical Electronics,
University of Electronic Science and Technology of China,
#4 Section II, Jianshe North Road, Chengdu 610054, P.R. China

bharatha_kumar@sutd.edu.sg, makaixue@uestc.edu.cn;

One of the efficient options to reduce the transceiver die area is to combine some building blocks operating at a similar frequency range from the transmitter and receiver chains to introduce a bi-directional signal flow capability. This chapter presents a high-linearity low-noise amplifier design, which is further extended to provide switchable directional control. Such bi-directional amplifiers are mainly used in the compact RF transceivers and a prominent application is the phase array systems used to achieve beam forming and beam scanning in the radar and defense communication systems.

Low-Power Wireless Communication Circuits and Systems: 60 GHz and Beyond
Edited by Kaixue Ma and Kiat Seng Yeo
Copyright © 2018 Pan Stanford Publishing Pte. Ltd.
ISBN 978-981-4745-96-3 (Hardcover), 978-1-315-15653-8 (eBook)
www.panstanford.com

8.1 Introduction

The bulkiest module or component in the RF transceiver system form-factor is the antenna. This will be a bigger concern when considering antenna arrays for beam-forming applications and phase arrays designed for wireless communication [1]. One benefit with the antenna design is they are bi-directional transducer components and the same design can work as transmitting as well as receiving antenna as shown in Fig. 8.1. By including either a T/R switch for time-domain multiplexing scheme as shown in Fig. 8.2 or using a diplexer for frequency domain multiplexing scheme as shown in Fig. 8.3 between the transceiver front end and the antenna, we can cut down on the number of antennas. The limitation of using T/R switches along the RF signal path in the series configuration introduces signal loss due to finite transistor ON resistance and in shunt configuration of the T/R switch then the OFF parasitic capacitance limits the transceiver operation frequency. Similarly, the stop-band roll-off of the diplexer is critical to achieve the isolation between the transmitter and receiver chain which in turn depends on the order of the diplexer filters. Hence, increased isolation can be achieved by increasing the diplexer filter order and therefore increases the system form factor.

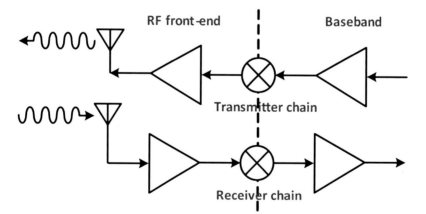

Figure 8.1 Conventional transceiver frontend with separate antennas.

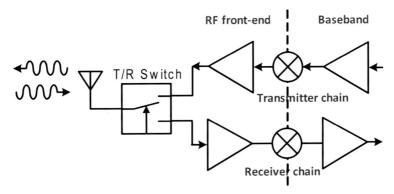

Figure 8.2 Transceiver frontend with single antenna using T/R switch.

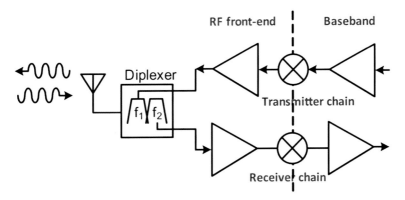

Figure 8.3 Transceiver frontend with single antenna using diplexer.

Another option to cut down on the number of antennas and with as smaller overall system form factor is by implementing bi-directional amplifiers (BDA) as shown in Fig. 8.4. The passive mixer design converts frequency between RF and baseband (BB) frequency with a conversion loss and can be easily implemented to achieve bi-directional frequency conversion capability. By realizing the amplifiers at the RF frontend as well as the baseband amplifiers with bi-directional capability, the overall transceiver can be reduced to a single chain. Just by using a digital configuration pin, switched in the time-division-multiplexing scheme, the whole system can operate in either the transmitter or the receiver mode [2–4].

However, unlike the passive mixer design, the bi-directional amplifiers (BDA) require active components for achieving amplification which are uni-directional devices. A detailed analysis on the design constraint and the limitation of such BDA are given in this chapter based on two designs fabricated in 65 nm CMOS process and 0.18 µm BiCMOS process.

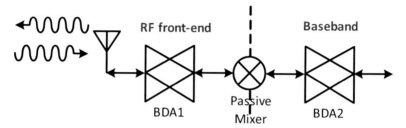

Figure 8.4 Transceiver frontend with single antenna using BDA (RF and Baseband) and passive mixer.

8.2   BDA Design Analysis

The proposed bi-directional amplifier (BDA) comprises two back-to-back connected low-noise amplifiers (LNA) using three-port interconnect traces as shown in the Fig. 8.5. A single antenna is connected to one end of the reference plane and the other end is connected to the mixer as shown in Fig. 8.4. Complementary switch input signals (RX and TX) in the time division multiplexing scheme are provided to the LNAs to select the direction of the signal flow. LNA#1 is functional, while LNA#2 is OFF in the transmitter mode and vice versa for the receiver mode. When the BDA as shown in Fig. 8.5 is operating in the transmitter mode, then Tx = ON activates the LNA#1 to enable signal flow to the antenna, meanwhile the Rx = OFF is set and the LNA#2 is turned OFF. Similarly, for the receiver mode, the operation status of LNA#1 and LNA#2 is interchanged. The design consideration for this implementation is to make sure that the interconnects provide low loss along the ON path, provide high isolation in the OFF path, and mitigate the impedance matching that may result from the ON/OFF states of the back-to-back connected LNAs.

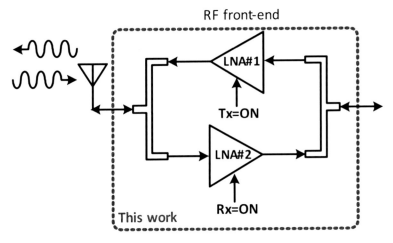

Figure 8.5 Typical amplifier topology to support variable gain.

In this section, we analyze the switch control achieved in the design. Then, we look into the aspect of designing the three-port interconnect network that provides low loss and also mitigates the input/output return loss degradations.

8.2.1 Signal Flow Direction Switch Control

Practically, transistors (MOSFET or BJT) provide uni-directional signal flow ignoring the leakage reverse signal, which is explored in our design. A latch-up condition due to negative feedback (out-of-phase loop signals) or the oscillation condition due to positive feedback (in-phase loop signals) of the back-to-back connected amplifiers may occur if both the amplifiers are ON. To avoid both these conditions, only one amplifier should be ON at a time and the other amplifier should be turned OFF. By controlling the mutually exclusive amplifiers ON/OFF conditions, the bi-directional control of signal flow can be achieved. The transistor bias operating point plays an important role in determining whether the amplifier is in ON/OFF condition as shown in Fig. 8.6. In this proposed BDA design, the amplifier transistors also function as the T/R switch and support the control of the signal flow direction. Therefore, this overcomes the series resistive loss or the shunt capacitive loading issues of the standalone T/R switch as discussed previously. Additionally, the amplifier transistors when biased properly has gain for frequencies below its transition frequency (f_T).

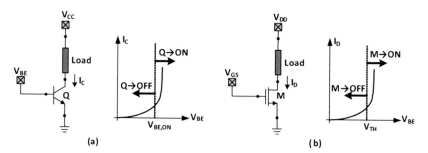

(a)   (b)

Figure 8.6 Transistor bias condition (a) BJT (b) MOSFET.

8.2.2 Interconnect Network Design

The interconnect network can be implemented by using either the micro-strip line (MSL) or the coplanar waveguide (CPWG) transmission line structure. The interconnect lines are desired to be low loss and compact size and also provide 50 Ω impedance matching irrespective of the amplifiers' ON/OFF condition during the bi-directional control. Among the two following examples, one BDA is based on the MSL and the second design is based on the CPWG structure. Since the three-port interconnect network is connected at both the input and the output reference planes, the overall BDA design becomes a two-port system as shown in Fig. 8.5.

The challenging aspect of the three-port interconnect network used in the BDA is the impedance matching to 50 Ω to the common input/output port (Port 1) based on the amplifier ON/OFF condition at the other two ports (Port 2 and Port 3). The two scenarios of the impedance transformation are shown in Fig. 8.7 for the two operating conditions of the BDA, namely receive (forward) and transmit (reverse) modes. If both the LNAs used in the BDA are identical, then both the scenarios as shown in Fig. 8.7 will be the same, hence resulting in a symmetric impedance requirement for the three-port network. To simplify the design of the three-port network, the amplifier input and output terminals can be matched to 50 Ω over the interested frequency range at both ON and OFF conditions. Hence, the three-port network will be symmetric structure about Port 1.

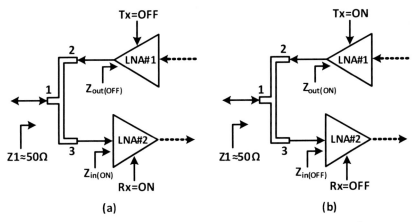

Figure 8.7 Three-port interconnect network impedance transformer: (a) Receive (forward) mode; (b) transmit (reverse) mode.

8.3 Bi-Directional Low-Noise Amplifier Examples

This section illustrates two BDA designs: one using a 65 nm CMOS process with MSL-based interconnect network (BDA1) and the other design using the bipolar SiGe HBT technology with CPWG-based interconnect network (BDA2). The design of the standalone LNA in the BDA examples is illustrated in Chapter 7 on 60 GHz low-noise amplifier as LNA1 version 2 and LNA2 for BDA1 and BDA2 designs, respectively.

8.3.1 BDA1—Based on 65 nm CMOS with Custom-Built Inductor and Micro-Strip Line Three-Port Interconnect Network

The proposed BDA1 consists of two LNAs (LNA1 version 2) back-to-back connected using the three-port MSL interconnect network as shown in Fig. 8.7. The interconnect three-port MSL network is designed by using Ansoft HFSS v15.0 EM simulator to provide low loss performance. The impedance of this MSL transmission line is controlled by optimizing the planar lateral dimensions (length and width). The resulting MSL dimension is very long and by using a serpentine structure, the transmission line can be implemented within a compact die area. By stacking several top metal layers using vertical vias for the signal trace and also similarly stacking some lower metal layers to form the ground plane of the MSL transmission line, we can achieve the desired impedance matching as shown in the 3D view of the line in Fig. 8.8.

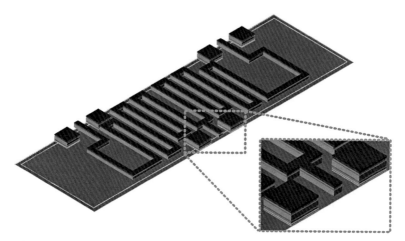

Figure 8.8 Interconnect transmission line (3D view).

The BDA is also fabricated in GLOBALFOUNDRIES 65 nm CMOS process with a die area (0.8 mm × 0.6 mm) as shown in Fig. 8.9. By using the back-to-back connected proposed LNA design as discussed in LNA1 version 2 along with the MSL interconnect transmission lines as shown in Fig. 8.8, the bi-directional functionality is experimentally verified by switching ON one LNA with transistor biasing greater than threshold voltage while biasing the other LNA in the OFF state by using on-wafer probing.

Based on the measured S-parameters as shown in Fig. 8.10, the proposed BDA1 has identical forward receive (blue) and reverse transmit (red) S-parameter characteristics. This symmetric result with an isolation of about 40 dB is achieved between the two modes, and the return loss is also not significantly affected and provides the evidence of the proposed bi-directional reconfigurability of amplifiers.

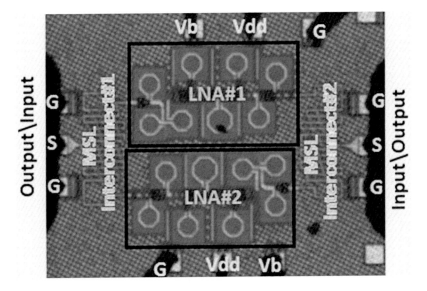

Figure 8.9 Die microphotograph of the BDA1.

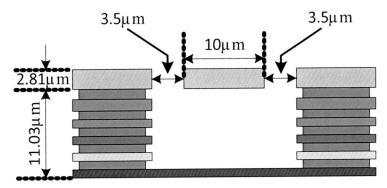

Figure 8.10 Cross-sectional view of CPWG used in LNA2 and BDA2 [5], © IEEE 2015.

However, the performance of the BDA1 is degraded from the standalone LNA1 version 2 design and can be ascertained to the interconnect losses of the transmission lines.

Based on Table 8.1, we find that the proposed BDA1 has comparable bandwidth, low noise figure, and input/output matching to the state-of-the-art designs. The proposed design does not incorporate SPDT switches and has low power consumption and smaller die area of 0.6 mm × 0.8 mm.

Table 8.1 Measured performance of the CMOS LNA1 version 2 and BDA1

Parameter	Units	LNA1 version 2	BDA1
Technology	—	65 nm CMOS	65 nm CMOS
Peak gain	(dB)	13.7	8.6
–3 dB Bandwidth	(Hz)	47.6 G to 67.1 G	55 G to 66 G
Noise Figure	(dB)	6.2* (Min.)	6.9* (Min.)
Output P_{1dB}	(dBm)	+1.0	–2.0
Core area	(mm^2)	0.24	0.48
DC power consumption	(mW)	27.6	27.6
Supply voltage	(V)	1.2	1.2
Topology	—	Single-ended	Single-ended

*Simulation result

8.3.2 BDA2—Based on 0.18 μm SiGe BiCMOS with Distributive Transmission Line Inductor and Interconnect Network Design

The proposed BDA2 is based on the four-stage cascode single-ended amplifier (LNA2) using the 0.18 μm SiGe BiCMOS process from TowerJazz Semiconductor. The design has impedance matching networks, amplifier interconnects, and load inductance and the three-port interconnects are implemented as coplanar waveguide (CPWG) transmission lines with the cross sectional structure as shown in Fig. 8.10. The structures are built and modeled by 2.5D EM simulation using Agilent ADS Momentum v2011. The proposed BDA2 design occupies an active die area of 0.85 mm^2 excluding measurement pads as shown in Fig. 8.11. The proposed physical design is a two-port symmetrical LNA and the direction can be selected by controlling the bias voltages provided at V_{B1} and V_{B2}.

The measured S-parameters obtained for the bias voltage V_{B1} = 1.8 V in the forward direction LNA#1 while V_{B2} = 0 V are shown in Fig. 8.12. The $|S_{21}|$ plot indicates a good gain flatness and the input $|S_{11}|$ and output $|S_{22}|$ return losses are better than 8 dB over the entire operating frequency range from 54 to 65 GHz. The reverse isolation $|S_{12}|$ is better than 35 dB, and hence the proposed BDA2 design provides a better uni-directional signal flow with improved stability.

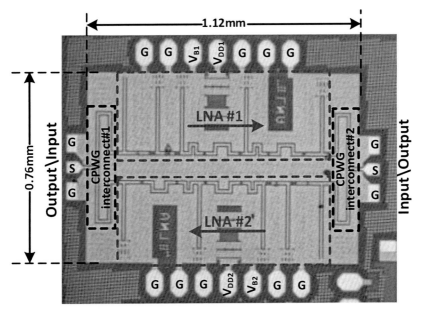

Figure 8.11 BDA2 die microphotograph [5], ©IEEE 2015.

The measured gain and noise figure (NF) comparison plots of BDA2 against the standalone LNA2 are shown in Fig. 8.12. The single-ended NF of the BDA2 and LNA2 is measured by using the NoiseCom NC5115-60G noise source based on the Y-factor method. The comparison gain plot indicates a minimum insertion loss of 1.5 dB that is contributed by the CPWG-based interconnect networks at both the input and the output ports.

Table 8.2 summarizes the on-wafer probing measured performance of the standalone LNA2 as compared to the proposed BDA2. The three-port CPWG interconnects provide a low loss signal path retaining the 50 Ω matching throughout the design. The proposed BDA2 has the three-port CPWG interconnect on both the IO ends and hence the actual insertion loss seen is doubled between the two RF IO ports.

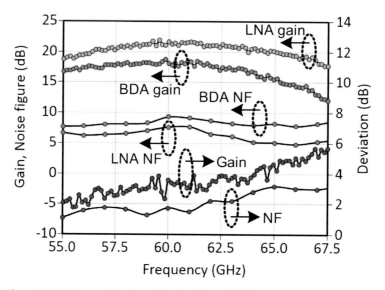

Figure 8.12 Measured gain and noise figure (NF) comparison of the BDA2 against the standalone LNA2 [5], © IEEE 2015.

Table 8.2 Measured performance of the SiGe LNA2 and BDA2

Parameter	Units	LNA2	BDA2 [5]
Technology	—	0.18 μm SiGe BiCMOS	0.18 μm SiGe BiCMOS
Peak gain	(dB)	21.9	18.8
–3 dB Bandwidth	(Hz)	55 G to 66.6 G	54 G to 65 G
Noise figure	(dB)	5.1 to 7.6	7.7 to 9.3
Input P_{1dB}	(dBm)	–20.5	–16.5
Die area	(mm²)	0.63	1.3
DC power consumption	(mW)	19.3	19.3
Supply voltage	(V)	1.8	1.8
Topology	—	Single-ended	Single-ended

Acknowledgments

The authors would like to thank TowerJazz Semiconductors for providing fabrication service of the design in 0.18 μm SiGe

BiCMOS and GLOBALFOUNDRIES in 65 nm CMOS process. The authors would also like to thank W. Yang of Nanyang Technological University (NTU), Singapore, for assisting in the on-wafer measurement of the proposed design.

References

1. Sim, S., Jeon, L., and Kim, J.-G. (2013). A compact X-band bi-directional phased-array T/R chipset in 0.13 µm CMOS technology, *IEEE Trans. Microw. Theory Techn.*, TMTT, vol. 61, no. 1, pp. 562–569.

2. Uzunkol, M., and Rebeiz, G. M. (2010). A low-loss 50–70 GHz SPDT switch in 90 nm CMOS, *IEEE J. Solid-State Circuits*, JSSC, vol. 45, no. 10, pp. 2003–2007.

3. Cohen, E., Ruberto, M., Cohen, M., Degani, O., Ravid, S., and Ritter, D. (2013). A CMOS bidirectional 32-element phased-array transceiver at 60 GHz with LTCC antenna, *IEEE Trans. Microw. Theory Techn.*, TMTT, vol. 61, no. 3, pp. 1359–1375.

4. Kuang, L., Chi, B., Jia, H., Ye, Z., Jia, W., and Wang, Z. (2014). Co-design of 60-GHz wideband front-end IC with on-chip T/R switch based on passive macro-modeling, *IEEE Trans. Microw. Theory Techn.*, TMTT, vol. 62, no. 11, pp. 2743–2754.

5. Kumar, T. B., Ma, K. and Yeo, K. S. (2017). A 60-GHz coplanar waveguide-based bidirectional LNA in SiGe BiCMOS, *IEEE Microw. Wireless Compon. Lett.*, MWCL, vol. 27, no. 8, pp. 742–744.

Success is ...
Think what others don't;
See what others can't; and
Do what others won't."

—Kiat Seng Yeo and Kaixue Ma

Chapter 9

Millimeter-Wave Mixer

Shouxian Mou,[a] **Kaixue Ma,**[a] **and Kiat Seng Yeo**[b]

[a]*School of Physical Electronics,*
University of Electronic Science and Technology of China,
#4 Section II, Jianshe North Road, Chengdu 610054, P. R. China
[b]*Engineering Product Development, Singapore University of Technology and Design,*
8 Somapah Road, Singapore 487372

moushouxian@gmail.com

The mixer is an important component, which is used in the demodulator and modulator designs to convert the RF (radio frequency) signals to and from baseband or IF (intermediate frequency) signals. In the receiver, this conversion is from RF to IF, while in the transmitter, the conversion is from IF to RF.

9.1 Mixer Fundamentals

9.1.1 Basic Mixer Operation

Basically, the mixer performs frequency translation by multiplying two signals, which at most of the time are called RF signals and LO (local oscillation) signals. According to the orders of the LO, mixers can be categorized into fundamental and sub-harmonic

Low-Power Wireless Communication Circuits and Systems: 60 GHz and Beyond
Edited by Kaixue Ma and Kiat Seng Yeo
Copyright © 2018 Pan Stanford Publishing Pte. Ltd.
ISBN 978-981-4745-96-3 (Hardcover), 978-1-315-15653-8 (eBook)
www.panstanford.com

types as shown in Fig. 9.1. By far the most common type of mixer is the fundamental-mode mixer, with its operation illustration in Figs. 9.1a,c. In this type of mixer, the sum and difference of the two input frequencies are produced at the output. For the case of down-conversion, the frequency component of $f_{RF} - f_{LO}$ will try to be retained, while the high-frequency component of $f_{RF} + f_{LO}$ will be filtered out. For the case of up-conversion, the high-frequency component of $f_{RF} + f_{LO}$ will be retained and the low frequency component of $f_{RF} - f_{LO}$ will be filtered out. Figure 9.1b is the illustration of a sub-harmonic mixer (SHM), which will be discussed in the final section of this chapter. The above-mentioned nonlinearity can be realized by diodes or transistors and be followed by a filter to remove the undesired frequency components. The nonlinearity operation mechanism can be illustrated by a mathematical expression. Let us suppose that two sinusoid signals $v_{RF} = A_{RF} \cos(\omega_{RF}t)$ and $v_{LO} = A_{LO} \cos(\omega_{LO}t)$, are multiplied together through a nonlinear device, the corresponding results can be expressed as

$$v_{RF} \cdot v_{LO} = A_{RF} \cos(\omega_{RF}t) \cdot A_{LO} \cos(\omega_{LO}t) = \frac{1}{2} A_{RF} A_{LO}$$
$$[\cos(\omega_{RF} - \omega_{LO})t + \cos(\omega_{RF} + \omega_{LO})t. \tag{9.1}$$

Equation (9.1) shows that the sum and difference frequencies of ω_{RF} and ω_{LO} are produced as desired for a fundamental mixer. The potential nonlinear devices that can be used to perform the mixing functions, are diodes and transistors, each of which has different circuit configurations. The mixing function can be easily demonstrated by a single diode, based on its *I–V* relationship expression. Applying two sinusoid signals of $v_{RF} = A_{RF} \cos(\omega_{RF}t)$ and $v_{LO} = A_{LO} \cos(\omega_{LO}t)$ to a single diode, the voltage across the diode can be described as

$$v_d = A_{RF} \cos(\omega_{RF}t) + A_{LO} \cos(\omega_{LO}t). \tag{9.2}$$

The corresponding diode current with Taylor series expansion form can also be expressed as

$$i_d = I_s(e^{v_d/V_T} - 1) = I_s\left(1 + \frac{v_d}{V_T} + \frac{1}{2!}\left(\frac{v_d}{V_T}\right)^2 + \frac{1}{3!}\left(\frac{v_d}{V_T}\right)^3 + \cdots - 1\right), \tag{9.3}$$

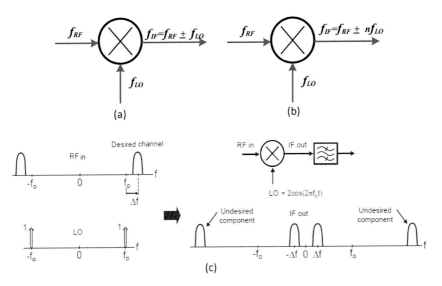

Figure 9.1 Simplified mixer diagram illustration: (a) a fundamental mixer; (b) a sub-harmonic mixer; and (c) the down-conversion illustration.

where I_S is the diode's saturation current in the reverse-bias condition; and V_T is thermal voltage, which is around 26 mV at room temperature. Equations (9.2) and (9.3) indicate that a large number of components with different frequencies are created due to the diode's nonlinearity. For example, the squared term in Eq. (9.3) will produce the sum and difference frequencies $\omega_{RF} + \omega_{LO}$ and $\omega_{RF} - \omega_{LO}$, respectively, as well as the second harmonics of $2\omega_{RF}$ and $2\omega_{LO}$. The cubic term will produce frequency components of $3\omega_{RF}$, $3\omega_{LO}$, and $2\omega_{RF} \pm 2\omega_{LO}$. The results suggest that a diode can be utilized to implement both the fundamental and the sub-harmonic mixing operations, which will be analyzed in the subsequent sections.

9.1.2 Controlled Transconductance Mixer

Mixers have various topologies. The input of some kinds of mixers, adopts a simple amplifier and the amplified current from this gain stage is then passed into a switching stage, as shown in Fig. 9.2. The switching stage steers the current to one side of the output or the other depending on the control signal v_2, which at most of the time is the LO signal and providing the nonlinear characteristics. If the control signal is assumed to be periodic, then this will have the effect of multiplying the current coming out of the gain stage (Q_1, Q_2) by ±1 (when it is a square wave for simplicity). Multiplying a signal by another signal will produce a large number of components with various frequencies at the output as already discussed. Therefore, the circuit in Fig. 9.2 can be used to perform frequency conversion of the signal v_1. The signal v_1 at most of the time is the RF signal for down-conversion or IF signal for up-conversion.

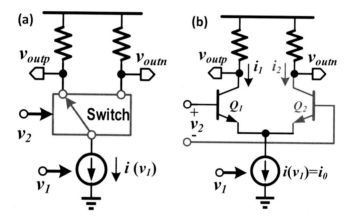

Figure 9.2 Illustration of a transconductance-controlled mixer: (a) Conceptual diagram, (b) basic circuit.

Figure 9.2b shows a transconductance-controlled mixer with a differential switching pair of bipolar transistors. For this configuration, the current is related to the input voltage v_2 by the transconductance g_{m1} and g_{m2} of the two input switching transistors Q_1 and Q_2. However, g_{m1} and g_{m2} are controlled by the tail current, which actually is controlled by the input voltage v_1. Hence, the output current will be dependent on both input voltages v_1 and v_2, i.e., both the RF and LO signals. Through derivation, the difference of the output current i_1 and i_2 can be simplified and calculated as [1, 2]

$$i_o = i_1 - i_2 = (I_0 + g_{mc}v_1)\tanh\frac{v_2}{2V_T} = I_0\tanh\frac{v_2}{2V_T} + g_{mc}v_1\tanh\frac{v_2}{2V_T}, \quad (9.4)$$

where the first term is v_2 (LO) feedthrough and the second term is the multiplication product, namely mixing products of v_1 and

v_2; g_{mc} is the transconductance of the current source. The differential feedthrough output voltage is equally above the common voltage, and can be eliminated in a double-balanced configuration as will be discussed later.

To remove the v_2 feed-through of Eq. (9.4), the output of the circuit in Fig. 9.2b can be combined with another similar circuit, which is driven by the 180° out-phased signals of v_1 and v_2, namely $-v_1$ and $-v_2$ as illustrated in Fig. 9.3. This presented mixer has four switching transistors Q_3 to Q_6 known as the switching quad. With the same analysis method, the output current of the second differential pair Q_5 to Q_6 can be derived and expressed as

$$i'_0 = i_6 - i_5 = (I_0 - g_{mc}v_1)\tanh\frac{v_2}{2V_T} = I_0\tanh\frac{v_2}{2V_T} - g_{mc}v_1\tanh\frac{v_2}{2V_T}, \quad (9.5)$$

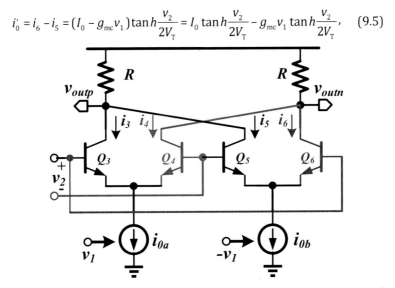

Figure 9.3 Illustration of a double-balanced transconductance-controlled mixer.

By subtraction of Eqs. (9.4) and (9.5), the total differential current of this topology can be obtained:

$$i_0 - i'_0 = 2g_{mc}v_1\tanh\frac{v_2}{2V_T} \quad (9.6)$$

Equation (9.6) indicates that with double-balanced topology, the LO feedthrough in Eq. (9.4) is eliminated, which helps to reduce the self-mixing and DC offset.

9.1.3 Transconductor Implementation

As discussed in the previous section that the RF input voltage V_{RF} can be converted to current $I_o = G_m V_{RF}$ by a transconductor. Then the current can be steered to either output nodes of the differential switching transistor pair, depending on the status of the LO signals as illustrated in Fig. 9.4. For simplicity, the LO signals in this case is assumed as periodic square waves.

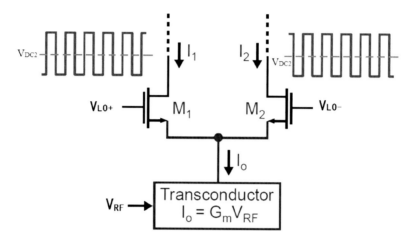

Figure 9.4 Simplified diagram of a single-balanced mixer.

Since mixer has linearity requirements, the transconductor must be proper designed, which is also has influence on the system's sensitivity and other performance. There are several configurations to implement the transconductor, as shown in Figs. 9.5a–c. A common source (CS) amplifier is illustrated in Fig. 9.5a, where the RF signal is applied to the gate. For a CS setup, at most of the time, transistor M1 operates in the saturation region for robust performance. The corresponding transconductance of this amplifier which converts the RF voltage to current, is the same as the transconductance of M_1. When increasing the gate bias voltage V_{bias}, the electrons in the channel of the NMOS transistor M_1 enter the velocity saturation region. As a result, a high linearity can be achieved.

Figure 9.5b illustrates a common gate (CG) configuration, where the RF signal is applied to the source node of the NMOS transistor M_1. The transconductance of this configuration is determined by the combination of the source resistor R_S and the transconductance g_m of M_1. It is smaller than that of the CS setup, and the CG amplifier is degenerated, so as to get higher linearity. The bias current I_{bias} can also be set higher for large current density through device to achieve higher linearity (velocity saturation).

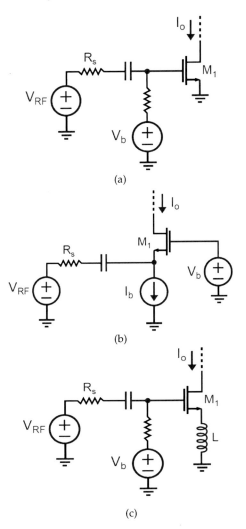

Figure 9.5 Transconductor implementation configuration: (a) Common source amplification; (b) common gate amplification; (c) common source amplification with source degeneration.

Just like the source inductive degeneration topology in LNA designs, which helps to get a high linearity, the source degenerated inductor can also benefit the linearity in the mixer designs as shown in Fig. 9.5c. The source inductor degrades the gain of the CS amplifier with its negative feedback. Thus, the linearity improves. The degeneration inductor can also be replaced with a resistor to reduce layout size. However, if chip area is permitted, an inductor is preferred rather than a resistor.

Ideally, the above-mentioned inductors do not contribute any noise to the system. Practically, all real inductors have parasitic resistance that generates thermal noise, but there can still be a significant reduction in the overall noise figure for the mixer with this technique. In addition, unlike the resistor, inductor does not have a voltage drop (or just in millivolt level, since its parasitic resistance is quite small), which is very important for the scaled-down low-V_{DD} semiconductor process and low power applications. Moreover, the inductor has increased impedance ($j\omega$L) at high frequencies, which helps filter out the undesired high-frequency components. The drawback for using degeneration inductors is the additional chip area they consumed. On-chip degeneration inductors will consume larger area than resistors, and thus will increase the cost. In mixer designs, this inductor is seldom to be used to resonate with C_{gs} like that in LNA designs. Power match usually is not required for IC implementation due to the proximity of LNA and mixer, compared with its discrete MMIC counterpart.

9.1.4   The Issue of Balance in Mixers

Commonly, a balanced signal has no DC component. Basically, there are two signals regarding the balance issues in mixer designs, namely the above-mentioned RF and LO signals. According to the various mixer designs in literature, LO feedthrough will appear due to unbalanced RF input signals; and RF feedthrough will appear due to unbalanced LO signal, as shown in Fig. 9.6. The feedthrough can be reduced by setting the DC bias point to zero, however, it is not practical since the transconductor transistor and the LO switching transistor pair do require a bias voltage to operate.

This issue can be released by combination of two mixer paths with LO signal 180° out of phase between the paths, i.e., with differential LO input signals. By subtraction between the two paths, the DC component owing to LO signal can be cancelled. The combination diagram is presented in Fig. 9.7 and the corresponding mixer is called a single-balanced mixer, just as the mixer shown in Fig. 9.4, which has differential LO input nodes and differential output nodes to reduce some issues that a single-end mixer cannot solve. For this configuration, the amplitude of the LO swing should be high enough to turn on and off the differential switching pair, but not so larger than that to fully turn on and off the transistors, otherwise the LO leakage and other effect might be severe. Ideally, square wave is the best format to minimize noise from M_1 and M_2. However, practically, it is difficult to realize square wave LO signals at millimeter-wave frequency.

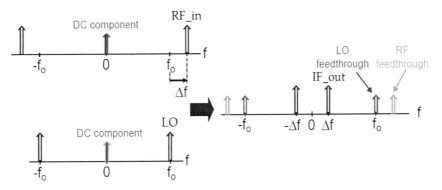

Figure 9.6 RF and LO unbalance illustration in a mixer.

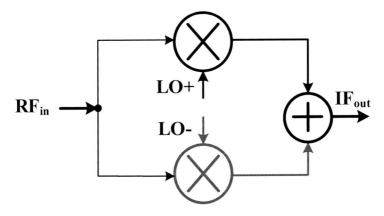

Figure 9.7 DC component cancellation diagram.

Although the single-balanced mixer as shown in Fig. 9.4 helps remove the unbalance effect due to LO signals, the RF unbalance issue still exists. It can be seen from Fig. 9.8a, when the RF input signal has DC component, even there is no DC component within the LO input signals, after the mixing operation of a single-balanced mixer, there is quite a high-power LO feedthrough in the output signal spectrum. The corresponding feedthrough can be removed by a low pass filter, at the cost of an extra chip area. Hence, we would better remove the feedthrough by eliminating the DC component in the RF input signals. As demonstrated in Fig. 9.8b, when there is no DC component in the RF input signals, the output spectrum indicates the LO feedthrough will be dramatically reduced (as at the frequency of f_0).

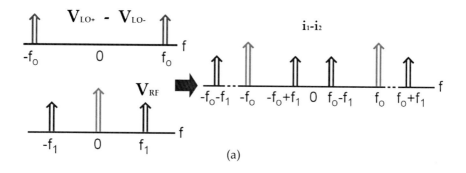

(a)

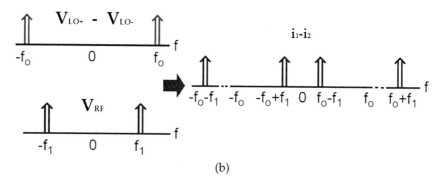

(b)

Figure 9.8 LO feedthrough in a single-balanced mixer: (a) with DC component in the RF input signals; and (b) no DC component in the RF input signals.

As presented in the previous paragraphs, using a differential LO input signals can reduce its unbalance effect, it also can be expected to try to realize a configuration with differential RF input signals to cancel its DC component. Thus the same method as with that dealing with the LO balancing can be adopted as presented in Fig. 9.9. At the combined IF output node, the DC components are cancelled and the useful signal components add together. The subtraction is realized by cross-coupling the output current of each stage. The corresponding mixer is called a double-balanced mixer. The simplified circuit block diagram of a double-balanced mixer is shown in Fig. 9.10 with an implementation of MOS transistors, which is similar to the BJT implementation as already illustrated in Fig. 9.3. The double-balanced mixer, has both differential RF input signals and differential LO input signals applied to two switching transistor pairs. The four outputs are combined to differential outputs. Basically, the double-balanced configuration is the most preferred mixer topology when a radio system is implemented on IC.

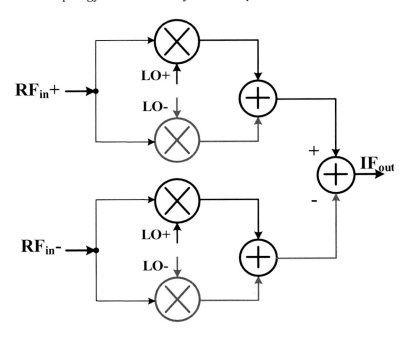

Figure 9.9 DC component cancellation diagram.

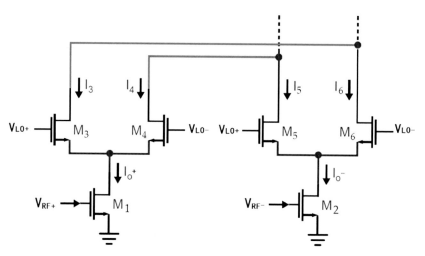

Figure 9.10 Simplified circuit diagram of a double-balanced mixer.

9.2 Fundamental Mixers

9.2.1 FET Resistive Mixer

As mentioned in the early sections that the mixer can be implemented with either diodes or FET/Bipolar junction transistors. Past research works on diode-based mixers were generally focused on RF and millimeter-wave frequencies, whereas mixers with Gilbert cell or with other complicated techniques were focused on the lower frequency operation range owing to the poor characteristics of the on-chip transistor at RF or millimeter-wave frequencies [3–10]. With fast scaling-down of semiconductor technology, the transistors' cutoff frequency can now reach up to hundreds of gigahertz, which makes it possible to implement millimeter-wave mixer with bipolar or field-effect transistors. Resistive FET mixer is one of the popular techniques [3] as shown in Fig. 9.11, which uses the nonlinearity of the FET resistance to perform mixing. Specifically, since the LO is generally a large signal, the FET resistance will be varied with the transistor's non-linear characteristics when the LO signal is changing. FET resistive mixers have a number of merits such as circuit simplicity (compared to the Gilbert cell–based mixers, which will be discussed in the next sections), high linearity, and low $1/f$ noise, which are achieved by operating the mixing transistors at zero drain biasing condition [4]. Commonly, it consumes no DC power. Therefore, the FET resistive mixers can be utilized in the applications of receivers desiring a large dynamic range with low power consumption.

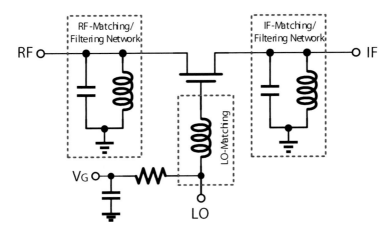

Figure 9.11 Illustration of a millimeter-wave FET resistive mixers.

Figure 9.11 illustrates the basic diagram of the FET resistive mixer, with LO signal applied to the gate. Normally the FET transistor should be biased in the resistive or triode region [3, 4] through an additional gate biasing voltage such as a RC network in the figure, which functions as a low pass filter and RF choke. The RF signal is applied to the source node of the transistor; and the down-converted IF signal is outputted from the transistor's drain node. Each port incorporates a matching and filtering network for interface connection and filtering out the unwanted signal. In literature [3], a FET resistive mixer based on this topology with a 90 nm CMOS silicon-on-insulator (SOI) technology was implemented, which achieves measured conversion loss of 9–13 dB from 26.5 GHz to 30 GHz and measured port-to-port isolations 22–33 dB with 5 dBm LO input power when LO frequency is 24.5 GHz and RF frequency of 27 GHz. In addition, the FET resistive mixer consumed quite a compact chip area of 0.38 mm × 0.32 mm, which further proved the feasibility of the FET resistive mixer topology.

Normally, with scaling-down of the semiconductor technology, for the corresponding scaled MOS transistors, the gate–source capacitances C_{gs} and the drain–source channel resistances R_{ds}

will decrease due to the shorted channel lengths [5]. R_{ds} can be approximated to the turn-on resistance of the transistor when it operates as a switch, which incorporation with C_{gs}, measures the conversion loss and the switching speed. Therefore, when doing mixer designs at millimeter-wave frequencies, transistors with short channel length are more preferred. However, compared to GaAs and InP based FET resistive mixers, the FET resistive mixers even based on scaled-down CMOS process, still suffer a high conversion loss because of the lossy substrates. Moreover, the layout of the transistor with n-fingers (n is integer) must be properly designed at RF and millimeter-wave frequency, since the parasitic gate resistance and parasitic capacitance will greatly degrade the conversion loss and switching speed (operating frequency), especially when frequency is high. It even has negative effect on the LO driven power level. To reduce the gate resistance, ring-type transistor layout are commonly used, where all the gate fingers are connected together from both sides of the transistor and form a ring [4, 5], as illustrated in Fig. 9.12a. The source and drain are placed on the opposite side of each other. Compared with the lateral ring-type structure in Fig. 9.12a, the vertical ring-type gate structure as depicted in Fig. 9.12b, has reduced gate resistance. However, both the lateral and vertical structures increase the parasitic capacitances between the transistor terminals, such as the source-to-drain capacitance C_{sd}, which can degrade the conversion loss of the mixers owing to the signal leakage path between source and drain, and prevent the transistors from switching off completely especially at millimeter-wave frequency [4]. The parasitic capacitances between the interconnection metal lines of drain terminal and the silicon substrates, and the capacitance between the drain fingers and source fingers all contribute to the degradation.

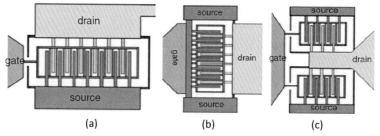

(a)   (b)   (c)

Figure 9.12 Comparison of various transistor layout structures: (a) Lateral ring-type gate; (b) vertical ring-type gate; and (c) symmetry type.

In literature [4], a modified symmetrical ring-type gate structure was proposed as shown in Fig. 9.12c to minimize the parasitic capacitances and the gate resistances. It is calculated that the symmetrical structure can reduce around 50% the length of the gate ring, and it has a smaller drain interconnection metal area compared to the lateral and vertical ring types of layout, which can definitely reduce the parasitic capacitances between the drain and the lossy substrates. Therefore, the conversion loss can be decreased as well. The only drawback of the symmetrical ring-type layout is that the source nodes must be tied out on both sides. In the case that the source nodes need to be tied to another component, the extra interconnection metal line might degrade the mixer performance. Fortunately, in [4], there are no extra devices to connect to the source nodes of the transistor, and the two source nodes can be connected to nearby ground layer, respectively. The proposed modified and optimized transistor layout configuration was adopted to implement a 94 GHz CMOS FET resistive mixer [4] based on a 65 nm CMOS process. Generally, the optimized transistor layout greatly reduces the conversion loss and the final measured conversion loss is only 8.8–9.2 dB with RF frequency range from 87 to 94 GHz and the LO power of less than 7.6 dBm. The drawback is that the port-to-port isolation is poor, which is 13 dB from LO port to the RF port.

9.2.2 Gilbert Cell

Basically, the mixers implemented with diodes or with FET resistive topology, have simple circuit configuration and generally consume no DC power. However, they suffer from high conversion loss and poor port-to-port isolation. Thereafter, many mixers have been implemented with active FET transistors so as to get a positive conversion gain. One of the most popular topologies is the Gilbert cell–based topology [6–8], as already shown in Figs. 9.3 and 9.10, which has several advantages such as excellent port-to-port isolation due to its double-balanced structure as well as the high conversion gain. The schematic diagram of a wideband 9–50 GHz down-conversion mixer implemented in literature [6] with a 0.13 um CMOS technology is illustrated in Fig. 9.13.

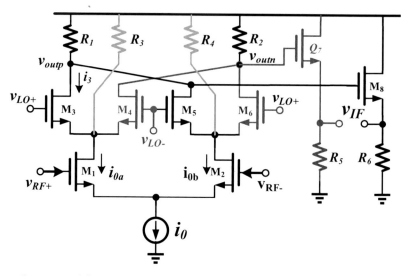

Figure 9.13 Schematic diagram of a double-balanced Gilbert cell mixer.

Basically, this type of mixer operates in the following manners. The differential RF signal is fed into the gate nodes of the two bottom transconductance transistors M_1 and M_2, which are biased at the saturation region so as to get a high gain for the RF input signal. M_1 and M_2 can also be biased in the velocity saturation region for a higher linearity purpose. The differential LO signal is applied to the upper switching quad transistors (M_3–M_6). The upper two pairs of cross-coupled transistors are biased near the pinch-off region, so as to be used as current switches, steering the currents to flow through the drain load. The load in this case are resistors R_1 and R_2. Sometimes, the load can be a LC parallel network to further increase the conversion gain, and reduce the voltage drop through the resistive loads in order to realize a low-V_{DD} application. The four outputs are combined and come out in differential format from nodes v_{outp} and v_{outn}, so as to perform the subtraction operation of the RF/LO DC components and the addition operation of the useful signal components. Besides, a current source is used under the differential transconductance transistor pair of M_1 and M_2 to properly control the total current consumption of the Gilbert cell. As presented in the previous section, degeneration inductor or resistor can also be connected with the source node of the bottom transistors to provide feedback and improve the linearity of the mixer.

9.2.3 Gilbert Cell–Based Mixer

Basically, it can be seen the presented mixer has two stacked transistors, and possibly three stacks if the current source is implemented with a transistor as shown in Fig. 9.13. Since the load of the switching transistor pairs is resistor R_1 and R_2, there will be extra voltage drop across them. Therefore, this circuit topology may not be suitable for a low-supply voltage and low-power application. Some methods can be adopted to solve this issue. Firstly, the current source can be eliminated by applying DC bias voltage to the gate of M_1 and M_2. The bad effect is that a slight change of the bias voltage might cause a significant mixer core current variation, since at most of the time M_1 and M_2 operate at saturation region and the drain current is much sensitive to V_{GS}. Regarding the load resistor R_1 and R_2, as mentioned in the previous section, they can be replaced with inductive load, due to the merit of inductors that they do not have a voltage drop, which is still quite low even with the associated parasitic resistance. The bad effect is that the bandwidth of the inductive-load mixer cannot be very broad and inductors occupy a large chip area compare to resistors or PMOS transistor load.

Another way to reduce the effect of R_1 and R_2 is to use current injection technique as shown in Fig. 9.13, which is implemented by M_1's and M_2's separate resistive loads R_3 and R_4, respectively, directly connected to V_{DD}. This extra injected currents lead to increased drain current for M_1 and M_2, so as to increase the transconductance without increasing the drain current of the switching quad M_3 to M_6. By keeping the two crossed-coupled switching transistor pair M_3 to M_6 working with low current, the voltage drop on the load resistors R_1 and R_2 will be lower, so that the voltage supply V_{DD} can be set lower for the convenience of using current fast-scaling-down CMOS process and being suitable for the popular ultra-low power applications. For Gilbert cell–based mixers, either the LO input nodes or the RF input nodes are inherently capacitive, so the reflection coefficient of each input port is very high. To obtain input impedance matching, a matching network is typically desired, which can be implemented using on-chip inductors and capacitors, or off-chip with packaged inductors/capacitors or transmission line structures. At the mixer output ports, output matching networks are also required. Sometimes, the amplification buffers such as shown in Fig. 9.13, two source follower buffers implemented with M_8 & R_5 and M_9 & R_6 are adopted to provide 50 Ω output matching for further system integration of off-chip measurement purpose.

Practically, the LO/RF input and IF output matching networks significantly influence the operating bandwidth of the Gilbert cell–based mixers. Therefore, as in [6], at the input nodes, two microstrip line transformers are adopted to convert the LO and RF signals from single-ended form to differential form, and used for an ultra-broadband input matching at the same time, which assist the mixer to realize an super wideband operating range of 9 to 50 GHz. As expected when adopting the Gilbert cell–based topology, the mixer has an active conversion gain conversion gain over 5 dB and the RF-to-IF port isolations is more than 40 dB, which definitely verified the advantage of a double-balanced Gilbert cell–based mixer. The drawback is that measured noise figure with RF signal of 15 GHz is 16.4 dB, which is high. The noise figure of this type of mixers is obviously technology-dependent, but it will normally be somewhat high since there are at least six active devices, which have various noise source such as channel current noise, gate induced noise, flicker noise, and node resistance thermal noise. In addition, there are possibly two or more load resistors, which will contribute thermal noise.

9.2.4 Some Techniques Used in Gilbert Cell–Based Mixers

Besides the current-bleeding or current-injection technique used in the broadband Gilbert cell–based double balanced down-conversion mixer illustrated in Fig. 9.13, some other techniques can also be adopted when doing mixer designs, as shown in Fig. 9.14, which is a narrow-band up-conversion mixer operating in the 60 GHz range, implemented based on a standard 90 nm

CMOS technology with high conversion gain and port-to-port isolation [7]. In this topology based on the idea in VCO designs, two PMOS transistors PM_7 and PM_8 are cross-coupled to realize negative resistance to compensate the loss so as to enhance the conversion gain. For the case without negative resistance compensation, the conversion gain CG_1 of the mixer can be expressed as [7]

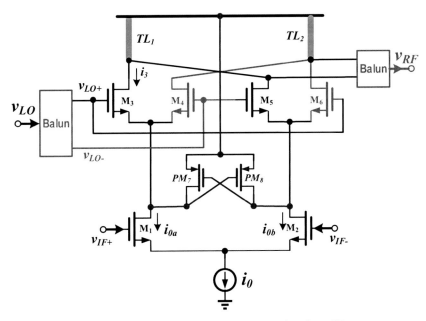

Figure 9.14 Schematic diagram of a narrow-band millimeter-wave double-balanced Gilbert cell up-conversion mixers.

$$CG_1 = \frac{2}{\pi} g_{m1,2} \omega_{RF} L_{TL},$$ (9.7)

where $g_{m1,2}$ is the transconductance of the differential IF signal input transistors pair of M_1 and M_2; L_{TL} is the inductance of the load inductors TL_1 and TL_2, which were implemented with transmission lines. For comparison, the mixer conversion gain CG_2 with negative resistance compensation can be expressed as [7]

$$CG_2 = \frac{2}{\pi} \frac{G_{m,LO}}{(G_{m,LO} - g_{m7,8})} g_{m1,2} \omega_{RF} L_{TL},$$ (9.8)

where $G_{m,LO}$ is the equivalent input conductance of the two pairs of cross-coupled LO switching transistors M_3 to M_6; and $-g_{m7,8}$ is the equivalent input conductance of the cross-coupled PMOS transistors PM_7 and PM_8, which are used for negative resistance compensation. By comparing Eqs. (9.7) and (9.8), it can be found clearly that the negative resistance compensation technique help improve the conversion gain. As mentioned in the previous section, the input/output ports matching relates to the operating band of the mixer, therefore as shown in Fig. 9.14, two baluns are integrated on chip to implement the single-end to differential conversion (for input IF signal) and differential to single-end (for RF output signals) conversion, which can also greatly benefit the mixer's port-to-port isolation performance. With the dedicated techniques, the mixer in [7] achieves measured active up-conversion gain of 4.5 dB with IF of 0.1 GHz and RF being 60 GHz and LO-to-RF port isolation of 57.5 dB with a LO power of 6 dBm, with a low power consumption of 15.1 mW from a 1.2 V voltage supply.

In addition to the current-bleeding technique, transistor cross-coupling compensation technique and the input/output transformers, the current-reusing technique that is commonly used in LNA designs, can also be introduced in mixer designs to enhance the conversion gain, as illustrated in Fig. 9.15, which is a narrow-band double-balanced Gilbert cell–based mixer operating at 60 GHz range, implemented in [8] with a standard 90 nm CMOS technology. The current-reusing technique incorporation with the transconductance transistors M_1 and M_2, realizes a current-reused RF single-to-differential converter to replace the Marchand balun in Fig. 9.14 so as to reduce the chip area.

As known for a common-source amplifier, the drain output has a phase difference of 180° from the input signal of the gate terminal [5]. Therefore, V_{RF1+} and V_{RF1-} of the drain terminals of M_1 and M_2, respectively, should be out of phase. M_1 and M_2 and their gate bias voltage must be chosen carefully to guarantee V_{RF1+} and V_{RF1-} to have equal amplitude. The adoption of a current-reuse topology of the single-to-differential converter rather than a cascode topology, is because of that current-reuse topology has higher gain so as to achieve a higher mixer down-conversion gain. In literature [8], the mixer has an average conversion gain of 13.58, 7.79, and 6.75 dB, respectively, corresponding to the current reuse topology, cascode topology and common-source topology (with removal of M_3 and M_4). The detailed mechanism why the current-reused converter could improve the conversion gain more effectively than the cascode topology, can be found in [8]. Basically, according to [8], the output drain current I_{D3R} can be derived and simplified as

$$|I_{D3R}| \approx \frac{\omega_{T3}}{\omega_{RF}}|I_{D1}| > |I_{D1}|, \tag{9.9}$$

$\omega_{T3} = 2\pi f_{T3}$, where f_{T3} is the cutoff frequency of M_3 and ω_{T3}/ω_{RF} is larger than 1. For the case of cascode topology, according to [8], the output drain current I_{D3C} can be derived and simplified as

$$|I_{D3C}| \approx \left| \frac{g_{m3}}{j\omega C_{gs3} + j\omega C_{ds1} + \dfrac{1}{R_{ds1}} + g_{m3}} \right| |I_{D1}| < |I_{D1}|. \tag{9.10}$$

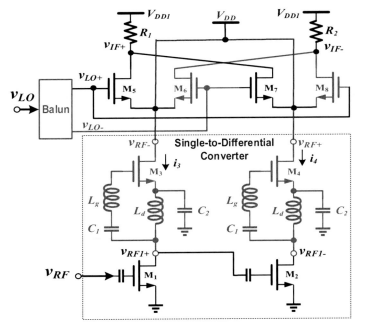

Figure 9.15 Schematic diagram of a narrow-band millimete-wave double-balanced Gilbert cell down-conversion mixers.

It is obvious from Eqs. (9.9) and (9.10) that the current-reused topology has a higher output current and therefore a higher conversion gain. Similar to the mixer presented in Fig. 9.13, this mixer illustrated in Fig. 9.15, also adopts current injection technique by directly connecting the drain terminals of M_3 and M_4 to supply voltage V_{DD} to further enhance the conversion gain and reduce the drain current of the two pairs of switching transistors. The introduced techniques has been demonstrated by the measured conversion gain of 13.87 ± 1.59 dB [8], which is quite high compared to the previous mixer designs.

9.3 Sub-Harmonic Mixers

9.3.1 LO Self-Mixing

Compared to the input RF or IF signal, the local oscillator (LO) signal generally has a much higher power; hence, it can easily leak or couple to various circuits on the chip. Therefore, there are some outstanding issues such as LO feedthrough/leakage and self-mixing in mixer designs, which will degrade the performance such as increased noise and intermodulation distortion.

As illustrated in Fig. 9.16, there are several LO feedthrough or self-mixing paths. The first path as LO feedthrough occurs from the LO port to the IF output port, due to parasitic capacitance and power supply coupling, etc. When the LO power is very high, the leakage is possible to desensitize the receiver. This leakage often can be reduced or removed by a low-pass filter at the IF output stage. The second path as reverse LO feedthrough occurs from the LO port to the RF input port due to parasitic capacitance coupling. LO component in the RF input can pass back through the mixer and modulate with the LO signal, which will lead to DC offset and $2f_{LO}$ component at the IF output spectrum. As known, the DC offset is troublesome for zero IF receivers. If the reversed LO leakage to the RF port is still strong and LNA's isolation is poor, it will further be coupled to the input of the LNA as path 3, which is also a great trouble since it will then be amplified along with the RF signal and enters the RF port of the mixer to have a self-mixing again to further worsen the DC offset issue. The LO signal can also be coupled to the antenna where it can be radiated out to be an interference. Generally, path 2 and path

3 generate static DC offsets, as demonstrated in Fig. 9.17. Even in the transmitting chain as an up-converter, the LO leakage should be minimized since an undesired carrier signal in the RF output spectrum can degrade the system performance. Generally, compared to the high-resistivity substrate based GaAs and other III–V semiconductor technologies, CMOS process is very susceptible to LO self-mixing due to the lossy substrate that easily allows signals to couple to other sub-circuits through the low-resistivity substrate and the corresponding parasitic capacitance.

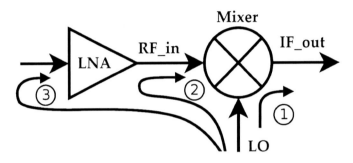

Figure 9.16 Possible LO feedthrough and self-mixing paths.

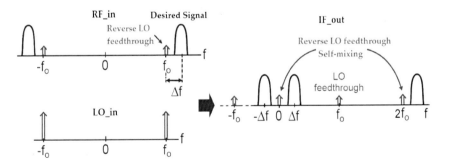

Figure 9.17 Illustration of self-mixing of reverse LO feedthrough.

9.3.2 Anti-Parallel Diode Pair

To combat the LO self-mixing, DC-offsets and other LO signal leakage issues, sub-harmonic mixers have been introduced and studied [9–23]. The sub-harmonic topology mixers, use second or higher order harmonics of the LO signal to reduce LO self-mixing and to perform up or down frequency conversion, namely $f_{IF} = f_{RF} \pm nf_{LO}$, where n is the order of the sub-harmonic mixer. For example, the use of a sub-harmonic mixer with order $n = 4$, permits the use of an LO with one-quarter of the frequency that is required in a fundamental-mode mixer. Therefore, the fundamental component of LO leakage does not appear or is very weak in the desired signal frequency bands. In fact, the LO leakage cannot be completely eliminated due to the non-ideality of the circuit, such as the imperfection of mismatch. However, the sub-harmonic mixing technique helps reduce LO leakage in the modulator and eliminate dc offset in the demodulator [9].

The reduction of LO frequency can potentially simplify the LO design and can improve the phase noise performance of the oscillator, which can ultimately improve the overall system performance. At millimeter-wave frequency, it is very difficult to design an oscillator with a low phase noise and high output power fundamental LO signal, since the quality factor of the on-chip components such as the inductor, varactor and capacitor is quite limited compared to their low frequency counterparts, and the operating frequency is close to the transistor's cutoff frequency. Therefore, the sub-harmonic technique can be used to build integrated RF frontends at millimeter-wave frequencies, helping the transceiver be less susceptible to LO pulling. At the same time, the design difficulty of some other blocks such as the frequency synthesizers and buffer amplifiers can be lowered, and some extra circuit blocks such as the frequency multipliers can be saved, so as to reduce circuit complexity and system cost.

As already discussed in the first section of this chapter, a diode can be used to perform mixing. The drawback is that as indicated in Eq. (9.3) that the amplitude of the harmonic components decreases fast with increasing of the order n. Basically at millimeter-wave frequency, most of the sub-harmonic mixers were implemented with diodes, since some dedicated diodes have higher cutoff frequency, such as the Schottky barrier diodes based on silicon process has achieved a cutoff frequency of over 1 terahertz [9]. The most popular type of the diode-based SHM is the anti-parallel diode pair (APDP) SHM, as shown in Fig. 9.18, where the RF and LO signals are applied to the APDP with the overall effect expression of $v_d = A_{RF} \cos(\omega_{RF}t) + A_{LO}\cos(\omega_{LO}t)$. The currents flowing through each of the diodes can still be calculated as Eq. (9.3) in the early section. Thus, the total mixing current that flows through the APDP can be derived and simplified with Taylor-series expansion to the third order as

$$i_d = i_{d1} - i_{d2} = I_s(e^{v_d/V_T} - e^{-v_d/V_T}) \approx I_s \left[2\left(\frac{v_d}{V_T}\right) + \frac{1}{3}\left(\frac{v_d}{V_T}\right)^3 \right]. \qquad (9.11)$$

By substituting $v_d = A_{RF}\cos(\omega_{RF}t) + A_{LO}\cos(\omega_{LO}t)$ into Eq. (9.11) and doing a simplification, the following simplified expression can be obtained:

$$i_d \approx I_s \left[\begin{array}{l} \frac{2}{V_T} A_{RF}\cos(\omega_{RF}t) + A_{LO}\cos(\omega_{LO}t)) + \frac{1}{2V_T^2} \\ (3A_{RF}A_{LO}^2\cos(\omega_{RF}t)\cos^2(\omega_{LO}t) + A_{LO}^3\cos^3(\omega_{LO}t)) \end{array} \right] \qquad (9.12)$$

It can be seen from Eq. (9.12), the mixing current i_d contains many frequency components such as ω_{RF}, ω_{LO}, $2\omega_{LO} + \omega_{RF}$, $2\omega_{LO} - \omega_{RF}$ and $3\omega_{LO}$. Especially the presence of the signal components $2\omega_{LO} + \omega_{RF}$ and $2\omega_{LO} - \omega_{RF}$ and proves the possibility of adopting the APDP to implement a sub-harmonic mixer. Since there are many intermodulation products generated by the diode (with high order Taylor-series expansion over 3), the system often requires a very high-performance filter. Practically, the APDP structure inherently eliminates the even-order intermodulation products as can be seen from Eq. (9.12) due to the symmetrical diode connection configuration. However, there still have the fundamental components of RF and LO signals in the output spectrum, which are called the RF feedthrough and the LO feedthrough as already discussed. In particular, the LO feedthrough still with a relatively high power. Therefore, the APDP sub-harmonic mixer requires a filter as mentioned in the output to filter out the unwanted signals. Sometimes the RF choke inductor can be replaced by a low-pass-filter, which exhibits high impedance characteristics at RF frequency.

9.3.3 Techniques Used in Sub-Harmonic APDP Mixer

Besides the simplicity of circuit implementation with APDP, since the diodes commonly have higher cutoff frequency than transistors [10], the passive APDP mixers, suffers less $1/f$ noise since there is no quiescent current. Therefore, APDP based SHMs are widely used in millimeter-wave frequencies. Since as shown in Fig. 9.18, both the RF and the IF signals share the same side of the APDP, their isolation might be poor. Modifications of the basic APDP SHM structure are necessary. In literature [11], a 60 GHz sub-harmonic mixer implemented with modified APDP structure based on an ordinary 0.18 um CMOS technology is demonstrated. The basic APDP core diagram is shown in Fig. 9.19. The APDP cores are implemented with two pairs of Schottky diodes. As known that the Schottky diode is a majority-carrier device with electrons, has the feature of much higher speed of frequency response to mixing operation and signal rectification, since there is no minority-carrier of holes' storage influence.

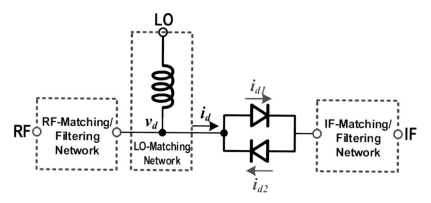

Figure 9.18 Diagram of a typical APDP based sub-harmonic mixer.

As shown in Fig. 9.19, there are two APDP mixer cores, which are connected in series. The middle common node is the virtual ground of the signals, which is also the output port of the down-converted IF signal. In addition, there is a dual-band phase-inverter rat-race coupler in the 60 GHz sub-harmonic mixer, which combines an RF signal divider and an LO balun together to reduce chip area and generate differential RF and LO signal for the APDP cores. The structure is like a balanced architecture, and a much better broadband LO-to-IF isolation compared to the conventional APDP based SHM designs can be achieved. It also can be expected that good broadband isolations between the RF and LO ports should be obtained due to the intrinsic isolation property of the wideband four-port coupler before the APDP cores. Moreover, as already mentioned in the previous section, the APDP SHM inherently rejects the even-order harmonics. In summary, excellent broadband 2LO-to-RF/IF isolations in [11] are expected to be achieved, and it is finally verified by the 60 dB 2LO-to-RF ports isolation performance, which definitely proves the merits of the modified APDP based SHM topology. The detailed configuration and techniques can be found in [11], which is a good try to implement the 60 GHz key modules with an outdated 0.18 um CMOS process.

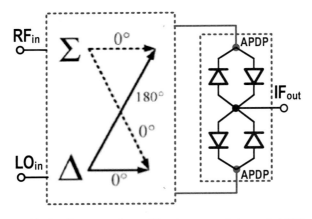

Figure 9.19 Basic diagram of a millimeter-wave balanced APDP down-conversion SHM.

Besides the presented modified balanced APDP-based down-conversion SHM in Fig. 9.19, double-balanced configuration that is common used in active FET/BJP mixers can also be adopted to realize the APDP based SHMs, so as to improve the mixer performance, as shown in Fig. 9.20, which is has been demonstrated in literature [11]. As illustrated in Fig. 9.20, there are four APDP cores, connected with double-balanced configuration. A trifilar transformer is adopted to feed the differential IF and LO inputs to the double-balanced APDP cores. A Marchand balun is used to convert the 60 GHz differential RF signal to single end form, so that the RF signal can be amplified by the final power amplifier, which is normally with single end form in the transmitter. The detailed information related to this double-balanced APDP based sub-harmonic up-converter can be found in [11]. Generally, both the APDP based down-conversion sub-harmonic mixer and the up-conversion sub-harmonic mixer implemented with an ordinary 0.18 um CMOS process in literature [11], further proved the feasibility of the APDP SHM designs in millimeter-wave frequency such as the 60 GHz range.

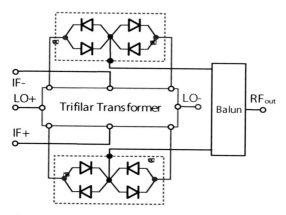

Figure 9.20 Basic diagram of a millimeter-wave double-balanced APDP up-conversion SHM.

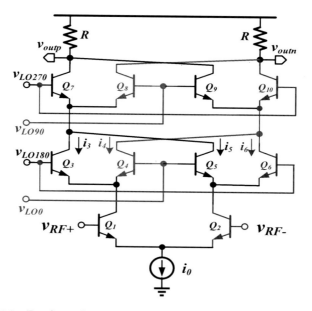

Figure 9.21 Topology of a second-order (2×) sub-harmonic mixer.

9.3.4 Topology of Transistor-Based Sub-Harmonic Mixer

Diode-based SHMs with simple circuit implementation configuration and almost no DC power consumption, are popular in implementing sub-harmonic mixers, however, they suffer from conversion loss and poor isolation with most of the diode-based configurations. There are now a lot of benefits of using transistors to implement SHMs, such as the positive conversion gain and high port-to-port isolation performance. The fast down-scaling of semiconductor technology, which leads to greatly increased cutoff frequency exceeding 200 GHz for the BJT and FET transistors, makes it possible to implement high-performance SHMs with on-chip BJT or FET transistors at millimeter-wave frequency [12–23].

Since Gilbert cell mixers have high isolation between ports and DC-offset elimination effect owing to their double-balanced structure. Therefore, it can be expected to realize the second order (2×) SHMs based on this architecture with some modification such as adding an additional level of LO switching transistors to the conventional fundamental Gilbert cell mixer, so as to adopt quadrature LO signals rather than differential LO signals [12, 13], for the purpose of generating the double LO frequency component 2LO, to perform sub-harmonic mixing with the RF signal as shown in Fig. 9.21. As the figure shows that this configuration requires three levels of transistors, with the bottom-level transistors being the differential transconductance transistor pair to obtain a high conversion gain for the RF signals, with middle-level two cross-coupled transistor pairs and upper-level two cross-coupled transistor pairs being the four quadrature LO switching transistor pairs. The mixer actually has four levels of transistors, when the current source is taken into account. Hence quite a high supply voltage is required to guarantee the normal operation of the transistors of each level, which makes it not suitable for low-voltage and low-power applications.

Therefore, another topology with only one level of LO switching pairs are expected, as shown in Fig. 9.22 to lower the supply voltage and to break the application limits, which is also demonstrated in literature [14]. By incorporating a distributed transconductance stage and high impedance compensation technique to compensate the parasitic capacitance of the CMOS transistors, the sub-harmonic mixer achieved an ultra-broadband operating range from 30 to 100 GHz. For this topology, the LO switching pairs totally have eight transistors, which will make the layout implementation much difficult.

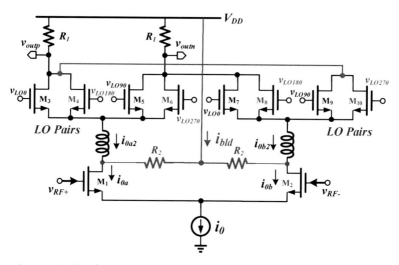

Figure 9.22 Another topology of a transistor-based 2× sub-harmonic mixer.

Therefore, some other topology with less switching transistors should be expected as shown in Fig. 9.23, where there are only two levels of stacked transistors excluding the current source [13]. There are only two LO switching transistor pairs, which is the same number as the normal fundamental double-balanced Gilbert cell mixer. The difference is that the differential RF transistor pair changes from two transistors to four transistors. Even with this difference, the total transistor numbers of this topology is only 8, compared to the total transistor numbers of 10 of Fig. 9.22. Another difference for the topology in Fig. 9.23, is that the position of the LO switching transistor pairs and the differential RF transistor pair are exchanged, namely the LO transistors pairs are on the bottom whereas the RF transistors are on the top level. For this topology, the quadrature LO signals are also required.

A comparison of the three illustrated topologies in Figs. 9.21–9.23 was presented in [13]. Basically, the first topology with the lowest maximum operating frequency, can operate with a low LO input power but requires a higher DC voltage supply. The second topology can achieve a higher conversion gain and higher 2LO-to-RF isolation. The third topology has advantages of power consumption, linearity, RF-to-IF port isolation, and lower noise figure over the other two topologies.

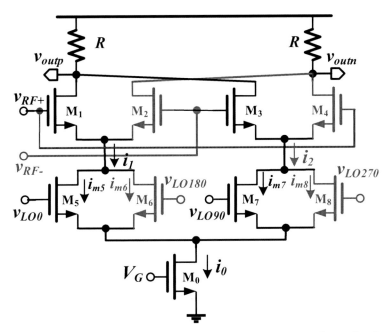

Figure 9.23 Another topology of a 2× sub-harmonic mixer with two-levels of stacked transistors.

9.3.5 Operation Mechanism of the Transistor-Based 2× HM

As discussed in the previous section, to implement a 2× active SHM, quadrature LO signals with relative phase shifts of 0°, 90°, 180°, and 270° are required to generate the required frequency components with twice the LO frequency to perform further mixing with the differential RF signals. The quadrature LO signals can be obtained from a quadrature VCO. Practically, most of the VCO designs only have differential outputs. A quadrature VCO will complicate the VCO designs and consume more the power and more chip area. Basically, the required quadrature LO signals can be generated with passive on-chip RC phase shifters, on-chip 90° hybrid coupler along with on chip baluns, and some specially-designed differential to quadrature converters. The balun can be active or passive. Generally, RC phase shifters and active balun have small chip area, but with lower accuracy and lower operating frequency, and are susceptible to the variation of the fabrication process. The passive hybrid coupler incorporation with passive baluns has better accuracy and higher power handling ability, but often requires a large chip area.

Let us consider the SHM topology as shown in Fig. 9.23, the generated currents i_1 and i_2 are actually switched at twice the LO frequency as analyzed in [15]. The frequency doubling operation mechanism can be better understood by monitoring the drain currents of the four switching transistors M_5 to M_8, where i_1 is the sum of the drain current of M_5 and M_6, and i_2 is the sum of the drain current of M_7 and M_8. Let us observe the drain current of M_5 and M_6 and their summed current i_1 only, as shown in Fig. 9.24a. Since the LO input generally has a high power, therefore has a large voltage amplitude. Transistors M_5 and M_6 will be turned on and off periodically according to the variation of the LO driving signals. As the 0° LO signal rises to the threshold value V_{TH}, transistor M_5 begins to turn on, its drain current i_{m5} will increase and be dominant in i_1. Since the gate voltage at M_6 is 180° out of phase and below V_{TH}, therefore M_6 is on the off state. When the amplitude of the 0° LO signal begins to drop and the 180° LO amplitude begins to rise, current i_{m5} starts to decrease, and transistor M_6 is still off, which leads to decreased sum current i_1. As the 180° LO signal rises over V_{TH} approaching to its peak amplitude and the 0° LO decreases to V_{TH} approaching to its notch, M_6 is turned on while M_5 is turned off. The current i_{m6} will increase and be dominant in i_1. In summary, during one period of the LO signal, i_{m5} has one cycle of increasing and one cycle of decreasing, while and i_{m6} have one cycle of decreasing and one cycle of increasing. Therefore, their sum current i_1 has two cycles of increasing and two cycles of decreasing, which indicates a doubling of the LO frequency, as illustrated in Fig. 9.24b. Another LO switching transistor pair M_7 to M_8, which are corresponding to the 90° and 270° LO driving signals, has the same operation mechanism. Current i_2 is 180° out of phase with current i_1, i.e., i_1 and i_2 are differential. Thereafter, the mixing operation of RF signals with the 2LO frequency components will be performed. Practically, compared to the fundamental Gilbert cell–based double-balanced mixer, the drawback of the sub-harmonic mixer is that it requires a higher LO driving power to get a reasonable conversion gain. However, the SHM has the significant advantage of using half the LO frequency to release the VCO design difficulty, as well as reducing LO self-mixing in direct-conversion receivers, as already discussed in the previous sections of this chapter.

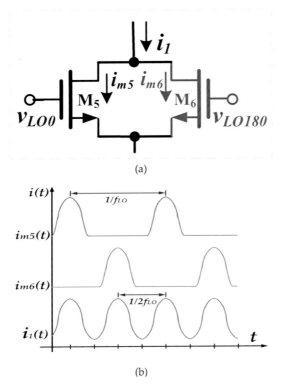

Figure 9.24 LO frequency doubling mechanism in a 2× SHM: (a) LO switching pair, and (b) switching current variation illustration.

9.3.6 A 60 GHz Transistor–Based 2× Sub-Harmonic Modulator

As discussed earlier, most of the Gilbert cell–based sub-harmonic mixers require quadrature LO driving signals to produce the

2LO components for further mixing operation. Practically in the transmitting chain, the input IF signals from the baseband module are often quadrature signals, which can be utilized to improve the image-rejection performance of a sub-harmonic modulation (or up-converter) [22], as shown in Fig. 9.25. Similar to the SHM topology shown in Fig. 9.22, there are four LO switching pairs totally eight BJT transistors in the upper level. The dedicated quadrature sub-harmonic QPSK modulator also comprise a miniaturized on-chip differential to quadrature converter (DQC) for LO driving signals, and an on-chip compensation hybrid coupler to transfer the differential up-converted RF signals to its single-end form, so as to provide to the single-end power amplifier. With the topology of Fig. 9.25, the sub-harmonic modulator has the feature of image rejection, as well as the merit of elimination of IF/LO feedthrough and LO self-mixing. By proper design of the hybrid coupler, the modulator offers an application flexibility, which can be utilized to realize low sideband (LSB) modulation when the USB port is tied to a 50 Ω load, or can be utilized to realize upper side band (USB) modulation, when the LSB port is terminated with a 50 Ω load.

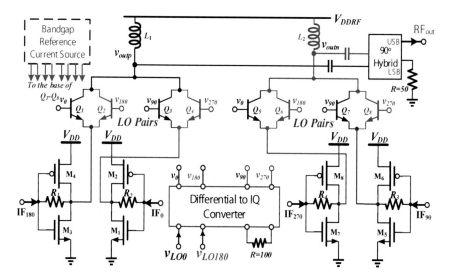

Figure 9.25 Diagram of a millimeter-wave sub-harmonic QPSK modulator.

Figure 9.25 demonstrates the simplified schematic diagram of the proposed quadrature sub-harmonic modulator. As mentioned in the previous paragraph, eight BJT transistors with a high cutoff frequency up to 200 GHz, are used to form the four differential LO switching pairs. As analyzed in Section 9.3.5, each switching pair can generate 2LO components and then mix with the IF signals to produce 2LO+IF terms for the frequency up-conversion case. For sub-harmonic conversion operation with a better LO feedthrough rejection, the quadrature LO driving signals are preferred to have balanced amplitude and accurate phase difference of 90°. Eight MOS transistors M_1 to M_8 incorporation with resistors R_1 to R_4, compose four inverter buffers, which are used to amplify the input quadrature IF signals as well as to provide an interface between the mixer and the baseband amplifiers. The resistors R_1 to R_4 tied between the input/output nodes of the inverters are for self-biasing purpose, which also help to realize a low-pass-filter response to filter out the unwanted signal components of the input IF signals. In addition, the inverter buffer amplifiers benefit the rejection characteristics of the signal leakage as well.

The 90° hybrid coupler is implemented on-chip with elaborate consideration of amplitude and phase compensation, so as to better deal with the orthogonal vector signals to single-end format and reject the image frequency components. Besides the hybrid coupler, the modulator also integrates a broadband on-chip differential to quadrature converter to transfer the 24 GHz fundamental differential LO input signal to the quadrature format.

The proposed sub-harmonic QPSK modulator was implemented based on a 0.18 um SiGe process with a measured conversion gain of 5±0.5 dB and measured input 1 dB compression point of –14 dBm over the 60 GHz operating band of 57–66 GHz. The double-balanced sub-harmonic modulator achieves more than 15 dBc sideband rejection. The fundamental LO feedthrough and the second LO harmonic feedthrough are suppressed more than 28 dB. The modulator has a current consumption of 15.3 mA from a 1.8 V supply with a very compact chip area of 0.4 mm × 0.7 mm, including the passive differential to quadrature converter and

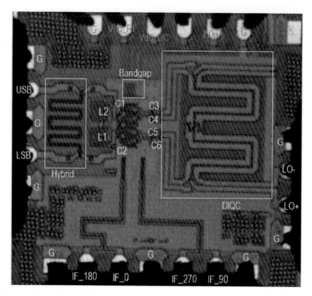

Figure 9.26 Die photo of the 60 GHz sub-harmonic QPSK modulator with chip area of 0.4 mm × 0.7 mm. [22] ©IEEE 2014.

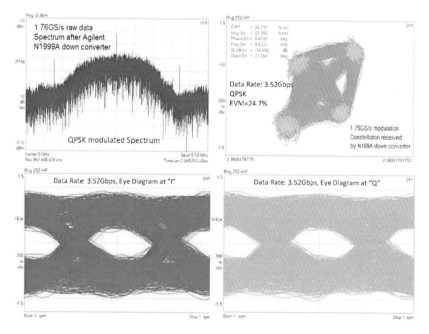

Figure 9.27 The measured QPSK modulation results. [22] ©IEEE 2014.

the 90° hybrid coupler as shown in Fig. 9.26. QPSK modulation test is also conducted, with the quadrature "I" and "Q" IF digital square wave signals being applied to the input pads of the four inverter buffers. The 60 GHz output spectrum from the LSB or USB pads is down converted to the 5 GHz frequency band off-chip, so as to be analyzed by the digital analyzer through the QPSK modulation testing. The corresponding QPSK modulation testing results are demonstrated in Fig. 9.27, which indicate a high data rate up to 3.52 Gbps, which was actually restricted by the testing equipment limitation. There are some non-ideality points related to the constellation and eye-diagram measurement results, which might be caused by the unbalance of the phase and amplitude of the off-chip LO and IF driving signals of the testing system [22].

Table 9.1 Measured performance of the QPSK modulator

Parameter	Units	This work	Ref. [23]	Ref. [9]
Technology	—	0.18 μm SiGe	0.13 μm SiGe	0.13 μm CMOS
IF Port	—	Quadrature	Differential	Quadrature
IF bandwidth	Hz	DC-1.9 G	8.3–9.1 G	—
RF bandwidth	Hz	57–67 G	57–64 G	35–65 G
Conversion gain	dB	5.1	6	–6
Input P_{1dB}	dBm	–14	–7	–5.6
LO power	dBm	4	–3	7
LO-RF isolation	dB	20	20	43
IF-RF isolation	dBc	40	—	—
2LO-RF isolation	dBc	28	—	50
Image rejection	dBc	2LO-IF@RF –15	—	2LO-IF@RF –20
Modulation	Gbps	QPSK 3.52	—	PRBS 1.0
Supply voltage	V	1.8	2.7	3.3
Power consumption	mW	27.5	51.8	75.9
Die area	mm^2	0.28	2.23	0.78

The detailed performance in comparison to some related up-converter designs in literature can be found in Table 9.1. In summary, compared to the related state-of-the-arts mixer designs, the quadrature QPSK sub-harmonic modulator shows advantages in terms of the image rejection, high data rate, compact chip area with fully passive and active devices integration, and low power consumption, which demonstrate the application feasibility of the proposed SHM topology at millimeter-wave frequency.

9.3.7 Some Techniques Used in Sub-harmonic Mixer Designs

As mentioned, a sub-harmonic mixer with Gilbert cell–based double-balance structure has high LO-to-RF and 2LO-to-RF isolation but requires quadrature LO driving signals, which either increases the design complexity with active converters or significantly increases the chip area with a passive network. Moreover, the converter has phase/amplitude imbalance and ohmic losses, which might degrade the system performance. Figure 9.28 illustrates the simplified diagram of a g_m-boosting Gilbert cell–based sub-harmonic mixer, which requires only differential rather than quadrature LO signals [24].

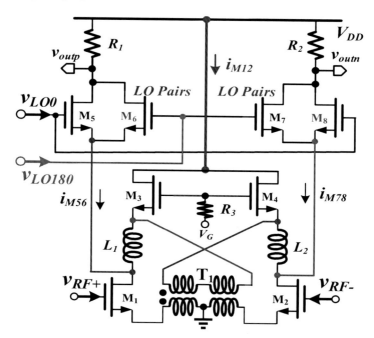

Figure 9.28 Schematic diagram of a millimeter-wave sub-harmonic mixer with g_m-boosting technique.

Besides the normal portions such as the transconductance stage M_1 to M_2, the LO switching transistor pairs M_5 to M_8, and the load resistors R_1 to R_2, there are a current-bleeding block and a g_m-boosting block. The inductors L_1 to L_2 are used to tune out the parasitic capacitances at the source nodes of the switching transistors at the operating frequency. The current-bleeding circuits are composed of two NMOS transistors M_3–M_4 rather than PMOS transistors for better g_m-boosting and noise suppression [24]. As discussed in Figs. 9.13 and 9.15 of previous sections, current-bleeding is used to alleviate the voltage headroom issues at the output nodes, without degrading g_m of the transconductance stage by keeping its current i_{m1} and i_{m2} nearly constant. Moreover, using this technique, the drain current i_{m56} and i_{m78} of the switching transistor pairs can be greatly reduced, so as to use a relatively large load resistor R_1 to R_2 avoiding a large voltage headroom drop. In literature [24], the NMOS transistors M_1 to M_4 are biased at 0.5 V, while the switching transistors M_5 to M_8 is biased at 0.2 V only to maximize the second harmonic of the LO signal, so as to realize sub-harmonic mixing without the commonly required quadrature LO driving signals. It can be found from Fig. 9.28, that an additional transformer-based feedback network is incorporated with the NMOS current-bleeding circuits to achieve additional g_m-boosting, without extra power consumption. With transformer T_1, the signals from the source nodes of M_3 and M_4 can be coupled to the source nodes of M_2 and M_1. Hence, transistors M_1 and M_2, which are originally used as common-source amplifiers, now also operate as common-gate amplifiers at the same time, since the coupled signal is now applied to their source terminals through the transformer, which means a further boosted g_m. Since there is one grounded common node in the transformer, therefore T_1 can also be considered to be two individual source degeneration inductors, which are commonly used in RF circuits to achieve better linearity and noise performance.

A millimeter-wave sub-harmonic mixer with the above-discussed techniques was demonstrated based on a 65 nm CMOS process in literature [24]. Based on the g_m-boosting technique, even with a low LO power of –5 dBm, the mixer still can achieve a measured conversion gain of 1.6 dB when the RF and LO signals are set to 79.5 and 39.5 GHz, respectively.

9.3.8 The 4× Sub-Harmonic Mixer

Most of the 4× SHMs were implemented with diodes or APDP structures [25]. Compared to the fundamental mixers and 2× SHMs, the 4LO components in 4× SHMs, has smaller amplitude, which requires an even higher fundamental LO input power level to obtain a reasonable conversion gain, which will definitely increase the current consumption of the oscillator's buffer amplifiers. As already discussed that quadrature LO driving signals are commonly desired for a 2× SHM to generate the 2LO components. It can be expected for a Gilbert cell–based 4× SHM, that LO driving signals with 8 different phase, i.e., 0°, 90°, 180°, 270°, and 45°, 135°, 225° and 315° will be required to generate the 4LO components. Figure 9.29 illustrates a basic schematic diagram of a 4× SHM, where there are two LO switching transistor groups with each group comprising four transistors. The phase of each of the LO signal applied to the gate nodes of the four transistors, has a difference of 90°. Namely LO signals with phase of 0°, 90°, 180°, 270° are fed into one switching group, and LO signals with phase of 45°, 135°, 225° and 315° are fed into another switching group.

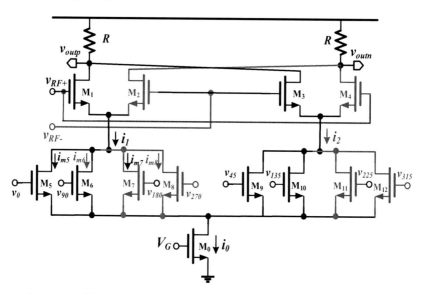

Figure 9.29 Illustration of transistor-based 4× sub-harmonic mixer.

With the same analysis method as that in Fig. 9.24, it can be summarized that during one period of the fundamental LO, the drain current of each of the four transistors in a switching group, has one cycle of increasing and one cycle of decreasing. Therefore, their sum current i_1 will have four cycles of increasing and four cycles of decreasing, which means a produced frequency component of 4× LO. Another LO switching transistor group, has the same operation mechanism. And current i_2 is 180° out of phase with i_1. Thereafter, mixing operation of RF signals and the generated 4× LO frequency components will be performed. To increase the 4× LO signal amplitude, inductors and other amplitude boosting techniques can be used between the transconductance stage and the LO switching stage.

9.4 Summary

In this chapter, design issues and techniques related to millimeter-wave mixer designs are presented and discussed. In the first section, the mixer fundamentals including the mixing mechanism, transconductance stage design and mixer balance issues are introduced. In the second section, techniques and topologies such as the FET resistive mixers and Gilbert cell–based double-balanced mixers, related to the fundamental mixer designs are discussed. Based on some outstanding issues, such as LO self-mixing and difficulty to design a higher-performance oscillator, which should operate at millimeter-wave frequency with low phase noise and high output power, techniques about the SHM designs, are presented and discussed in the third section.

SHM can perform mixing operations with the LO's second harmonic (2×) or high order harmonic frequency components ($n×$, where n is integer). Therefore, the oscillator can be designed with a lower oscillation frequency, which will greatly simplify the VCO designs. With SHM, the LO-to-RF and LO-to-IF isolation can be improved as well. Hence, in the third section of the chapter, the sub-harmonic mixing mechanism and SHM topologies are presented in detail, including the diode-based passive APDP SHM technique, Gilbert cell–based active SHM technique and the 2× LO components generation mechanism. In the final part of this section, the 4× SHM ideas, which commonly desire eight different phase of LO driving signals, i.e., 0°, 90°, 180°, 270°, and 45°, 135°, 225° and 315° to generate the 4× LO components, are also introduced.

In the chapter, some techniques incorporation with some state-of-the-art millimeter-wave designs are also discussed, which can be used to enhance the mixer's conversion gain or port-to-port isolation such as the current-injection technique and g_m-boosting technique and, etc.

References

1. B. Razavi, *RF and Microelectronics*. Upper Saddle River, NJ: Prentice-Hall, 1998.

2. R. John and P. Calvin, *Radio Frequency Integrated Circuit Design*. Artech House, 2003.

3. F. Ellinger, 26.5–30-GHz Resistive mixer in 90-nm VLSI SOI CMOS technology with high linearity for WLAN, *IEEE Trans. Microwave Theory Tech.*, vol. 53, no. 8, pp. 2559–2565, Aug. 2005.

4. J. Kim and Y. Kwon, Low conversion loss 94 GHz CMOS resistive mixer, *Electron. Lett.*, vol. 51, no. 18, pp. 1464–1466, Sep. 2015.

5. B. Razavi, Design of Analog CMOS Integrated Circuits. McGraw-Hill, 2001.

6. C.-S. Lin, P.-S. Wu, H.-Y. Chang, and H. Wang, A 9–50-GHz Gilbert cell down-conversion mixer in 0.13-um CMOS technology, *IEEE Microw. Wireless Compon. Lett.*, vol. 16, no. 5, pp. 293–295, May 2006.

7. T. M. Tsai and Y. S. Lin, 15.1 mW 60 GHz Up-conversion mixer with 4.5 dB gain and 57.5 dB LO-RF isolation, *Electron. Lett.*, vol. 48, no. 14, pp. 844–845, Jul. 2012.

8. J. H. Lee and Y. S. Lin, 60 GHz CMOS downconversion mixer with 15.46 dB gain and 64.7 dB LO-RF isolation, *Electron. Lett.*, vol. 49, no. 4, pp. 264–266, Feb. 2013.

9. J. H. Tsai and T. W. Huang, 35–65-GHz CMOS broadband modulator and demodulator with sub-harmonic pumping for MMW wireless gigabit applications, *IEEE Trans. Microw. Theory Techn.*, vol. 55, no. 10, pp. 2075–2085, Oct. 2007.

10. Y. Sun and C. J. Scheytt, A 122 GHz sub-harmonic mixer with a modified APDP topology for IC integration, *IEEE Microwave and Wireless Components Letters*, vol. 21, no. 12, pp. 679–681, Dec. 2011.

11. H. J. Wei, C. Meng, T. W. Wang, T. L. Lo, and C. L. Wang, 60-GHz dual-conversion down-/up-converters using Schottky diode in 0.18 μm foundry CMOS technology, *IEEE Trans. Microw. Theory Techn.*, vol. 60, no. 6, pp. 1684–1698, Jun. 2012.

12. L. Sheng, J. C. Jensen, and L. E. Larson, A wide-bandwidth Si/SiGe HBT direct conversion sub-harmonic mixer/downconverter, *IEEE J. Solid-State Circ.*, vol. 35, no. 9, pp. 1329–1337, Sept. 2000.

13. T.-H. Wu, S.-C. Tseng, C.-C. Meng, and G.-W. Huang, GaInP/GaAs HBT Sub-harmonic Gilbert mixers using stacked-LO and leveled-LO Topologies, *IEEE Trans. Microw. Theory Techn.*, vol. 55, pp. 880–889, May 2007.

14. J. H. Tsai, H. Y. Yang, T. W. Huang, and H. Wang, A 30–100 GHz wideband sub-harmonic active mixer in 90 nm CMOS technology, *IEEE Microw. Wireless Components Lett.*, vol. 18, no. 8, pp. 554–556, Aug. 2008.

15. K. Nimmagadda and G. Rebeiz, A 1.9 GHz double-balanced subharmonic mixer for direct conversion receivers, *IEEE Radio Frequency Integrated Circuits (RFIC) Symposium*, pp. 253–256, 2001.

16. B. G. Perumana, C.-H. Lee, J. Laskar, and S. Chakraborty, A Subharmonic CMOS mixer based on threshold voltage modulation, *IEEE MTT-S International Microwave Symposium Digest*, pp. 33–36, June 2005.

17. S. K. Lin, J. L. Kuo, and H. Wang, A 60 GHz sub-harmonic resistive FET mixer using 0.13 um CMOS Technology, *IEEE Microw. Wireless Components Lett.*, vol. 21, no. 10, pp. 562–564, Oct. 2011.

18. Y. Yan, M. Bao, S. E. Gunnarsson, V. Vassilev, and H. Zirath, A 110–170-GHz multi-mode transconductance mixer in 250-nm InP DHBT technology, *IEEE Trans. Microw. Theory Techn.*, vol. 63, no. 9, pp. 2897–2904, Sept. 2015.

19. H. K. Chiou, S. C. Kuo, and H. Y. Chung, 14–30 GHz low-power sub-harmonic single-balanced gate-pumped mixer with transformer combiner in 0.18 μm CMOS, *Electron. Lett.*, vol. 50, no. 16, pp. 1141–1143, Jul. 2014.

20. J. Kim and Y. Kwon, Low conversion loss 94 GHz CMOS resistive mixer, *Electron. Lett.*, vol. 51, no. 18, pp. 1464–1466, Sep. 2015.

21. P. Y. Chiang, C. W. Su, S. Y. Luo, R. Hu, and C. F. Jou, Wide-IF-band CMOS mixer design, *IEEE Trans. Microw. Theory Techn.*, vol. 58, no. 4, pp. 831–840, Apr. 2010.

22. K. Ma, S. Mou, Y. Wang, J. Yan, K. S. Yeo, and W. M. Lim, A miniaturized 28 mW 60 GHz differential quadrature sub-harmonic QPSK modulator

in 0.18 um SiGe BiCMOS, *2014 IEEE MTT-S International Microwave Symposium (IMS2014)*, Tampa, FL, 2014, pp. 1–4.

23. S. K. Reynolds, A 60-GHz superheterodyne downconversion mixer in silicon-germanium bipolar technology, *IEEE J. Solid-State Circ.*, vol. 39, no. 11, pp. 2065–2068, Nov. 2004.

24. J. Jang, J. Oh, C. Y. Kim, and S. Hong, A 79-GHz adaptive-gain and low-noise UWB radar receiver front-End in 65-nm CMOS, *IEEE Trans. Microw. Theory Techn.*, vol. 64, no. 3, pp. 859–867, Mar. 2016.

25. M. W. Chapman and S. Raman, A 60-GHz uniplanar MMIC 4× subharmonic mixer, *IEEE Trans. Microw. Theory Techn.*, vol. 50, no. 11, pp. 2580–2588, Nov. 2002.

The rules for success are constantly changing. Those who can see the changes and make the change first will be the ones who define the future.

—Kiat Seng Yeo and Kaixue Ma

Chapter 10

Voltage-Controlled Oscillator

Zou Qiong,[a] Kaixue Ma,[b] and Kiat Seng Yeo[a]

[a]*Engineering Product Development, Singapore University of Technology and Design,*
8 Somapah Road, Singapore 487372
[b]*School of Physical Electronics,*
University of Electronic Science and Technology of China,
#4 Section II, Jianshe North Road, Chengdu 610054, P. R. China

qiong_zou@sutd.edu.sg

As a key building block, the voltage-controlled oscillator (VCO) has great influence on the overall performance of a synthesizer and also the transceiver. The most widely used topology of VCO is the LC-tank based VCO, which is termed LC-VCO. In this chapter, first we will study some VCO basics and then focus on the LC-VCO and discuss the properties of the LC-tank and tank components. Finally, some typical topologies of LC-VCO and their advantages and disadvantages to be applied in millimeter-wave frequency will be introduced.

Low-Power Wireless Communication Circuits and Systems: 60 GHz and Beyond
Edited by Kaixue Ma and Kiat Seng Yeo
Copyright © 2018 Pan Stanford Publishing Pte. Ltd.
ISBN 978-981-4745-96-3 (Hardcover), 978-1-315-15653-8 (eBook)
www.panstanford.com

10.1 VCO Basics

10.1.1 Overview of VCO Architectures

For millimeter-wave frequency, there are two types of oscillators: the resonator-based oscillator and the resonator-less oscillator. RC ring oscillators are a well-known type of resonator-less oscillators. As shown in Fig. 10.1a, the ring oscillator is always made up of three or more stages of inverters or delay cells with the output feedback to the input. The oscillation frequency of a ring oscillator is determined by the delay of each stage. Hence, the oscillation frequency of a ring oscillator can be tuned by varying the delay of each stage [1]. The LC oscillator is probably the most widely used resonator-based oscillator. The topology of an LC-VCO with a cross-coupled pair is shown in Fig. 10.1b. The cross-coupled NMOS transistors provide a negative resistance and add energy into the circuit to sustain the oscillation. The oscillation frequency is determined by the LC-tank. When the added energy is larger than the energy dissipated in the LC-tank, the oscillation can be excited.

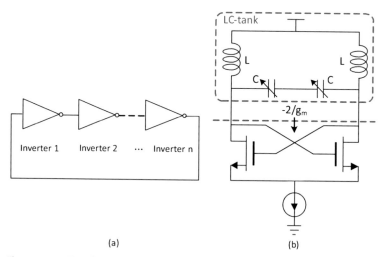

(a) (b)

Figure 10.1 Topology of typical oscillator: (a) RC-ring oscillator, (b) LC oscillator.

An RC ring oscillator is popular for low frequency low cost application due to its wide tuning range, multi-phase outputs, and low power consumption. However, the phase noise of ring oscillators suffers from the low open loop Q and the noisy active devices in the signal path [2]. In addition, the frequency of ring oscillator relies on the delay of each stage; thus, it is difficult to be applied to millimeter-wave frequency. In contrast, with a simple and symmetrical structure, LC-VCOs provide many advantages for high–speed and differential designs with low power consumption and reasonable tuning range, making it an attractive solution for millimeter-wave VCO design.

10.1.2 Oscillator Theory

The oscillator behavior can be explained by either a feedback model or a negative resistance model [3] as shown in Fig. 10.2. The feedback model treats the oscillator as a linear feedback system, while the negative resistance model separates the oscillator into two one-port networks (resonator and active circuit) connected to each other. Considering the simple linear feedback system in Fig. 10.2a, the overall transfer function can be written as

$$\frac{V_{out}(s)}{V_{in}(s)} = \frac{A(s)G(s)}{1 - A(s)G(s)} \tag{10.1}$$

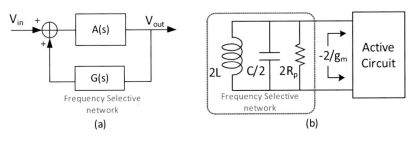

Figure 10.2 Oscillator models: (a) the feedback model, (b) the negative resistance model.

For steady oscillation, the loop gain and phase shift must satisfy the Barkhausen criteria [3]:

(1) The loop gain, $|A(s)G(s)| \geq 1$.
(2) The total phase shift around the loop, $\angle A(s) + \angle G(s) = 0°$ or $360°$.

By solving the above conditions for oscillation, we can obtain the oscillation frequency and the required gain. In most RF oscillators, $G(s)$ in the feedback loop can be a frequency selective network, which is also called a "resonator." It should be noted that Barkhausen's criteria is necessary but not sufficient [4] for oscillation. For instance, the circuit may latch up rather than oscillate, when the phase shift of the loop equals to 360° and the loop gain is sufficient.

The negative resistance model can be depicted as in Fig. 10.2b, where the oscillator is divided into two parts: the active circuit and the resonator. The operation of the LC-VCO can be easily understood by using the negative resistance model. The resonator is symbolized as parallel resonant LC-tank consisting of an inductor $2L$ and a capacitor $C/2$. Generally, the LC-tank determines the frequency of oscillation, while the active circuit provides a negative resistance $-2/g_m$ to compensate the loss of the resonator ($2R_p$ in Fig. 10.2b) and sustain the oscillation, where g_m is trans-conductance of the cross-coupled transistors. The startup condition of the oscillation and the oscillation frequency can be given by

$$\omega_o = \frac{1}{\sqrt{LC}} \tag{10.2}$$

$$g_m \geq \frac{1}{R_p}. \tag{10.3}$$

In practice, g_m is usually designed as 2~3 times of $1/R_p$ to ensure a robust oscillation against process, voltage and temperature (PVT) variations.

10.1.3 Performance Parameter

As one of the most important building blocks in a RF transceiver, the performance of VCO will significantly influence the overall performance of transceiver. For example, the phase noise of VCO dominates the phase noise of LO, and thus greatly influences the transceiver's selectivity and signal to noise ratio. Therefore, in this section, we will introduce some important performance parameters of VCO.

Phase noise

Phase noise is probably the most important specification of a VCO. The output of an ideal oscillator is an ideal sinusoidal signal:

$$V_{out}(t) = V_0 \cos\left[2\pi f_0 t + \phi\right], \qquad (10.4)$$

with constant amplitude V_0, center frequency f_0, and a fixed phase φ. In the frequency domain, it should be a single impulse, as shown in Fig. 10.3a. However, in practical, there are inevitably fluctuations on signal amplitude and phase. Thus, a real oscillator signal is given by

$$V_{out}(t) = V_0(t)\cos\left[2\pi f_0 t + \phi(t)\right]. \qquad (10.5)$$

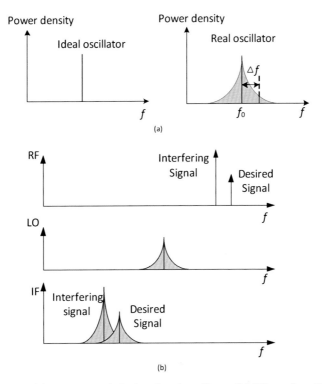

Figure 10.3 (a) Spectrum of ideal and real oscillator. (b) Effect of oscillator phase noise in a receiver.

In frequency domain, the fluctuations $V_0(t)$ and $\varphi(t)$ are transferred into a symmetrical "skirts" shape sideband around the oscillating frequency f_0 [5]. The phase noise is the signal sideband noise spectral density in a unit bandwidth at an offset of Δf from the center frequency f_0 divided by the carrier signal power. It is defined as

$$L(\Delta f) = 10 \log \left(\frac{P_{noise}(f_0 + \Delta f, 1\,\text{Hz})}{P_{carrier}} \right) \text{(dBc/Hz)}. \tag{10.6}$$

In a practical oscillator, the amplitude is limited by non-linear active devices and $L(\Delta f)$ is dominated by the phase part of the phase noise [5]. Figure 10.3b depicts the frequency conversion situation in a receiver to describe the importance of phase noise. Supposing there is a large power unwanted signal in an adjacent channel from the wanted signal, and the LO signal used for down-conversion has a noisy spectrum, then after mixing with the LO, the down-converted spectrum consists of two overlapped spectra because the LO sideband down-converts both the desired signal and the interfering signal. As a result, the desired signal suffers from significant noise. Therefore, stringent phase noise specifications have to be met in wireless communication systems in order to detect the signal accompanied with interferers.

The phase noise of LC-VCO is described by the insightful model first presented by Leeson [6]:

$$L(\Delta f) = 10 \log \left\{ \frac{2FKT}{P_s} \left[1 + \left(\frac{f_o}{2Q\Delta f} \right)^2 \right] \left(1 + \frac{\Delta f_{1/f^3}}{|\Delta f|} \right) \right\}, \tag{10.7}$$

where K is the Boltzmann constant, F is the excess noise factor, T is the temperature, f_o is the oscillation frequency, Δf is frequency offset, $\Delta f_1/f_3$ is the corner frequency between $1/f_3$ and $1/f_2$ phase noise regions, P_s is the power of carrier signal, and Q is the Q of the LC-tank. Figure 10.4 plots a general phase noise based on Lesson's phase noise model. There are three regions: $1/f_3$ region, $1/f_2$ region, and flat noise floor region. The phase noise in the $1/f_3$ region is declined in a slope of −30 dBc/decade, and is mainly contributed by AM-PM noise and flicker noise. The $1/f_2$

region is between the $1/f_3$ region and the noise floor and roles off with −20 dBc/decade. The flat noise floor at large frequency offset is mainly contributed by thermal noise. Since a PLL exhibits a high pass for the noise from VCO, the $1/f_2$ region noise usually dominates the phase noise. From Leeson formula, the phase noise of the $1/f_2$ region could be reduced by enhancing the LC-tank Q or the voltage amplitude of carrier signal. However, increasing the signal power is usually at the expense of larger power consumption. Thus, the effective way to reduce phase noise should be improving the Q of LC-tank.

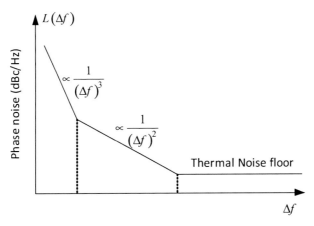

Figure 10.4 Typical phase noise plot.

Frequency Tuning Range

The frequency tuning range is the next important specification of LC-VCO. The oscillation frequency of VCO is determined by the tank inductor and capacitor, thus changing either of them could change the oscillation frequency. However, in practical, inductor is difficult to be varied continuously. The normal method for frequency tuning is using varactor. The tuning range of a VCO is defined as

$$TR(\%) = \frac{\Delta f}{f_{center}} \times 100, \qquad (10.8)$$

where $\Delta f = f_{max} - f_{min}$, $f_{center} = (f_{max} + f_{min})/2$. If the inductor is fixed, f_{max} and f_{min} are determined by the minimum and maximum capacitances of varactor. Considering the fixed capacitance of LC-tank as C_{fix}, and the maximum and minimum capacitance of varactor as C_{vmax} and C_{vmin}, then Eq. (10.8) can be rewritten as

$$TR(\%) = \frac{\sqrt{\dfrac{C_{vmax}}{C_{vmin}} + \dfrac{C_{fix}}{C_{vmin}}} - \sqrt{1 + \dfrac{C_{fix}}{C_{vmin}}}}{\sqrt{\dfrac{C_{vmax}}{C_{vmin}} + \dfrac{C_{fix}}{C_{vmin}}} + \sqrt{1 + \dfrac{C_{fix}}{C_{vmin}}}} \times 200. \qquad (10.9)$$

It should be noted that the parasitic capacitance of transistors will contribute to the capacitance of LC-tank and degrade the tuning range. This situation will become even worse at millimeter-wave frequency, because the increasing transistors size to sustain oscillation at such a high frequency will inevitably increase the transistors parasitic capacitance, which will further limit the frequency tuning range.

Figure of merit

To compare the performance of VCOs with different center frequencies, power consumption, and phase noise over offset frequency, a popular figure of merit (FOM) is widely used:

$$FOM = L(f_m) - 20\log\left(\frac{f_0}{f_m}\right) + 10\log(P_{DC}), \qquad (10.10)$$

where $L(f_m)$ is the phase noise from the oscillator frequency (f_0) at a frequency offset of f_m, and P_{DC} is the DC power consumption of VCO in milliwatt. For a wide tuning range VCO, a FOM that also takes into account frequency tuning range is commonly used:

$$FOM_T = L(f_m) - 20\log\left(\frac{f_0}{f_m}\right) + 10\log(P_{DC}) - 20\log\left(\frac{FTR}{10\%}\right), \qquad (10.11)$$

where FTR stands for the frequency tuning range of the VCO.

10.2 LC-Tank

Since LC-VCOs are based on LC-tank, the performance of LC-tank is important for the VCO performance. Quality factor (Q) is usually used to describe the loss of an LC-tank. As mentioned in Section 10.1, Q of LC-tank is crucial to VCO phase noise. Many Q definitions are used in different applications, such as resonators and filters. In this section, we will first introduce several useful definitions of Q of LC-tank and then look at the properties of tank components.

10.2.1 Quality Factor

The fundamental definition of Q is from the energy view, which is given by the energy stored divided by the energy dissipated per cycle.

$$Q = 2\pi \frac{\text{Energy stored}}{\text{Energy loss in one oscillation cycle}} \tag{10.12}$$

For the LC-VCO shown in Fig. 10.1b, the impedance of the LC-tank is expressed as

$$Z(j\omega) = \frac{1}{\dfrac{1}{j\omega L} + j\omega C + \dfrac{1}{R_p}}. \tag{10.13}$$

The magnitude and phase response of the LC-tank is shown in Fig. 10.5. It can be seen that the oscillation occurs at the frequency where the phase shift of the LC-tank is zero. The magnitude response of the LC-tank is like the bandpass characteristic of a filter, therefore the Q of the LC-tank can also be defined as the ratio between the center frequency and the 3 dB-bandwidth:

$$Q = \frac{\omega_o}{\omega_{3dB}} \tag{10.14}$$

Since the magnitude response of an LC-tank is easy to obtain from the S-parameter, this definition of Q provides a convenient way to observe the Q of the LC-tank based on the magnitude response of the LC-tank.

Another useful definition of Q is the phase steepness of the oscillator open loop transfer function at the resonance [7]. Considering the oscillator as a feedback system and the phase shift of the open loop transfer function ϕ, the Q is then defined as

$$Q = -\frac{\omega_0}{2}\frac{\partial\phi}{\partial\omega}\bigg|_{\omega=\omega_0}. \tag{10.15}$$

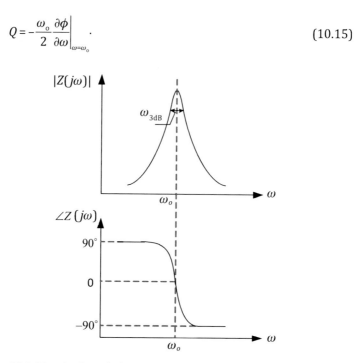

Figure 10.5 Magnitude and phase response of the LC-tank.

In addition to the three different definitions of Q described above, the overall Q of an LC-tank can be expressed by the Q of individual devices in an LC-tank, i.e., the inductor and the capacitor:

$$Q_{Tank} = \frac{Q_L Q_C}{Q_L + Q_C}, \tag{10.16}$$

where Q_L and Q_C are the Q of the inductor and the capacitor, respectively. This expression has provided an insight into the relationship between the LC-tank Q and the individual devices Q. It can be seen that the device with lower Q will dominate the overall Q of the LC-tank. Generally, when the frequency is low, the Q of a capacitor is much higher than the Q of an inductor. Thus, the loss of capacitors can be ignored, and the overall Q of an LC-tank is determined by the Q of the inductor. When the frequency is high, such as at millimeter-wave frequency, the Q of capacitors is comparable or even lower than the Q of inductors, then the loss of capacitors cannot be ignored, and the Q of an LC-tank is determined by the Q of both the inductor and the capacitor.

10.2.2   Tank Components

The capacitance in an LC-tank can be divided into two parts: One is the fixed capacitance provided by the linear capacitor, and the other is the variable capacitance, which is usually provided by varactors. Most CMOS processes offer linear capacitors in the form of a metal-insulator-metal (MIM) capacitor. Due to the use of top metal, MIM capacitor provides good Q and less parasitic. However, it requires extra masks, and the minimum capacitance of MIM capacitor is usually much larger than the typical capacitances needed for 60 GHz VCOs. Alternatively, another linear capacitor that can be realized with the standard metal layers is MOM (metal-oxide-metal) capacitor. The typical structure of an MOM capacitor is depicted in Fig. 10.6. It is composed of a large number of parallel fingers connected to either port of the device. With a combination of fringing capacitance and area capacitance between metal layers, this kind of capacitor features large capacitance but only occupies small area. Although the parasitic capacitance of an MOM capacitor is usually larger than that of an MIM capacitor, an MOM capacitor can support small capacitance value, which is required by high-frequency VCO design. Also, an MOM capacitor provides convenient connections to other devices because its two ports both use multi metal layers. The capacitance of an MOM capacitor needs trade-off with its quality factor Q. For example, as the length of the fingers increases, the series resistance also increases, leading to the decreasing of Q.

The variable capacitance in LC-tank is usually provided by varactors. Although linear capacitors combined with switches can provide capacitance varied in certain steps to switch frequency band, the continuous frequency tuning of VCO still relies on varactors. The most widely used varactors are MOS varactors. The Q of a MOS varactor and the maximum capacitance variation versus its control voltage are trade-off between each other, which is a major limitation to the design of wide tuning range VCOs at millimeter-wave. An admittance transforming technique can be used to reduce the load effect of varactor on the overall tank [8].

3D view   Top view

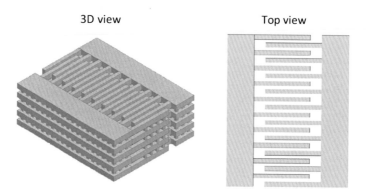

Figure 10.6 The typical structure of an MOM capacitor.

By inserting inductive elements in series connection with the varactor, the equivalent shunt conductance of the tank can be effectively reduced at higher frequencies, leading to a larger Q of the tank. However, this technique will also reduce the variation of capacitance in LC-tank, resulting in a small tuning range.

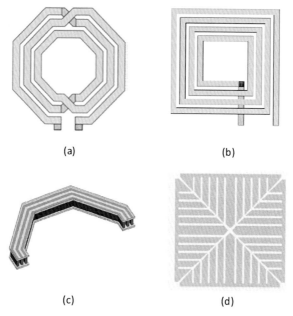

Figure 10.7 Typical layout of spiral inductor: (a) octagon and (b) square. (c) Two shunt-connected metal layers of inductor. (d) Patterned ground shield.

The typical layouts of octagon and square spiral inductor in standard CMOS process are shown in Figs. 10.7a,b. The loss of an inductor is mainly contributed by the lossy substrates and series resistance of winding [1, 9]. Modern CMOS processes offer 4 to 9 metal layers, the top thick metal is usually used for an inductor for less loss on metal and smaller coupling from substrate. In some cases, two metal layers are in shunt connection to reduce the series resistance of the winding, as shown in Fig. 10.7c. The substrate loss of inductor can be reduced by using patterned ground shield [10]. Figure 10.7d shows an example of patterned ground shield. The slots are cut into the plane perpendicular to the direction of magnetic current flow, thus the current flow into substrate can be prevented. However, the patterned ground shield would introduce parasitic capacitance to the inductor. Therefore, the ground shield should be placed far away from the inductor.

10.3 LC-VCO Topologies for Millimeter-Wave Frequency

10.3.1 Cross-Coupled LC-VCO

Since the transistor gain is degraded significantly in the millimeter-wave frequency region, the cross-coupled LC-VCO, which adopts a pair of cross-coupled transistors (Fig. 10.1b), is an attractive VCO topology due to its easy start-up and moderate phase noise and tuning range performance.

Figures 10.8a–d show four modified cross-coupled LC-VCO topologies based on the LC-VCO in Fig. 10.1b. Figure 10.8a is a cross-coupled LC-VCO that utilizes PMOS transistors instead of NMOS transistors as cross-coupled pair. Since PMOS transistors have lower flicker noise, using PMOS instead of NMOS will reduce phase noise. However, for the same required negative resistance, double width of transistor is needed for PMOS compared to NMOS. Therefore, tuning range of VCO will be reduced.

Figure 10.8b is a top-biased NMOS cross-coupled LC-VCO topology. One important advantage of this topology is the output DC voltage level can be designed at VDD/2. Since the tuning voltage of varactor is usually varied from 0 to VDD in PLL, this topology is able to utilize the whole tuning range of varactor, resulting in a wide tuning range. This topology has been widely used in low frequency VCO design, and also millimeter-wave frequency VCO [11].

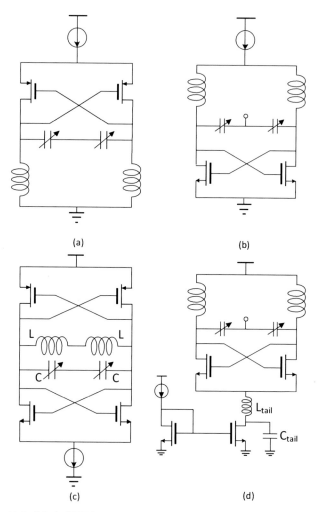

Figure 10.8 (a) A PMOS cross-coupled LC-VCO, (b) a top-biased NMOS cross-coupled LC-VCO, (c) a complementary LC-VCO with current source to ground, (d) a modification of NMOS LC-VCO with tail noise filter.

The complementary LC-VCO topology shown in Fig. 10.8c use both NMOS and PMOS cross-coupled pair to generate negative resistance, therefore, if the requirement of the negative resistance is same, then the power consumption can be reduced by half. However, the voltage swing is limited to the supply voltage. Although the PMOS only cross-coupled LC-VCO and complementary LC-VCO have better phase noise and lower power performance compared to NMOS only cross-coupled LC-VCO, the double width of PMOS transistor would bring double parasitic capacitance, making it is even difficult to design a wide-tuning-range millimeter-wave VCO.

The noise from the bias current source can disturb the voltage at the common source node of the cross-coupled pair and modulate with the oscillation frequency of the nonlinear VCO, degrading the close-in phase noise [12]. One approach to reduce the noise of current source is illustrated in Fig. 10.8d, where a noise filter is used in the tail [13]. Despite the use of inductor that would require larger chip area, it can lead to a very low noise bias, leading to low-phase-noise designs.

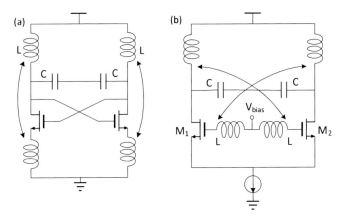

Figure 10.9 LC-VCOs with transformer-based feedback: (a) drain-to-source feedback, (b) drain-to-gate feedback.

Transformer-based feedback technique can be added into cross-coupled LC-VCO to enhance the voltage swing of oscillator and improve the phase noise. Figure 10.9a shows an LC-VCO with transformer-based drain-to-source feedback [14]. This topology allows the drain voltage higher than VDD and the source voltage could be lower than GND. Since the drain voltage is in phase with source voltage, the oscillation amplitude can be enhanced. Consequently, the phase noise would be reduced. Figure 10.9b shows another topology of an LC-VCO with transformer-based feedback, where the NMOS transistors are cross-coupled connected through the transformer-based drain-to-gate feedback. It will bring an advantage that the gate and drain of transistors can be separately biased in DC. By properly design the turn ratio of transformer, the voltage swing at the gate of transistor can be much smaller than that at the drain. Hence, the voltage swing of VCO output could be increased for same bias current, resulting in an improvement of phase noise.

The LC-tank of the cross-coupled LC-VCO can be replaced by the switched transformer to realize multi-mode operation and extend the frequency tuning range. In [15], a cross-coupled LC-VCO with wide tuning range of 41.1% from 57.5 to 90.1 GHz was reported. The circuit schematic is shown in Fig. 10.10. The mode switching is realized by changing the magnetic coupling coefficient between the primary and secondary coils in the transformer tank.

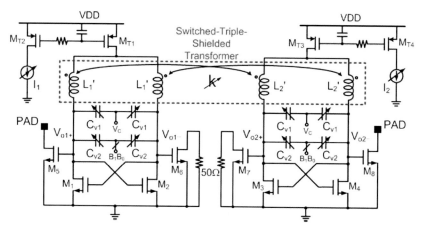

Figure 10.10 Multi-mode LC-VCO based on switched-transformer [15].

10.3.2 Colpitts VCO

Another category of LC-VCO is Colpitts VCO [16–18]. Different from the cross-coupled LC-VCO, Colpitts VCO provides negative resistance based on capacitive feedback. The Colpitts oscillator was first proposed in the 1920s using only one transistor [19], as shown in Fig. 10.11a. The operation of the Colpitts oscillator can be easily understood by examining the resonance circuit shown in Fig. 10.11b. By investigating the small signal equivalent circuit, the admittance looking into the gate-drain port of the circuit can be expressed as

$$Y_{eq,b} = \frac{-C_1 C_2 \omega^2 g_m}{g_m^2 + \omega^2 (C_1 + C_2)^2} + \frac{jC_1 C_2 \omega^3 (C_1 + C_2)}{g_m^2 + \omega^2 (C_1 + C_2)^2}, \qquad (10.17)$$

which is equivalent to a negative conductance in parallel with a capacitor. If the negative admittance is large enough to compensate the loss on the tank, the circuit may oscillate. Due to their non-differential structure, the single-ended Colpitts VCOs were rarely adopted as an integrated circuit. The differential common gate and common drain Colpitts oscillator topology are shown in Figs. 10.10c,d. The differential Colpitts oscillator shows a good close-in phase noise [20]; however, the poor start-up characteristic requires high-power dissipation.

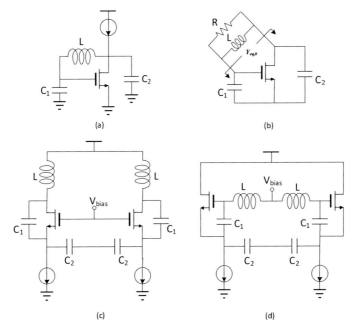

Figure 10.11 (a) A traditional Colpitts oscillator, (b) one-port view of Colpitts oscillator, (c) differential common gate Colpitts oscillator, (d) differential common drain Colpitts oscillator.

To ease the start-up condition of traditional differential Colpitts oscillator, [18] combined the cross-coupled LC-VCO and Colpitts VCO, as shown in Fig. 10.12a. The positive feedback is generated by connecting the gates of $M_{3,4}$ to the gates of opposite switching transistors $M_{1,2}$. The positive feedback enhances the overall small-signal loop gain of VCO, increasing the negative conductance and reducing the start-up current.

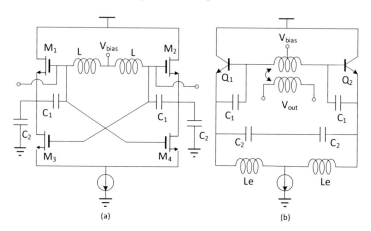

(a)   (b)

Figure 10.12 (a) An improved differential Colpitts VCO with gate-to-source feedback. (b) A W-band Colpitts VCO.

The Colpitts LC-VCO is a promising topology for high frequency because of the better performance in terms of phase noise and tuning range at a given bias current [21]. A W-band Colpitts VCO is realized in the 0.13 µm BiCMOS technology using the topology depicted in Fig. 10.12b [22]. A transformer is used as inductive component in LC-tank at the base of transistor, and providing output for VCO. The inductors connected to emitter provide high impedance path.

Colpitts VCO based on BJT transistor can be used together with push-push technique to achieve oscillation frequency up to sub terahertz (THz) [23], as shown in Fig. 10.13. Compared to a BJT cross-coupled pair, Colpitts topology has proved to achieve a higher maximum oscillation frequency. By using push-push technique, second harmonic signal can be extracted at common-mode node (collector) of the VCO. Fabricated in SiGe 0.13 µm BiCMOS technology, the VCO has achieved −7 dBm output power at 200 GHz oscillation frequency.

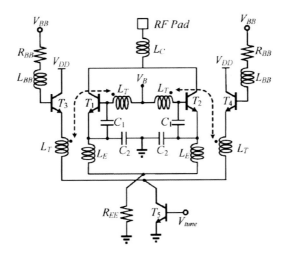

Figure 10.13 A push–push 200-GHz Colpitts VCO.

10.4 Summary

In this chapter, starting from the basic theory of an oscillator, we focus on the discussion of LC-VCO. As a key portion of LC-VCO, the LC-tank has been discussed, including the tank Q and tank components. The typical topologies of LC-VCO for millimeter-wave frequency have been presented.

References

1. J. M. W. Rogers, J. W. M. Rogers, and C. Plett, *Radio frequency Integrated Circuit Design*. Norwood, MA: Artech House, 2010.

2. Y. A. Eken and J. P. Uyemura, multiple-GHz ring and LC VCOs in 0.18 μm CMOS, in *IEEE Radio Freq. Integr. Circuits Symp.*, 2004, pp. 475–478.

3. B. Razavi, *RF Microelectronics*. Upper Saddle River, NJ: Prentice Hall, 2012.

4. N. M. Nguyen and R. G. Meyer, Start-up and frequency stability in high-frequency oscillators, *IEEE J. Solid-State Circuits*, vol. 27, no. 5, pp. 810–820, 1992.

5. A. Hajimiri and T. H. Lee, *The Design of Low Noise Oscillators*. Norwell, MA: Kluwer, 1999.

6. D. B. Leeson, A simple model of feedback oscillator noise spectrum, *Proc. IEEE*, vol. 54, no. 2, pp. 329–330, 1966.

7. B. Razavi, A study of phase noise in CMOS oscillators, *IEEE J. Solid-State Circuits*, vol. 31, no. 3, pp. 331–343, 1996.

8. H.-H. Hsieh, Y.-H. Chen, and L.-H. Lu, A millimeter-wave CMOS LC-tank VCO with an admittance-transforming technique, *IEEE Trans. Microw. Theory Tech.*, vol. 55, no. 9, pp. 1854–1861, 2007.

9. C. P. Yue and S. S. Wong, Physical modeling of spiral inductors on silicon, *Electron Devices, IEEE Trans.*, vol. 47, no. 3, pp. 560–568, 2000.

10. C. P. Yue and S. S. Wong, On-chip spiral inductors with patterned ground shields for Si-based, *IEEE J. Solid-State Circuits*, vol. 33, no. 5, pp. 743–752, 1998.

11. S. Elabd, S. Balasubramanian, Q. Wu, T. Quach, A. Mattamana, and W. Khalil, Analytical and experimental study of wide tuning range mm-wave CMOS LC-VCOs, *IEEE Trans. Circuits Syst. I: Reg. Papers*, vol. 61, no. 5, pp. 1343–1354, 2014.

12. J. J. Rael and A. A. Abidi, Physical processes of phase noise in differential LC oscillators, in *Proc. IEEE Custom Integr. Circuits Conf.*, May 2000, pp. 569–572.

13. E. Hegazi, H. Sjoland, and A. A. Abidi, A filtering technique to lower LC oscillator phase noise, *IEEE J. Solid-State Circuits*, vol. 36, no. 12, pp. 1921–1930, 2001.

14. K. Kwok and H. C. Luong, Ultra-low-Voltage high-performance CMOS VCOs using transformer feedback, *IEEE J. Solid-State Circuits*, vol. 40, no. 3, pp. 652–660, 2005.

15. J. Yin and H. C. Luong, A 57.5–90.1-GHz Magnetically tuned multimode CMOS VCO, *IEEE J. Solid-State Circuits*, vol. 48, no. 8, pp. 1851–1861, 2013.

16. M.-D. Tsai, Y.-H. Cho, and H. Wang, A 5-GHz low phase noise differential Colpitts CMOS VCO, *IEEE Microw. Wireless Compon. Lett.*, vol. 15, no. 5, pp. 327–329, 2005.

17. J.-A. Hou and Y.-H. Wang, A 7.9 GHz low-power PMOS Colpitts VCO using the gate inductive feedback, *IEEE Microw. Wireless Compon. Lett.*, vol. 20, no. 4, pp. 223–225, 2010.

18. J.-P. Hong and S.-G. Lee, Low phase noise G_m-boosted differential gate-to-source feedback Colpitts CMOS VCO, *IEEE J. Solid-State Circuits*, vol. 44, no. 11, pp. 3079–3091, 2009.

19. E. H. Colpitts and O. B. Blackwell, Carrier current telephony and telegraphy, *Am. Inst. Electrical Eng., Trans.*, vol. 40, no. 5, pp. 410–421, 1921.

20. P. Andreani, W. Xiaoyan, L. Vandi, and A. Fard, A study of phase noise in Colpitts and LC-tank CMOS oscillators, *IEEE J. Solid-State Circuits*, vol. 40, no. 5, pp. 1107–1118, 2005.

21. S. T. Nicolson, K. H. K. Yau, P. Chevalier, A. Chantre, B. Sautreuil, K. W. Tang, and S. P. Voinigescu, Design and scaling of W-band SiGe BiCMOS VCOs, *IEEE J. Solid-State Circuits*, vol. 42, no. 9, pp. 1821–1833, 2007.

22. G. Sapone, E. Ragonese, A. Italia, and G. Palmisano, A 0.13-μm SiGe BiCMOS Colpitts-based VCO for W-band radar transmitters, *IEEE Trans. Microw. Theory Tech.*, vol. 61, no. 1, pp. 185–194, 2013.

23. C. Pei-Yuan, O. Momeni, and P. Heydari, A 200-GHz inductively tuned VCO With −7-dBm output power in 130-nm SiGe BiCMOS, *IEEE Trans. Microw. Theory Tech.*, vol. 61, no. 10, pp. 3666–3673.

Small success depends on intelligence. Big success depends on ethics.

—Kiat Seng Yeo and Kaixue Ma

Chapter 11

Microwave and Millimeter-Wave Switches

Fanyi Meng,[a] Kaixue Ma,[a] and Kiat Seng Yeo[b]

[a]School of Physical Electronics,
University of Electronic Science and Technology of China,
#4 Section II, Jianshe North Road, Chengdu 610054, P. R. China
[b]Engineering Product Development, Singapore University of Technology and Design,
8 Somapah Road, Singapore 487372

meng.fanyi@gmail.com

A switch is one of the basic elements of modern radiofrequency/ millimeter-wave (RF/mmW) systems. It is commonly used for signal routing, transceiver time-domain duplex switching, and imager fluctuation reduction (in Dicke radiometer). Depending on its contact terminology, the switch can be denominated as N-poles M-throws (NPMT) where there are N number of poles and M number of throws. Here, the number of poles refers to the number of electrically separate switches which are controlled by a single physical actuator, where the number of throws refers to the number of separate wiring path choices other than "open"

Low-Power Wireless Communication Circuits and Systems: 60 GHz and Beyond
Edited by Kaixue Ma and Kiat Seng Yeo
Copyright © 2018 Pan Stanford Publishing Pte. Ltd.
ISBN 978-981-4745-96-3 (Hardcover), 978-1-315-15653-8 (eBook)
www.panstanford.com

that the switch can adopt for each pole. For example, Fig. 11.1 depicts the single-pole double-throw (SPDT) switches that can be used as T/R and Dicke switches.

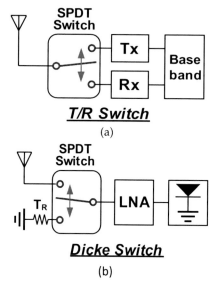

Figure 11.1 SPDT switches used as (a) T/R switch and (b) Dicke switch.

The following sections will start with the analysis of CMOS FET transistors, which are essential for switching functions in RF/mmW ICs. Then, it will discuss the analysis and design of the most adopted SPDT switch topology. NPMT designs can be easily migrated from SPDT design skills. Next, a new switch topology named magnetic switchable artificial resonator will be introduced. Last, a comparison between state-of-the-art SPDTs will be presented.

11.1 CMOS FET Transistor

In Fig. 11.2, the shunt n-type field-effect-transistor (nFET) switch transistor is analyzed using a small-signal circuit model, which comprises an intrinsic FET [1] and extrinsic/parasitic components [2]. Since the transistor is configured in the shunt connection, its intrinsic part is modeled as C_{ch} and R_{ch} according to [3] and [1], where C_{ch} is the channel capacitance and R_{ch}

is the channel resistance as shown in Fig. 11.2a. The extrinsic components are modeled as the gate-drain capacitance C_{GD}, the gate-source capacitance C_{GS}, the drain-bulk junction capacitance $C_{jun,D}$, the source-bulk junction capacitance $C_{jun,S}$, the resistance to substrate R_{sub}, and the gate resistance r_{gate}. In most of the millimeter-wave switch designs, including this work, a large resistor R_G or a $\lambda_g/4$ T-line is added at the gate terminal to effectively float the transistor gate terminal and reduce RF signal leakage. Thus, the model is reduced into Fig. 11.2b, where the equivalent shunt resistance and capacitance are derived in Eqs. (11.1) and (11.2) as follows:

$$R_{eq} = \frac{R_{ch}\left(4R_{sub}^2\omega^2C_j^2 + 1\right)}{\left(4 + \dfrac{R_{ch}}{R_{sub}}\right)R_{sub}^2\omega^2C_j^2 + 1} \tag{11.1}$$

$$C_{eq} = C_{ch} + \frac{C_j}{2} + \frac{C_j(2R_{sub}^2\omega^2C_j^2 + 1)}{4R_{sub}^2\omega^2C_j^2 + 1}, \tag{11.2}$$

where $C_j = C_{jun,S} = C_{jun,D}$.

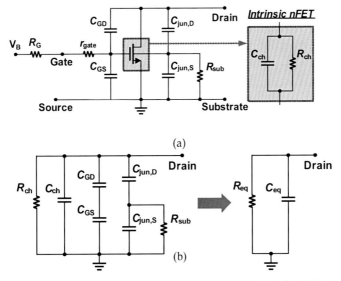

(a)

(b)

Figure 11.2 Small-signal equivalent circuit model of nFET switch transistor: (a) Transistor intrinsic and extrinsic components; (b) simplified model of shunt transistor.

The equivalent shunt resistance in Eq. (11.1) has two expressions depending on the gate bias voltage V_B. In the condition, $V_B = V_{DD}$, the transistor operates in triode region and $R_{ch\_ON} \ll R_{sub}$. Thus, this equivalent resistance is approximated in Eq. (11.3) as follows:

$$R_{eq\_ON} \approx \frac{R_{ch\_ON}\left(4R_{sub}^2\omega^2 C_j^2 + 1\right)}{(4+0)R_{sub}^2\omega^2 C_j^2 + 1} = R_{ch\_ON}, \tag{11.3}$$

which is frequency-independent but relates to the transistor size and process characteristics. In another condition $V_B = 0$ V, transistor is off with $R_{ch\_OFF} \gg R_{sub}$, and the shunt resistance becomes frequency-dependent as

$$R_{eq\_OFF} \approx \frac{R_{ch\_OFF}\left(4R_{sub}^2\omega^2 C_j^2 + 1\right)}{\dfrac{R_{ch\_OFF}}{R_{sub}}R_{sub}^2\omega^2 C_j^2 + 1} \approx \left. R_{ch\_OFF}\right|_{\text{at low frequency}} . \tag{11.4}$$

$$\left. 4R_{sub}\right|_{\text{at high frequency}}$$

In Fig. 11.3a, the equivalent shunt resistances in both conditions are plotted based on transistors from GLOBALFOUNDRIES (GF) 65 nm bulk CMOS technology. As predicted, R_{eq_ON} remains about 6 Ω from 20 to 200 GHz, while the R_{eq_OFF} is >1 kΩ at 20 GHz but decreases rapidly to only 170 Ω at 200 GHz. Generally in switch designs, the smaller R_{eq_ON} of shunt transistor leads to better isolation as it creates lower impedance at drain terminal. The R_{eq_OFF} directly influences the insertion loss of switches, as the finite impedance at drain terminal presents a leakage path for RF signals. Thus, switches in a same technology tend to have higher insertion loss when operated at higher frequencies.

If we use R_{eq_OFF}/R_{eq_ON} as a figure-of-merit (FoM) to evaluate the shunt transistors, this process has a value of 58 at 100 GHz. In the 90 nm SiGe HBT technology [3], this FoM is up to 800 at 94 GHz that resulted in very low insertion loss with high isolation of the switch designs.

The equivalent shunt capacitance in Eq. (11.2) is approximated to Eq. (11.5) as

$$C_{eq} \approx \frac{C_j}{2} + \frac{C_j(2R_{sub}^2\omega^2C_j^2 + 1)}{4R_{sub}^2\omega^2C_j^2 + 1} \approx \begin{cases} 1.5C_j \big|_{\text{at low frequency}} \\ C_j \big|_{\text{at high frequency}} \end{cases}$$ (11.5)

because $C_{ch} \ll C_j$. According to Eq. (11.5), C_{eq} decreases with frequency. It is noted that the junction capacitance C_j has additional contribution from gate-channel capacitances in the triode region. Thus, the C_{eq_ON} is slightly larger than C_{eq_OFF} as shown in Fig. 11.3b.

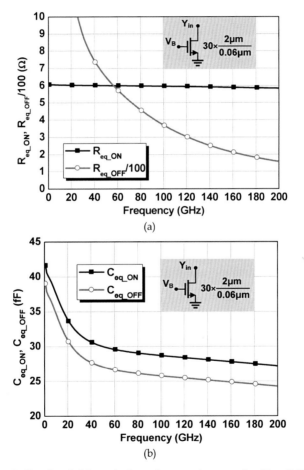

Figure 11.3 Simulated (a) equivalent shunt resistances for $V_B = 0/V_{DD}$, (b) equivalent shunt capacitance for $V_B = 0/V_{DD}$.

11.2   SPDT Switches Based on $\lambda_g/4$ T-line Topology

In the literature, millimeter-wave SPDT switches [3–7] mostly adopt $\lambda_g/4$ transmission-line (T-line) topology as shown in Fig. 11.4, where λ_g is the guided wavelength at operating frequency. When control voltage V_C is set high, the top transistor is turned on, which creates low impedance at point A. The $\lambda_g/4$ T-line transforms this low impedance into high impedance at a common point T, which prevents signal flowing to the top path. Thus, the bottom path becomes a low-loss path with bottom transistor turned off. Shunt T-lines T_M are added to resonate out the parasitic capacitance of transistors. It operates in a similar fashion when V_C is set low.

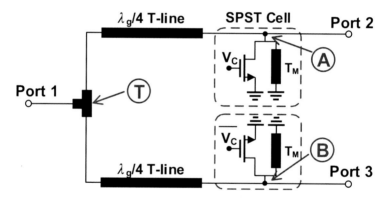

Figure 11.4 Conventional $\lambda_g/4$ T-line topology for millimeter-wave SPDT switches.

The design procedures are straightforward, just to satisfy the below two conditions:

- Condition 1: Length of main transmission line is $\lambda_g/4$ at centre operating frequency of switches.
- Condition 2: Matching transmission line matches out the C_{eq} of switching transistors.

Both conditions can be easily achieved by hand-calculation or EDA tools. For extension to NPMT designs, similar concept can be adopted. However, it is noted that the isolation and insertion loss are generally poorer due to additional poles and throws.

11.3 SPDT Switches Based on Magnetically Switchable Artificial Resonator Topology

The complete configuration of the proposed SPDT switch by using magnetically switchable artificial resonator is shown in Fig. 11.5. In the operation mode with Port 2 as the signal through port and Port 3 as the isolation port, the control voltages are set as follows: $V_1 = V_a = 0$ V and $V_2 = V_b = V_{DD}$. Another operation mode can be set with alternated control voltages. It comprises three main coupled lines 1–3 for the switching function, and two auxiliary coupled lines for isolation enhancement.

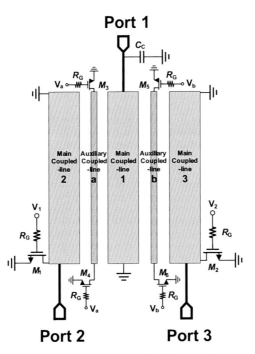

Figure 11.5 Configuration of the proposed SPDT switch using magnetically switchable artificial resonator.

11.4 Main Coupled Lines

In Fig. 11.6a, the proposed SPDT switch adopts the artificial resonator concept, which comprises three coupled-lines, two switch transistors M_{1-2}, one lump capacitor C_C, and bias resistors R_G. Auxiliary coupled-lines, which only affect the magnetic coupling between the three main coupled-lines in Fig. 11.6a, have almost no effect on SPDT "on" throw but improve isolation for the "off" throw and will be introduced and studied at the end of this section.

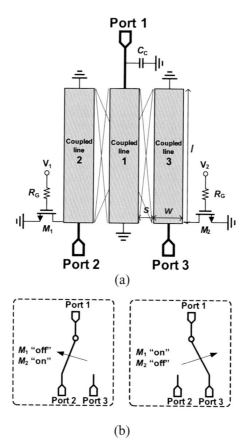

(a)

(b)

Figure 11.6 Proposed SPDT switch using artificial resonator: (a) Configuration; (b) two operation modes.

Figure 11.6b shows the two operation modes of the switch. In the operation mode when transistor M_2 is turned on, it creates low impedance at Port 3, which isolates Port 3 from Port 1. Meanwhile, transistor M_1 is turned off, whose parasitic components and coupled-lines form an artificial resonant network with a bandpass transmission response from Port 1 to Port 2.

For simplicity, the equivalent resistances of shunt switch transistors are neglected and assumed as short-/open-circuit as $R_{eq\_ON} \ll 50\ \Omega \ll R_{eq\_OFF}$ (see Fig. 11.3a). In reality, as previously described, these resistances have determinative effects on the insertion loss and the isolation performance of the designed switches. However, the R_{eq_OFF}/R_{eq_ON} ratio is basically a process-determined factor and is hard to improve by proper circuit design techniques. Thus, the following analysis focuses on the resonance property of the proposed SPDT switches, which models the switch transistors as C_{eq_ON} and C_{eq_OFF}.

In Fig. 11.7a, the small-signal equivalent circuit model is built for the operation mode where Port 2 is the through port and Port 3 is the isolation port, i.e., $V_1 = 0$ V and $V_2 = V_{DD}$ as shown in Fig. 3. The opposite mode has a similar circuit model. In the model, the three coupled-lines are modeled as lump inductors L_1, L_2, L_3, and lump capacitors C_1, C_2, C_3, according to the transcendental T-line model equations as follows [8]:

$$L = L_1 = L_2 = L_3 = \frac{Z_C \tan(\beta l)}{\omega}, \tag{11.6}$$

$$C = C_1 = C_2 = C_3 \approx \frac{\varepsilon_0 \varepsilon_r w\ l}{h}, \tag{11.7}$$

where Z_C and β are the characteristic impedance and propagation phase constant, respectively, of the standalone T-line with length l and width w, ε_r is the effective dielectric constant of the stacked dielectric materials, and h is the distance between signal line and metal ground. The magnetic coupling between coupled-lines can be extracted using electromagnetic (EM) simulator using (11.8) as

$$k_{i,j} = \frac{1}{L_i L_j} \left[\frac{\text{Im}(Z_{i,j})_{\text{DUT}}}{\omega} \right]_{\text{Low frequency}}. \tag{11.8}$$

As shown in Fig. 11.8b, the reduced small-signal equivalent circuit resembles a magnetic-coupled LC resonator, with the equivalent coupling coefficient derived as in [9] as follows:

$$k_{eq} = k_{1,2} - k_{2,3}k_{1,3} = k_{1,2}(1 - k_{2,3}).$$ (11.9)

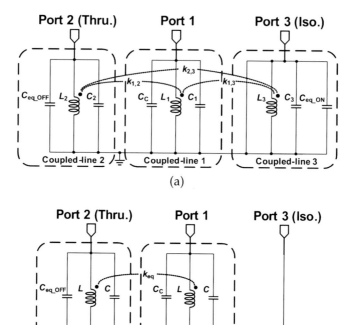

(a)

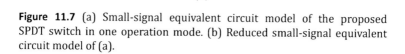

(b)

Figure 11.7 (a) Small-signal equivalent circuit model of the proposed SPDT switch in one operation mode. (b) Reduced small-signal equivalent circuit model of (a).

Thus, a second-order bandpass frequency response from Port 1 to Port 2 is expected. The transmission responses are simulated by assuming L = 35 pH, C = 5 fF, C_{eq_OFF} = 20 fF, and C_C = 30 fF, and plotted in Fig. 11.8 for different equivalent coupling coefficients. It is noticed that the two transmission poles are separated apart with a stronger coupling, but become closer by reducing the coupling strength. The optimum response is achieved at around k_{eq} = 0.5 for this example.

Further, the locations of the two transmission poles which are the resonance frequencies can be derived in Eq. (11.10) as follows:

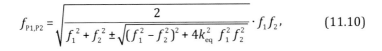

$$f_{\text{P1,P2}} = \sqrt{\frac{2}{f_1^2 + f_2^2 \pm \sqrt{(f_1^2 - f_2^2)^2 + 4k_{\text{eq}}^2 f_1^2 f_2^2}}} \cdot f_1 f_2, \qquad (11.10)$$

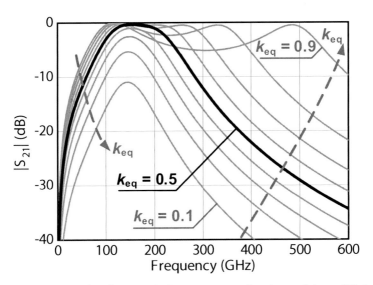

Figure 11.8 Simulated transmission responses for k_{eq} = 0.1 to 0.9 in steps of 0.1.

$$f_{\text{P1,P2}} = \sqrt{\frac{2}{f_1^2 + f_2^2 \pm \sqrt{(f_1^2 - f_2^2)^2 + 4k_{\text{eq}}^2 f_1^2 f_2^2}}} \cdot f_1 f_2, \qquad (11.10)$$

where f_{P1} and f_{P2} denote the first and second resonance poles, respectively, with

$$f_1 = \frac{1}{2\pi \sqrt{L(C_{\text{eq\_OFF}} + C)}}, \qquad (11.11)$$

$$f_2 = \frac{1}{2\pi \sqrt{L(C_{\text{c}} + C)}}. \qquad (11.12)$$

The two transmission poles are calculated and plotted in Fig. 11.9, which agree well with the transmission responses in Fig. 11.8.

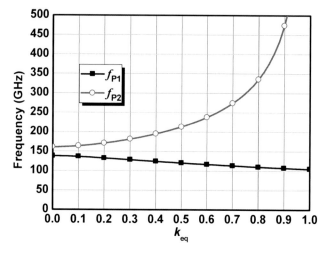

Figure 11.9 Calculated transmission poles for the design in Fig. 11.8.

11.5 Auxiliary Coupled Lines

In the above investigation, the coupling coefficients between adjacent coupled-lines are assumed to be equal, i.e., $k_{1,2} = k_{1,3}$ which represents the symmetry of the three coupled-lines.

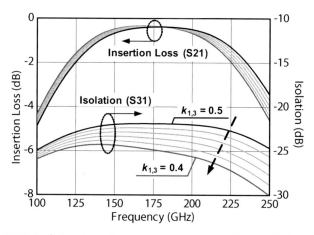

Figure 11.10 Isolation investigation by reducing coupling coefficient $k_{1,3}$.

However, it is surmised that the switch isolation can be improved by reducing the magnetic coupling to the couple-line connected to isolation port, i.e., $k_{1,3}$ in the above example. Assuming $L = 35$ pH, $C = 5$ fF, $C_{eq\_OFF} = 20$ fF, $C_C = 30$ fF, $k_{1,2} = 0.5$, $k_{2,3} = 0.15$, switch performance is studied with $k_{1,3}$ reduced from 0.5 to 0.4 in steps of 0.02. In addition, $R_{eq\_ON} = 5$ Ω is added in parallel to Port 3 in order to get meaningful isolation results. In Fig. 11.9, it is observed that by reducing $k_{1,3}$ from 0.5 to 0.4, the insertion loss almost remains the same, while the isolation is improved by 3 to 4 dB.

Therefore, in the proposed SPDT switch, switchable auxiliary coupled-line is inserted between main coupled-lines to control the magnetic coupling between them, as shown in Fig. 11.11a. Switch transistors are placed in series at each end of the auxiliary coupled-line. The two operating states are depicted

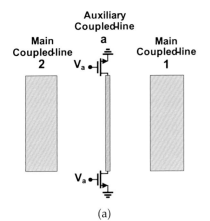

(a)

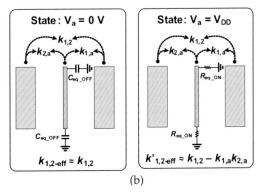

(b)

Figure 11.11 Switchable auxiliary coupled-line between main coupled-lines: (a) Schematic; (b) two operating states.

Table 11.1 Performance summary of the state-of-the-art SPDT switches

	[6] JSSC 2010	[10] IMS 2015	[11] JSSC 2012	[3] TMTT 2014	[5] MWCL 2014	[7] MWCL 2012	[12] ISSCC 2015
Technology	90 nm CMOS	90 nm CMOS	0.18 μm SiGe BiCMOS	90 nm SiGe HBT	0.13 μm SiGe HBT	45 nm SOI	65 nm Bulk CMOS
f_T (GHz)	130	130	200		300	485	220
Transistor $R_{ON} \times C_{OFF}$ (fs)	180	180	132	Not Mentioned	83.7	75.6	147
Frequency (GHz)	50–67	40–110	75–110	73–110	96–163	140–220	130–180
Insertion loss (dB)	1.5–2#	<4	2.8–3.1#	1.1#	2.6–3	3–4.5	3.3–4
Return loss (dB)	>8	>10	>10	>10	>10	>10	>10
Isolation (dB)	25–27.5	>20	21–22	22	23.5–29	20–30	21.1–23.7
P_{1dB} (dBm)	13.5†	10	Not Mentioned	17	17 @ 94 GHz†	10†	11.4†
Size excluding pads (mm²/1000 × λ_0^2)^	0.27/10.3	0.11/2.55	0.114/10.8	0.213/19.8	0.228/42.5	0.10/36	0.0035/0.94
P_{DC} (mW)	0	0	0	5.9	6	0	0
Topology*	$\lambda_g/4$ TL + SS-SPST	Traveling-wave	$\lambda_g/4$ TL + SS-SPST	$\lambda_g/4$ TL + DS-SPST	$\lambda_g/4$ TL + DS-SPST	$\lambda_g/4$ TL + DS-SPST	Magnetically switchable artificial resonator

*TL, transmission line; SS, single-shunt; DS, double-shunt.
#Pad loss de-embedded.
†Simulation.
^λ_0 is the free space wavelength at center operating frequency.

in Fig. 11.11b. In the state $V_a = 0$ V, the equivalent capacitance of the switches present impedances much larger than series resistance of the auxiliary coupled-line, which makes the auxiliary coupled-line a floating line. Thus, the effective coupling coefficient between main coupled-lines $k_{1,2\text{-eff}}$ is approximately equal to $k_{1,2}$. In the state $V_a = V_{DD}$, the small resistance of switches shorts the auxiliary coupled-line to ground. Subsequently, the effective coupling coefficient $k'_{1,2\text{-eff}}$ is approximated to $k_{1,2} - k_{1,a}k_{2,a}$.

11.6 State-of-the-Art Switches

Table 11.1 shows the performance summary of the state-of-the-art SPDT switches. It is clear that due to superior transistor performance, the switches in HBT and SOI generally have better insertion loss and isolation. For the CMOS switches, conventional $\lambda_g/4$ topology is good at frequencies around 60–110 GHz, while the switches based on magnetically switchable artificial resonator topology are better suitable for frequency beyond 110 GHz.

References

1. J. Mayer, MOS models and circuit simulation, *RVA Rev.*, vol. 32, pp. 42–63, 1971.

2. C. C. Enz and C. Yuhua, MOS transistor modeling for RF IC design, *IEEE J. Solid-State Circuits*, vol. 35, pp. 186–201, 2000.

3. R. L. Schmid, P. Song, C. T. Coen, A. C. Ulusoy, and J. D. Cressler, On the analysis and design of low-loss single-pole double-throw W-band switches utilizing saturated SiGe HBTs, *IEEE Trans. Microw. Theory Tech.*, vol. 62, pp. 2755–2767, 2014.

4. E. Shumakher, J. Elkind, and D. Elad, Key components of a 130 GHz Dicke-radiometer SiGe RFIC, in *IEEE Silicon Monolith. Integr. Circuits in RF Syst. (SiRF)*, 2013, pp. 255–257.

5. A. C. Ulusoy, *et al.*, A low-loss and high isolation D-band SPDT switch utilizing deep-saturated SiGe HBTs, *IEEE Microw. Wireless Compon. Lett.*, vol. 24, pp. 400–402, 2014.

6. M. Uzunkol and G. M. Rebeiz, A low-loss 50-70 GHz SPDT switch in 90 nm CMOS, *IEEE J. Solid-State Circuits*, vol. 45, pp. 2003–2007, 2010.

7. M. Uzunkol and G. M. Rebeiz, 140–220 GHz SPST and SPDT switches in 45 nm CMOS SOI, *IEEE Microw. Wireless Compon. Lett.*, vol. 22, pp. 412–414, 2012.

8. D. M. Pozar, *Microwave Engineering*, 4th ed, New York: Wiley, 2012.

9. U. Decanis, A. Ghilioni, E. Monaco, A. Mazzanti, and F. Svelto, A low-noise quadrature VCO based on magnetically coupled resonators and a wideband frequency divider at millimeter waves, *IEEE J. Solid-State Circuits*, vol. 46, pp. 2943–2955, 2011.

10. L. Wen-Chian and C. Huey-Ru, A 40-110 GHz high-isolation CMOS traveling-wave T/R switch by using parallel inductor, in *IEEE MTT-S Int. Microw. Symp. Dig.*, 2015, pp. 1–3.

11. Z. Chen, C.-C. Wang, H.-C. Yao, and P. Heydari, A BiCMOS W-band 2×2 focal-plane array with on-chip antenna, *IEEE J. Solid-State Circuits*, vol. 47, pp. 2355–2371, 2012.

12. F. Meng, K. Ma, and K. S. Yeo, A 130-to-180 GHz 0.0035 mm^2 SPDT switch with 3.3 dB loss and 23.7 dB isolation in 65 nm bulk CMOS, in *IEEE Int. Solid-State Circuits Conf. (ISSCC) Dig.*, 2015, pp. 34–36.

Regardless of employment or university admission, don't look at just one's grades, skills, and qualifications, but also the motivation, persistence, passion, and enthusiasm.

—Kiat Seng Yeo and Kaixue Ma

Chapter 12

Millimeter-Wave Beam Forming

Fanyi Meng,[a] Kaixue Ma,[a] and Kiat Seng Yeo[b]

[a]*School of Physical Electronics,*
University of Electronic Science and Technology of China,
#4 Section II, Jianshe North Road, Chengdu 610054, P. R. China
[b]*Engineering Product Development, Singapore University of Technology and Design,*
8 Somapah Road, Singapore 487372

meng.fanyi@gmail.com; makaixue@uestc.edu.cn, kiatseng_yeo@sutd.edu.sg

Beam-forming systems that are used for electrical beam steering to various directions within the predefined field view have become the major solution for millimeter-wave (mm-wave) systems, especially those operating at the unlicensed 60 GHz. Thus, systems typically utilize phased-array technique at mm-wave frequencies and emulate the high-gain antenna with the advantages of array gain, high directivity, and spatial coverage, as shown in Figs. 12.1 and 12.2.

In addition, phased-array allows non-line-of-sight communication which cannot be established in conventional mm-wave transceivers due to high barrier loss at 60 GHz. Theoretically

Low-Power Wireless Communication Circuits and Systems: 60 GHz and Beyond
Edited by Kaixue Ma and Kiat Seng Yeo
Copyright © 2018 Pan Stanford Publishing Pte. Ltd.
ISBN 978-981-4745-96-3 (Hardcover), 978-1-315-15653-8 (eBook)
www.panstanford.com

the performance of transceiver improves as the number of elements (*N*) in phased-arrays, as follows [1]:

$$\text{RX SNR improvement} = 10 \times \log(N) \qquad (12.1)$$

$$\text{TX Array Gain} = 20 \times \log(N) \qquad (12.2)$$

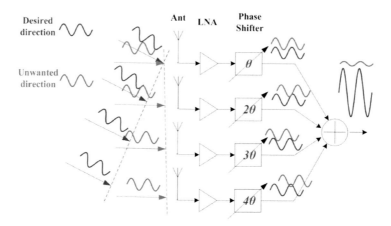

Figure 12.1 High directivity property of beam-forming technique.

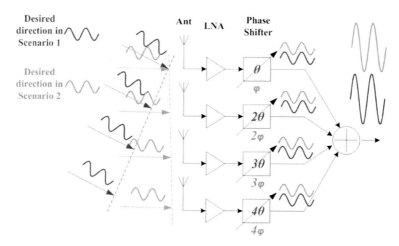

Figure 12.2 Wide coverage property of beam-forming technique.

12.1   Current Tread

The full integration of phased-array systems with digital baseband in silicon-based technologies leads to numerous improvements in cost, size, power consumption, and reliability. Meanwhile, it provides feasibility to perform fully on-chip signal processing and controlling, without any off-chip components, resulting in additional savings in cost and power. The multiple channels, operating in harmony, provide benefits at both system and circuit levels. For example, a 60 GHz integrated phased-array will make gigabit-per-second directional point-to-point communication feasible. At the circuit level, the division of the signal into multiple parallel paths relaxes the signal handling requirements of individual blocks, especially power amplifiers.

Despite its high functionality, a phased-array is still a costly solution. Multiple elements arise total power consumption, circuit size, complexity of RF and IF circuits routing and inter-element isolation, and system calibration algorithm. Thus, great challenges stills exist for the phased-array to be used in the commercial and mobile applications where power and cost are primarily concerned.

12.2   Recent Implementations

Lossy silicon substrate and poor power-handling capability have to be considered wisely in circuit designs. Besides, other than the traditional building blocks like low-noise amplifier [2], power amplifier [3], frequency synthesizer [4, 5], modulator [6], on-chip filter [7], switches [8], etc., in a single element transceiver [9], new building blocks like the variable phase shifters [10], RF variable gain amplifiers [11], and power combining/splitting circuits [12] have to be designed and co-designed on-chip to provide beam-steering capability. These designs must also feature compact size and low power consumption characteristics. Such systems have been demonstrated in 2-, 4-, 16-, and 32-element phased-arrays [1, 13–23].

In the early works of mm-wave phased-arrays, four-elements receivers and transmitter are successfully implemented in

0.12 µm SiGe BiCMOS [22] and 65 nm CMOS [24], respectively. In [22], the receiver array uses passive RF phase shifting topology, achieving full spatial coverage with peak-to-null ratio higher than 25 dB using with power consumption of ~65 mW per element. In the transmitter array [24], active phase shifting was adopted due to lower gain per stage in CMOS. The array achieves fully differential signal processing with independent tuning of both vertical and horizontal polarizations with ~20 dB gain, 11 dBm output Psat, and power consumption of ~150 mW per element.

A fully integrated 16-element phased-array receiver was reported in [1]. The arrays use aperture-coupled patch-antennas packaged with RX IC in multi-layer organic and LTCC, demonstrating EVM better than –18 dB in both line-of-sight and non-line-of-sight (using write board as reflector) links of ~7.8 m and ~9 m spacing, respectively. In [23], a 32-element phased-array TX/RX chip with a 2-bit phase shifter and IF converter to/from 12 GHz was implemented. The array achieves 12.5 dB gain, 11 dB noise figure, –17 dBm RX IP1 dB, and 8 dBm TX array Psat, with total power consumption of ~500 mW.

The most recent works of 60 GHz phased-array include very low power and compact designs that target for short-range (<1 m) and portable devices applications [13, 14], and fully integrated TX/RX chipset with state-of-the-art EVM performance (better than –20 dB) in [16].

12.3 Variable Phase Shifters

Variable phase shifters are commonly adopted in phased-arrays or beam-steering systems to adjust the signal phase in each antenna path and steer beam pattern.

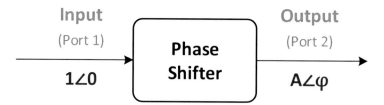

Figure 12.3 Simplified plot of a signal passing through a phase shifter.

Ideally, as shown in Fig. 12.3, phase shifter is a device that changes the insertion phase (phase of S21, φ). In a variable phase shifter, this insertion phase typically has a variable range from φ_1 to φ_2, which is defined as the total phase range φ_{total} ($\varphi_2 - \varphi_1$) of the phase shifter. In a phased-array, we definitely want the phase shifter to achieve φ_{total} as large as possible (typical maximum is 360°), to obtain a better phase control capability and beam coverage. However, as engineers (or potential engineers), we know it well: "Nothing comes for free." It must have certain trade-off. In phase shifter designs, large φ_{total} usually comes with bulky circuit size, high power consumption, and/or high level of insertion loss.

It is noted that the insertion phase (φ) is the absolute phase shift when a signal passes through the phase shifter. However, to adjust signal phase to a different insertion phase state, what matters is actually the relative phase shift across output states. It implies that in a phased-array system, phase shifter with various insertion phase states in Fig. 12.4a works in same as the phase shifter with phase performance in Fig. 12.4b, due to the simple fact that their ability to adjust signal phase is the same as shown in Fig. 12.4c. However, please take note that the poor phase linearity (large group delay variation) in Fig. 12.4a can cause serious system performance degradation.

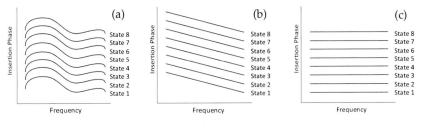

Figure 12.4 (a) Insertion phase of a 3-bit phase shifter PS1. (b) Insertion phase of another 3-bit phase shifter PS2. (c) Relative phase shift of PS1 and PS2.

If you read Fig. 12.3 carefully, you might notice some part missing in the above discussion and the following questions come in mind: (1) Why is there an "A" in the output signal? (2) Are phase shifters supposed to change the phase only? (3) Why the amplitude? My answer is: Please bear with it! In IC designs, we need to use some circuit blocks to achieve phase shifting.

If we use passive blocks, insertion loss occurs with $A < 1$. In case of active blocks, the signal is usually amplified with $A > 1$. Someone might suggest to use passive blocks followed by active ones or vice versa and obtain neither loss nor gain in the signal amplitude ($A = 1$). And some others might prefer to design phase shifters with signal gain as they like "gain" more than "loss." In fact, however, the amplitude change does not bother much for a phase shifter design to be successful as long as it fulfills these two conditions: (1) The variation in the amplitude (A) is small when the insertion phase (φ) changes. (2) The amplitude is flat in the operation bandwidth in any phase states. It is noted that tunable amplification blocks (e.g. variable gain amplifier, VGA) after phase shifters are used to compensate the variation in the signal amplitude in different states for phase shifting. It is better illustrated graphically in Fig. 12.5. From the above discussion, phase shifter with insert loss/gain in Fig. 12.5b is preferred over the one in Fig. 12.5a. Definitely, we want the amplitude variation as small as possible to relax our RF VGA design constraints. Thus, Fig. 12.5c is mostly preferred among these three.

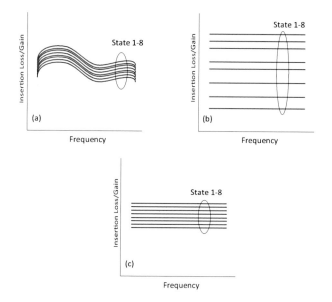

Figure 12.5 (a) Insertion phase of a 3-bit phase shifter PS4. (b) Insertion phase of another 3-bit phase shifter PS5. (c) Insertion phase of another 3-bit phase shifter PS6.

In the following, we will explore the four main types of phase shifters that are popular at mm-wave frequencies. They are reflective-type phase shifter (RTPS), switched-type phase shifter (STPS), vector-summation phase shifter (VSPS), and loaded-line phase shifter (LLPS).

12.4 Reflective-Type Phase Shifter

A typical RTPS comprises a 3 dB coupler and two identical reflective loads as shown in Fig. 12.6. The operation mechanism is studied in Fig. 12.7, showing a slow-motion of how the signal phase is tuned.

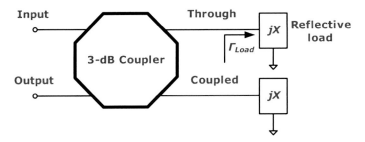

Figure 12.6 Schematic of a reflective-type phase shifter.

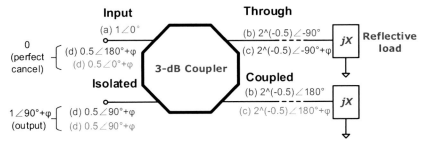

Figure 12.7 Study of RTPS operation mechanism.

A typical RTPS comprises a 3 dB coupler and two identical reflective loads as shown in Fig. 12.6. The operation mechanism is studied in Fig. 5.7, showing a "slow-motion" of how the signal phase is tuned.

Prior to the investigation, we need to know more about the 3 dB coupler or 90° directional coupler. It is a four-port network with the following scattering-parameters:

$$[S] = \begin{bmatrix} S_{11} & S_{12} & S_{13} & S_{14} \\ S_{21} & S_{22} & S_{23} & S_{24} \\ S_{31} & S_{32} & S_{33} & S_{34} \\ S_{41} & S_{42} & S_{43} & S_{44} \end{bmatrix} = \frac{-1}{\sqrt{2}} \begin{bmatrix} 0 & j & 1 & 0 \\ j & 0 & 0 & 1 \\ 1 & 0 & 0 & j \\ 0 & 1 & j & 0 \end{bmatrix}. \tag{12.3}$$

Assuming an input signal $1\angle 0°$ is injected into the input port as in step (a), it is split into two signals with equal amplitude and 90° phase difference at through and coupled port as in step (b). With short-circuit reflective loads, these two signals are reflected back into the coupler in step (c). If we treat them as input signals, each signal is split to another two signals at input and isolated port as in step (d). The split components from the reflected signals actually cancel each other at the input port, which provides a good matching condition. At the isolated port, these two signals are in phase and added up as the output.

Typically, we design the reflective loads with controllable reactance so that the RTPS insertion phase is also variable. The relation between insertion phase and load reactance is

$$\varphi_{out} = -\frac{\pi}{2} - 2\arctan\left(\frac{X}{Z_0}\right). \tag{12.4}$$

Thus, the total phase shift range is determined by the maximum and minimum reactance values as

$$\varphi_{total} = 2\left|\arctan\left(\frac{X_{max}}{Z_0}\right) - \arctan\left(\frac{X_{min}}{Z_0}\right)\right|. \tag{12.5}$$

Figure 12.8 shows the four types of reflective loads, commonly used in the mm-wave frequency range. They are capacitive load, resonant load, dual resonant load, and dual resonant load with impedance transformation. Using Eq. 12.5, the theoretical total phase shift ranges can be calculated with known loads.

In CMOS technology, the typical tuning range (C_{MAX}/C_{MIN}) of a varactor (variable capacitor) is between 3 and 5. To obtain the largest total phase shift range, in each type of reflective loads, its reactance is designed with $X_{max} = -X_{min}$.

Generally for CMOS design reference, at frequency between 30–90 GHz, the achievable total phase shift range for each type of reflective loads is summarized in Table 12.1. It is noted that in Fig. 12.8d, the impedance transformation network is used to reduce the insertion loss variation as discussed in Fig. 12.5.

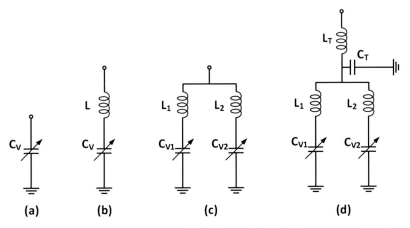

Figure 12.8 The popular types of reflective loads: (a) Capacitive load; (b) resonant load; (c) dual resonant load; (d) dual resonant load with impedance transformation.

Table 12.1 Practical phase shift range for four types of reflective loads in CMOS designs

	φ_{total} (°)
Capacitive load	40–90
Resonant load	90–200
Dual resonant load	Larger than 360
Dual resonant load with impedance transformation	Larger than 360

12.5   Switched-Type Phase Shifter

Figure 12.9 shows the general schematic of an STPS. It consists of N stages of STPS cells with different phase shifting, e.g., Stage 1 for 0/180° phase shift, Stage 2 for 0/90° phase shift, etc.

In this manner, it formed a complete N-bit 360° phase shifter. At mm-wave frequencies, N is usually less than 5 due to increased insertion loss with more stages.

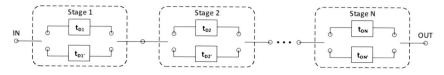

Figure 12.9 Schematic of a switched-type phase shifter.

Each stage is formed by SPDT switches at input and output ports and two networks with different phase delays, labeled as t_D and $t_{D'}$. The SPDT switches are different from T/R switches, which need to match to 50 Ω. Instead, in STPS, the matching network is co-designed during designing networks t_D and $t_{D'}$, facilitates the design procedures, and provides 50 Ω matching for cells to be cascaded.

Figure 12.10 shows the major topologies of the phase delay/advance networks used in STPS. Thus, we can select the correct network topology based on the phase difference between any two topologies and required phase shift. The basic design equations are also included in the figure.

Besides using SPDT switches for network selection to achieve desired phase shift, the switches are able to be designed "inside" or co-designed with passive networks. For example, the bridged T-type topology is prevailing in mm-wave STPSs, especially in designs with small phase shifts of less than 90°. In Fig. 12.11a, the capacitor-based bridged T-type phase shifter comprises two capacitors (C_p), inductors ($L_{1,2}$) and two MOS switches ($M_{1,2}$). Its phase shift is the output phase difference in the two operation states as indicated in Figs. 12.11b,c, respectively. By properly choosing design parameters as in Fig. 12.10, the required phase shift can be obtained as described in [25]. However, these capacitor-based phase shifter designs generally have poor design accuracy, as the fabrication tolerance of metal–insulator–metal (MIM) and metal–oxide–metal (MOM) capacitors are typically 5–10% in advanced CMOS [26, 27].

To tackle the aforementioned issue, the two capacitors (C_p) can be replaced with inductors (L_1) that are better modeled using electromagnetic (EM) simulators as shown in Fig. 12.11d. Reference [28] analyzed the circuits and provided design equations (see Fig. 12.10) under the conditions that the on-resistance and off-capacitance of transistor M_1 can be ignored as shown in Figs. 12.11e,f. The equations were used in the realizations of Ku-/V-band phase shifters [11, 28].

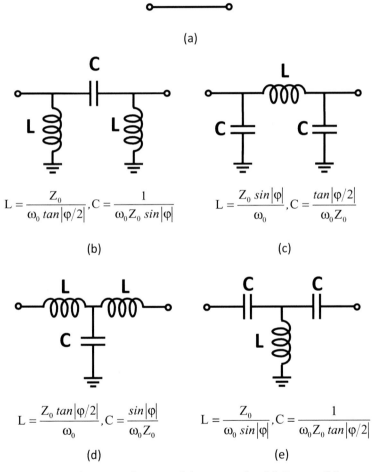

(a)

$$L = \frac{Z_0}{\omega_0 \, tan \, |\varphi/2|}, C = \frac{1}{\omega_0 Z_0 \, sin \, |\varphi|}$$

(b)

$$L = \frac{Z_0 \, sin \, |\varphi|}{\omega_0}, C = \frac{tan \, |\varphi/2|}{\omega_0 Z_0}$$

(c)

$$L = \frac{Z_0 \, tan \, |\varphi/2|}{\omega_0}, C = \frac{sin \, |\varphi|}{\omega_0 Z_0}$$

(d)

$$L = \frac{Z_0}{\omega_0 \, sin \, |\varphi|}, C = \frac{1}{\omega_0 Z_0 \, tan \, |\varphi/2|}$$

(e)

Figure 12.10 Schematic of various delay networks: (a) Bypass; (b) π-type high-pass; (c) π-type low-pass; (d) T-type low-pass; (e) T-type high-pass.

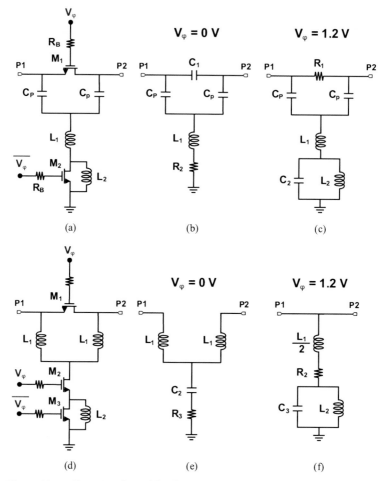

Figure 12.11 Capacitor-based bridged T-type phase shifter—(a) Topology; (b) operation state when $V_\varphi = 0$ V; (c) operation state when $V_\varphi = 1.2$ V—and inductor-based bridged T-type phase shifter—(d) topology; (e) operation state when $V_\varphi = $ GND; and (f) operation state when $V_\varphi = V_{DD}$. (R_1, R_2, and R_3 denote the on-resistances of M_1, M_2, and M_3, respectively; C_1, C_2, and C_3 denote the off-capacitances of M_1, M_2, and M_3, respectively; R_B is a large value biasing resistor.)

12.6 Vector-Modulation Phase Shifter

Phase shift is also achievable by the summation of two weighted orthogonal vectors as in Fig. 12.12. This is the vector-modulation method and can be realized by two variable-gain amplifiers (VGAs). Mathematically, the output is tenable within 90° phase shifting range. Further, these VGAs can be designed to change its polarity, for instance, by exchanging its positive and negative path in a differential topology, to support a full 360° operation.

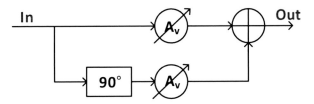

Figure 12.12 Basic operation principle of a vector-modulation phase shifter.

12.7 Loaded-Line Phase Shifter

Figure 12.13 shows the schematic of a basic LLPS. Its operation mechanism is very straightforward. By switching the shunt impedance, the impedance looking from input to output will change, leading to certain degree of phase shift.

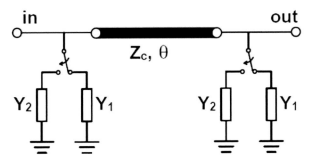

Figure 12.13 Schematic of a loaded-line phase shifter.

Thus, to obtain a large phase shift, multiple of the cells in the figure need to be cascaded in series, similar to STPS. However, different from STPS, each of LLPS cells has the same structure and phase shift. So, LLPS implementation usually leads to a large space occupation.

Table 12.2 Performance comparison of state-of-the-art mm-wave phase shifters

Ref.	Tech.	Freq. (GHz)	IL_MAX (dB)	Total phase shift (°)	RMS gain error (dB)	RMS phase error (°)	Core area (mm²)	P_1dB (dBm)	FoM** (°/dB)	DC power (mW)	Topology†
[29] MWCL 2009	CMOS 90 nm	50–65	8	90	*	*	0.08	4	11.25	0	RTPS
[30] RFIC 2009	BiCMOS 0.13 µm	57–64	8	180	0.2	2.7	0.18	*	22.5	0	RTPS
[10] MWCL 2014	CMOS 65 nm	54–66	6.9	90	*	5.2	0.034	*	13	0	Digital RTPS
[5] JSSC 2007	CMOS 0.18 µm	15–26	4	360	1.1–2.1	6.5–13	0.14	>−0.8	90	7.8	4-bit/VMPS
[6] IMS 2012	CMOS 45 nm	40–67	6	360	0.9–1.2	11–13	0.06	>0	60	23	4-bit/VMPS
[31] ESSCIRC 2008	CMOS 65 nm	60	12	180 diff.	*	*	0.2	*	15	0	3-bit/LLPS
[25] TCAS-II 2014	CMOS 65 nm	75–85	27.1	360	1–1.8	7.2–11.2	0.122	>15	13.3	0	4-bit/STPS
[32] IMS 2012	CMOS 90 nm	57–64	15.6	360	1.3	*	0.28	*	23.1	0	4-bit/STPS
[33] CISC 2009	BiCMOS 0.12 µm	67–78	30	360	1.5–2.8	3.5–12	0.135	>8	12	0	4-bit/STPS
[11] TMTT 2013	CMOS 90 nm	57–64	18	360	1.6–1.8	2–10	0.34	*	20	0	5-bit/STPS
[34] T-VLSI 2015	CMOS 65 nm	57–64	16.3	360	0.5–1.1	4.4–9.5	0.094	9.5–12.5	22.1	0	5-bit/STPS and RTPS

*Not mentioned.
**Total phase shift/maximum insertion loss.
†VMPS, vector-modulation phase shifter; LLPS, loaded-line phase shifter; STPS, switched-type phase shifter; RTPS, reflective-type phase shifter.

12.8 Comparison

Table 12.2 shows the performance comparison of the state-of-the-art phase shifters. RTPS is compact in size but has a limited phase shift range. STPS is commonly used as stages can be desired separately, but its size and level of insertion loss is moderate to high. VMPS has the lowest insertion loss (possibly power gain), but its bandwidth is narrow and phase accuracy is poor. When the system operating frequency goes higher, close to the transistor cut-off frequency, VMPS is more suitable because the signal power is not expendable to any loss. LLPS is an easy solution, but its performance is not good in most of the specifications.

References

1. A. Natarajan, et al., A fully-integrated 16-element phased-array receiver in SiGe BiCMOS for 60-GHz communications, *IEEE J. Solid-State Circ.,* vol. 46, pp. 1059–1075, 2011.

2. F. Meng, K. Ma, K. S. Yeo, S. Xu, C. C. Boon, and W. M. Lim, A 60-GHz 26.3-dB gain 5.3-dB NF low-noise amplifier in 65-nm CMOS using Q-factor enhanced inductors, in *URSI General Assembly and Scientific Symp.,* 2014, pp. 1–4.

3. T. B. Kumar, M. Kaixue, Y. Kiat Seng, and L. Wei Meng, A 12-GHz high output power amplifier using 0.18 μm SiGe BiCMOS for low power applications, *IEEE Asia Pacific Conference on Circuits and Systems (APCCAS),* 2012, pp. 180–183.

4. N. Mahalingam, M. Kaixue, Y. Kiat Seng, and L. Wei Meng, Coupled dual LC tanks based ILFD with low injection power and compact size, *IEEE Microw. Wireless Compon. Lett.,* vol. 24, pp. 105–107, 2014.

5. N. Mahalingam, M. Kaixue, Y. Kiat Seng, and L. Wei Meng, K-band high-PAE wide-tuning-range VCO using triple-coupled *LC* tanks, *IEEE Trans. Circ. Syst. II, Exp. Briefs,* vol. 60, pp. 736–740, 2013.

6. K. Ma, S. Mou, Y. Wang, J. Yan, and K. S. Yeo, A miniaturized 28 mW 60 GHz differential quadrature sub-harmonic QPSK modulator in 0.18 um SiGe BiCMOS, *IEEE MTT-S Int. Microw. Symp. Dig.,* 2014, pp. 344–345.

7. K. Ma, S. Mou, and K. S. Yeo, Miniaturized 60-GHz on-chip multimode quasi-elliptical bandpass filter, *IEEE Electron Device Lett.,* vol. 34, pp. 945–947, 2013.

8. K. Ma, S. Mou, and K. S. Yeo, A miniaturized millimeter-wave standing-wave filtering switch with high P1dB, *IEEE Trans. Microw. Theory Tech.*, vol. 61, pp. 1505–1515, 2013.

9. K. Ma, et al., An integrated 60 GHz low power two-chip wireless system based on IEEE802.11ad standard, *IEEE MTT-S Int. Microw. Symp. Dig.*, 2014, pp. 1–4.

10. F. Meng, K. Ma, K. S. Yeo, S. Xu, C. C. Boon, and W. M. Lim, Miniaturized 3-bit phase shifter for 60 GHz phased-array in 65 nm CMOS technology, *IEEE Microw. Wireless Compon. Lett.*, vol. 24, pp. 50–52, 2014.

11. W. T. Li, Y. C. Chiang, J. H. Tsai, H. Y. Yang, J. H. Cheng, and T. W. Huang, 60-GHz 5-bit phase shifter with integrated VGA phase-error compensation, *IEEE Trans. Microw. Theory Tech.*, vol. 61, pp. 1224–1235, 2013.

12. K. Ma, N. Yan, K. S. Yeo, and W. M. Lim, Miniaturized 40–60 GHz on-chip balun with capacitive loading compensation, *IEEE Electron Device Lett.*, vol. 35, pp. 434–436, 2014.

13. K. Lingkai, Dongjin, S., and Alon, E., A 50 mW-TX 65 mW-RX 60 GHz 4-element phased-array transceiver with integrated antennas in 65 nm CMOS, *IEEE Int. Solid-State Circuits Conf. (ISSCC) Dig.*, 2013, pp. 234–235.

14. V. Vidojkovic, et al., A low-power radio chipset in 40 nm LP CMOS with beamforming for 60 GHz high-data-rate wireless communication, *IEEE Int. Solid-State Circuits Conf. (ISSCC) Dig.*, 2013, pp. 236–237.

15. J.-L. Kuo, et al., 60-GHz four-element phased-array transmit/ receive system-in-package using phase compensation techniques in 65-nm flip-chip CMOS process, *IEEE Trans. Microw. Theory Tech.*, vol. 60, pp. 743–756, 2012.

16. M. Boers, et al., A 16TX/16RX 60 GHz 802.11ad chipset with single coaxial interface and polarization diversity, *IEEE Int. Solid-State Circuits Conf. (ISSCC) Dig.*, 2014, pp. 344–345.

17. W. Shin, B. H. Ku, O. Inac, Y. C. Ou, and G. M. Rebeiz, A 108–114 GHz 4×4 wafer-scale phased array transmitter with high-efficiency on-chip antennas, *IEEE J. Solid-State Circ.*, vol. PP, pp. 1–15, 2013.

18. F. Golcuk, Kanar, T., and Rebeiz, G. M., A 90-100-GHz 4 × 4 SiGe BiCMOS polarimetric transmit/receive phased array with simultaneous receive-beams capabilities, *IEEE Trans. Microw. Theory Tech.*, vol. 61, pp. 3099–3114, 2013.

19. S. Donghyup, K. Choul-Young, K. Dong-Woo, and G. M. Rebeiz, A high-power packaged four-element X-band phased-array transmitter in 0.13-μm CMOS for radar and communication systems, *IEEE Trans. Microw. Theory Tech.,* vol. 61, pp. 3060–3071, 2013.

20. M. Elkhouly, S. Glisic, C. Meliani, F. Ellinger, and J. C. Scheytt, 220–250-GHz phased-array circuits in 0.13-μm SiGe BiCMOS technology, *IEEE Trans. Microw. Theory Tech.,* vol. 61, pp. 3115–3127, 2013.

21. S. Shahramian, Y. Baeyens, N. Kaneda, and Y. K. Chen, A 70–100 GHz direct-conversion transmitter and receiver phased array chipset demonstrating 10 Gb/s wireless link, *IEEE J. Solid-State Circ.,* vol. 48, pp. 1113–1125, 2013.

22. A. Natarajan, B. Floyd, and A. Hajimiri, A bidirectional RF-combining 60 GHz phased-array front-end, *IEEE Int. Solid-State Circuits Conf. (ISSCC) Dig.,* 2007, pp. 202–597.

23. E. Cohen, C. Jakobson, S. Ravid, and D. Ritter, A thirty two element phased-array transceiver at 60 GHz with RF-IF conversion block in 90 nm flip chip CMOS process, *IEEE Radio Frequency Integrated Circuits Symp. (RFIC) Dig.,* 2010, pp. 457–460.

24. W. L. Chan, J. R. Long, M. Spirito, and J. J. Pekarik, A 60 GHz-band 2 × 2 phased-array transmitter in 65 nm CMOS, *IEEE Int. Solid-State Circuits Conf. (ISSCC) Dig.,* 2010, pp. 42–43.

25. H. Lee and B. Min, W-band CMOS 4-Bit phase shifter for high power and phase compression points, *IEEE Trans. Circuits Syst. II, Exp. Briefs,* vol. PP, pp. 1–1, 2014.

26. F. Meng, K. Ma, and K. S. Yeo, A 130-to-180 GHz 0.0035 mm^2 SPDT switch with 3.3 dB loss and 23.7 dB isolation in 65 nm bulk CMOS, *IEEE Int. Solid-State Circuits Conf. (ISSCC) Dig.,* 2015, pp. 34–36.

27. K.-J. Koh and G. M. Rebeiz, 0.13-μm CMOS phase shifters for X-, Ku-, and K-band phased arrays, *IEEE J. Solid-State Circ.,* vol. 42, pp. 2535–2546, 2007.

28. D.-W. Kang, H.-D. Lee, C.-H. Kim, and S. Hong, Ku-band MMIC phase shifter using a parallel resonator with 0.18-μm CMOS technology, *IEEE Trans. Microw. Theory Tech.,* vol. 54, pp. 294–301, 2006.

29. B. Biglarbegian, M. R. Nezhad-Ahmadi, M. Fakharzadeh, and S. Safavi-Naeini, Millimeter-wave reflective-type phase shifter in CMOS technology, *IEEE Microw. Wireless Compon. Lett.,* vol. 19, pp. 560–562, 2009.

30. M.-D. Tsai and A. Natarajan, 60 GHz passive and active RF-path phase shifters in silicon, *IEEE RFIC Symp. Dig.,* 2009, pp. 223–226.

31. Y. Yu, et al., A 60 GHz digitally controlled phase shifter in CMOS, in *European Solid-State Circuits Conf. (ESSCIRC) Dig.*, 2008, pp. 250–253.

32. Y.-C. Chiang, W.-T. Li, J.-H. Tsai, and T.-W. Huang, A 60 GHz digitally controlled 4-bit phase shifter with 6-ps group delay deviation, *IEEE MTT-S Int. Microw. Symp. Dig.*, 2012, pp. 1–3.

33. S. Y. Kim and G. M. Rebeiz, A 4-Bit Passive phase shifter for automotive radar applications in 0.13 μm CMOS, *IEEE Compound Semiconductor Integrated Circuit Symp. (CSIC) Dig.*, 2009, pp. 1–4.

34. F. Meng, K. Ma, K. S. Yeo, and S. Xu, A 57-to-64-GHz 0.094-mm^2 5-bit passive phase shifter in 65-nm CMOS, *IEEE Trans. Very Large Scale Integr. Syst.*, vol. 24, pp. 1917–1925, May 2015.

*Invest in CREDIT (**C**reativity, **R**esearch, **E**nterprise, **D**esign, **I**nnovation and **T**echnology) to prevent DEBIT (**D**ebt, **E**rror, **B**urden, **I**nterest and **T**ax).*

—Kiat Seng Yeo and Kaixue Ma

Chapter 13

Frequency Synthesizer

Nagarajan Mahalingam,[a] Kaixue Ma,[b] and Kiat Seng Yeo[a]

[a]*Engineering Product Development, Singapore University of Technology and Design,
8 Somapah Road, Singapore 487372*
[b]*School of Physical Electronics,
University of Electronic Science and Technology of China,
#4 Section II, Jianshe North Road, Chengdu 610054, P. R. China*

mahalingam@sutd.edu.sg, makaixue@uestc.edu.cn, kiatseng_yeo@sutd.edu.sg

The frequency synthesizer is one of the most important and indispensible blocks in any radio frequency (RF) communication system as shown in Fig. 13.1. The basic function of the frequency synthesizer is to generate a stable, clean, and programmable local oscillator (LO) signal for frequency translation in the transmit and receive path of a RF transceiver. The aim of this chapter is to provide a brief introduction to the design of high-performance frequency synthesizers with system architecture techniques and building block architectures.

Low-Power Wireless Communication Circuits and Systems: 60 GHz and Beyond
Edited by Kaixue Ma and Kiat Seng Yeo
Copyright © 2018 Pan Stanford Publishing Pte. Ltd.
ISBN 978-981-4745-96-3 (Hardcover), 978-1-315-15653-8 (eBook)
www.panstanford.com

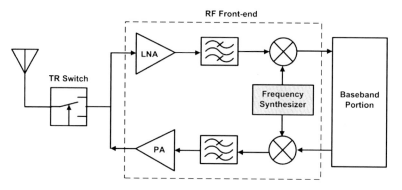

Figure 13.1 Block diagram of typical RF wireless transceiver.

13.1 Introduction to Concept of Frequency Synthesis

The frequency synthesizer is typically an electronic device that can generate multiple frequencies from a single reference frequency. The choice of the frequency synthesizer architecture is exhaustive and is dependent on the application requirement. The frequency synthesizer can be either analog or digital and is broadly classified as direct and indirect synthesizers based on the circuit architecture for frequency generation. In the direct frequency synthesizers, the output is synthesized by continuous mixing, multiplication, and division of the single reference signal [1]. However, achieving the spectral purity is an issue due to the existence of the spurious components and the synthesizer can be power hungry and bulky due to the large number of components. In comparison, the indirect frequency synthesis using phase-locked loops (PLL) is more popular frequency synthesizer architecture. In the PLL-based frequency synthesizer, the output frequency is generated by phase locking the voltage-controlled oscillator (VCO) phase to the reference phase. Therefore, PLL-based indirect frequency synthesizers are the most preferred architecture for high-frequency applications with low power consumption. In addition, all the components in the frequency synthesizer can be integrated in any low-cost IC processes and are highly area efficient. In the remainder of this chapter, we will focus in-depth on the implementation of PLL-based frequency synthesis.

13.2 Phase-Locked Loop Frequency Synthesizer

The block diagram of PLL-based indirect frequency synthesizer in RF communication system is shown in Fig. 13.2. The main components in the synthesizer are the VCO, feedback divider, phase frequency detector (PFD), charge pump, and loop filter. The frequency synthesizer is a feedback system and the PLL operation starts with the comparison of the VCO and reference phase in the PFD. The PFD outputs a voltage pulse which is equivalent to the phase difference between the VCO and reference signal. These voltage pulses are converted to current pulses by charge pump. The loop filter cleans and converts the current pulses to a constant DC voltage to be applied to the VCO. Based on the applied voltage, the VCO phase is adjusted until it is the same as the reference phase. The frequency synthesizer is in locked state when the VCO and reference phase are equal.

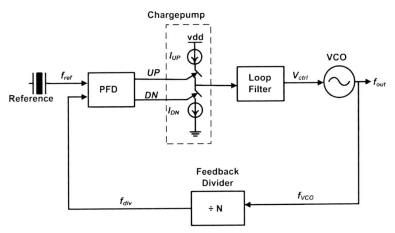

Figure 13.2 Block diagram of PLL based frequency synthesizer.

13.2.1 Performance Parameters

The performance parameters of the frequency synthesizer are mainly dependent on the performance of the individual sub-blocks.

Some of the important synthesizer performance parameters are presented in this section.

13.2.1.1 Frequency tuning range

The basic performance parameter of the frequency synthesizer is the frequency tuning range it can cover which is specified in units of Hz. The frequency tuning range is determined by the frequency range of the VCO and the sensitivity of the divider block in the PLL chain.

13.2.1.2 Phase noise

Phase noise (also spectral purity) is an important specification for the frequency synthesizer to be employed in communication system. Ideally, the output of the frequency synthesizer is a single frequency tone. However, due to the non-idealities in the frequency synthesizer building blocks, the output spectrum is degraded. Phase noise is the measure of spectral purity of the synthesizer output typically defined as the ratio between the total carrier power and the noise power in 1 Hz bandwidth at a frequency offset from the carrier as shown in Fig. 13.3a. In the frequency synthesizer, the overall phase noise is determined by the phase noise of the reference and phase noise of the VCO. Typically, inside the loop bandwidth, the synthesizer phase noise is determined by reference phase noise and outside the loop bandwidth, the synthesizer follows the VCO phase noise as shown in Fig. 13.3b.

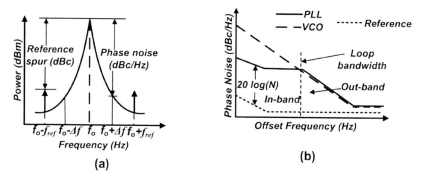

Figure 13.3 Frequency Synthesizer (a) phase noise spectrum, and (b) Typical synthesizer phase noise characteristics.

The importance of phase noise on the transceiver performance is illustrated in Fig. 13.4. In the receiver, the desired signal is down-converted by the mixer. In the presence of large interferer, if the LO signal with large phase noise is used in the mixer, both the desired and the interfering signal fall in the same frequency band. Since the interfering signal is typically larger than the desired signal, the desired signal is masked by the interferer and the signal to noise ratio (SNR) of the receiver is degraded. This phenomenon is known as reciprocal mixing as illustrated is Fig. 13.4a. In the transmit portion, the noise–skirt due to the phase noise in the transmitted signal can fall within the bandwidth of the pass-band filter along with the desired signal. This is represented in Fig. 13.4b.

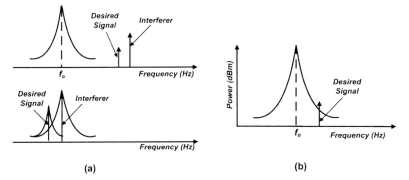

Figure 13.4 Effect of phase noise on frequency synthesizer performance (a) receiver, and (b) transmitter.

13.2.1.3   Spurious signals

The spurious signals or spurs are unwanted signals that are generated within or outside the frequency synthesizers. Unlike phase noise, spurs are generally considered as interferers and have different amplitudes at different frequency offsets. The most common type of spur in the synthesizer is the reference spur due to the switching noise and mismatch between the up and down currents in the charge pump circuit. In the locked condition, ideally the output from the charge pump is zero and a constant voltage is maintained at the VCO control line. However, due to the relatively high rise and fall times in the voltage pulses from the PFD, small amount of charge is leaked into the synthesizer loop by the parasitic resistance and capacitance in the charge pump current switches. This leakage in turn modulates the VCO control voltage and up-converts to the carrier frequency in the lower and upper side-bands at the intervals of reference frequency.

Similar to phase noise, the effect of spurs can be explained as in Fig. 13.5. If the desired signal in the presence of large interference is down-converted with LO signal that has spurs, the interfering signal can end up at the same intermediate frequency (IF) as the desired signal degrading the signal-to-noise ratio of the desired signal. Though spurs cannot be totally eliminated in the synthesizer, it can be reduced with careful design of the charge pump and by choosing a small bandwidth in the frequency synthesizer loop filter.

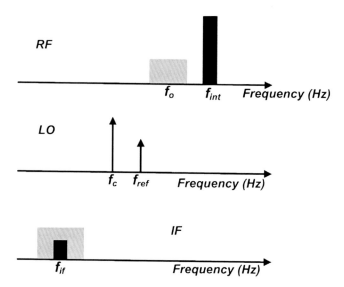

Figure 13.5 Effect of spurs on frequency synthesizer performance.

13.2.1.4 Frequency resolution and settling time

Frequency resolution is the smallest step size the synthesizer can achieve and has a direct influence on the architectural selection of the synthesizer. In the integer-N synthesizer, the frequency resolution is same as the channel spacing and reference frequency. Therefore, the performance of integer-N synthesizer is greatly influenced by the required frequency resolution. However, in comparison, fractional-*N* synthesizer can achieve a small frequency resolution with higher reference frequency.

Settling time in the frequency synthesizer is the time it takes for the synthesizer loop to settle within a specified frequency tolerance after a change in frequency control word. In the transmitting and receiving modes, the settling time is determined by the system specification of the particular communication standard. In most cases, the worst case settling time is used as PLL settling time as only one synthesizer is used in the transceiver for frequency translation to save power and area. Since frequency synthesizer is a feedback system with the loop filter limiting its bandwidth, the synthesizer settling time is directly related to the bandwidth of the PLL loop. The wider the loop bandwidth, the settling time of the synthesizer is reduced.

13.2.1.5 Loop bandwidth

The loop bandwidth is one of the key design parameters in the frequency synthesizer. The choice of loop bandwidth is typically a trade-off between reference frequency, settling time and phase noise. In general, the loop bandwidth is less than 1/10 of the reference frequency for loop stability considerations [2]. As discussed earlier, the phase noise of the PLL is dominated by the reference or VCO based on the PLL loop bandwidth. The condition for optimum PLL bandwidth which produces equal phase noise from the reference and the VCO is given by [3]

$$B_{pll} = \sqrt{\frac{a_{vco}\left[L(\Delta f)_{add} - 1\right]}{L(\Delta f)_{ref}(n_{mf}2\zeta f_n)}} \cdot \sqrt{1 + 2\zeta^2 + \sqrt{(1 + 2\zeta^2)^2 + 1}}, \quad (13.1)$$

where B_{pll} is the loop bandwidth of PLL, ζ is the PLL damping factor, $L(\Delta f)_{ref}$ is the reference phase noise, a_{vco} is the VCO slope constant calculated from VCO phase noise, f_n is the PLL natural frequency, $L(\Delta f)_{add}$ is the additive phase noise equal to 3 dB and n_{mf} is the division ratio of PLL.

13.2.1.6 Power consumption and output power

With power management becoming essential in recent trends, the overall power consumption is an important specification especially for the frequency synthesizer used in the wireless transceiver for mobile applications. In the mobile applications, reduction in synthesizer power consumption can increase the battery life due to overall reduction in power consumption of the transceiver. In the frequency synthesizer, a large part of power dissipation occurs in the high-frequency blocks (VCO, fixed prescaler, and divider chain). Therefore, reducing the power consumption of high-frequency blocks is essential to reduce the overall power consumption of the synthesizer.

Often a fringe but an important specification of the synthesizer is its output power. The synthesizer output power is related to the drive strength and power consumption of the transceiver. In the transceiver, the synthesizer output typically drives the up and down conversion mixers in the transmitter and receiver path, respectively. Therefore, the synthesizer must deliver high output power to eliminate or reduce the power consumption in the inter-stage LO drive amplifiers between the synthesizer and mixer stages in the transceiver. In the frequency synthesizer, since the output is typically extracted from the VCO or fixed prescaler stage, the power efficiency of the blocks needs to be maximized.

13.2.2 Phase-Lock Loop Modeling

The PLL-based frequency synthesizer is a highly nonlinear feedback system and it is difficult to accurately model the PLL behavior [2]. However, once the PLL loop has settled, the input and the output are constant and the frequency synthesizer can be analyzed based on the linear model [4]. The linear analysis of the PLL-based frequency synthesizer is presented in this section.

13.2.2.1 Linearized PLL analysis

The linear model of the frequency synthesizer is shown in Fig. 13.6. The operation principle of the PLL is based on the phase change within the feedback loop. When the PLL system is in locked state, there is no phase change in the VCO output and the PLL remains in steady state. The output frequency of the VCO for a change in DC control voltage is given by

$$\omega_{out} = 2\pi f_{out} = \omega_{free} + K_{VCO} \cdot V_{control}, \qquad (13.2)$$

where ω_{free} is the initial free running frequency of the VCO in rad/s units and K_{VCO} is gain of the VCO in rad·Hz/V. Since phase is the integral of frequency, the VCO output phase is

$$\varphi_{out} = \int 2\pi f_{out} \cdot dt = \int K_{VCO} \cdot V_{control} \, dt. \qquad (13.3)$$

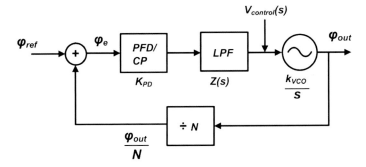

Figure 13.6 Linear model of PLL-based frequency synthesizer.

Therefore, in the linear model we represent the VCO as an integrator. The frequency divider in the synthesizer divides the VCO output down to the reference frequency. Therefore, the phase of the divider signal can be represented as

$$\varphi_{div} = \frac{\varphi_{out}}{N}. \qquad (13.4)$$

The phase of the reference is compared with the VCO output divided down phase by the PFD and converted to current pulses using the charge pump. Therefore, the PFD and charge pump are combined in the linear model and the gain of the PFD is represented as K_{PD} given by

$$K_{PD} = \frac{I_{CP}}{2\pi}. \qquad (13.5)$$

The loop filter in the synthesizer performs the current to voltage conversion of the charge pump current output to VCO tuning voltage and removes the unwanted high-frequency components from modulating the VCO tuning voltage. The transfer function of the loop filter is given by $Z(s)$.

The open-loop transfer function of the PLL loop in Fig. 13.6 can be written as

$$G(s) \cdot H(s) = \frac{K_{PD} \cdot Z(s) \cdot K_{VCO}}{s} \cdot \frac{1}{N} \qquad (13.6)$$

The magnitude and phase of the open-loop transfer function is an important parameter in the synthesizer design typically determined by the loop filter. The frequency at which the magnitude of open-loop transfer function drops to unity (i.e.) $|G(s) \cdot H(s)| = 1$ is defined as the PLL loop bandwidth. The arg $\{G(s) \cdot H(s)\}$ when the open-loop gain crosses unity is defined as the phase margin.

The most common passive loop filter configuration employed in the synthesizer are the second and third-order loop filter as shown in Fig. 13.7 The transfer function of the second-order loop filter in Fig. 13.7a is given by

$$Z_{Lf2}(s) = \left(R_2 + \frac{1}{sC_2} \right) \left\| \frac{1}{sC_1} \right. \qquad (13.7)$$

$$= \frac{1 + sR_2C_2}{s^2 R_2 C_1 C_2 + s(C_1 + C_2)}. \qquad (13.8)$$

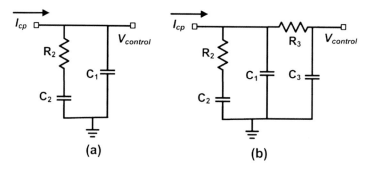

(a)   (b)

Figure 13.7 Loop filter configuration (a) second order, and (b) third order.

Rearranging Eq. (3.8), Z_{Lf2} can be given as

$$Z_{Lf2}(s) = \frac{1 + sR_2C_2}{s(C_1 + C_2)\left(1 + sR_2\dfrac{C_1C_2}{C_1 + C_2}\right)}. \qquad (13.9)$$

The zero and pole frequency of the second-order loop filter are

$$\omega_z = \frac{1}{R_2C_2} \qquad (13.10)$$

$$\omega_{p2} = \frac{C_1 + C_2}{R_2C_1C_2}.$$

For the third-order loop filter in Fig. 13.7b, the transfer function is given by

$$Z_{Lf3}(s) = \left(R_2 + \frac{1}{sC_2}\right) \left\|\frac{1}{sC_1} + \left(R_3 + \frac{1}{sC_3}\right)\right. \qquad (13.11)$$

$$= \frac{1 + sR_2C_2}{s^3 R_2R_3C_1C_2C_3 + s^2(R_2C_2(C_1 + C_3) + R_3C_3(C_1 + C_2)) + s(C_1 + C_2 + C_3)}. \qquad (13.12)$$

Rearranging Eq. (13.12), Z_{Lf3} can be given as

$$Z_{Lf3}(s) = \frac{1 + sR_2C_2}{s(C_1 + C_2 + C_3)\left(1 + s\dfrac{R_2C_2(C_1 + C_3) + R_3C_3(C_1 + C_2)}{C_1 + C_2 + C_3} + s^2\dfrac{R_2R_3C_1C_2C_3}{C_1 + C_2 + C_3}\right)}. \qquad (13.13)$$

Simplifying Eq. (13.13) assuming $C_2 \gg C_1, C_3$ and $R_2 > R_3$, the poles and zeros of the third-order loop filter is given by

$$\omega_z = \frac{1}{R_2C_2}$$

$$\omega_{p2} \approx \frac{1}{R_2(C_1 + C_3)}$$

$$\omega_{p3} \approx \frac{(C_1 + C_3)}{R_3C_2C_3}. \qquad (13.14)$$

The phase margin of the third-order loop filter is given by

$$\varphi_m = \varphi_z - \varphi_{\omega p2} = \varphi_{\omega p3} = \tan^{-1}\left(\frac{\omega_c}{\omega_z}\right) - \tan^{-1}\left(\frac{\omega_c}{\omega_{p2}}\right) - \tan^{-1}\left(\frac{\omega_c}{\omega_{p3}}\right) \quad (13.15)$$

where ω_c is the PLL open-loop bandwidth given by

$$\omega_c \approx \frac{K_{PD}K_{VCO}R_2}{N} \cdot \frac{C_2}{C_1 + C_2 + C_3}. \quad (13.16)$$

Typically, in the third-order loop filter the phase margin is determined by the location of the zero as it provides the positive phase. Also, the high-frequency poles due to R_3 and C_3 are added for extra attenuation of the reference spur and have little impact on the phase margin as its frequency is far away from the zero frequency. Therefore, the maximum phase margin is a function of the capacitor ratios given by $m = C_2/(C_1 + C_3)$ and occurs around the value of ω_c given by

$$\omega_{c,\varphi m} \approx \sqrt{\omega_z \omega_{p2}}. \quad (13.17)$$

The closed loop transfer function of the PLL synthesizer with a third-order loop filter is given by

$$H_{cl,4}(s) = \frac{N \cdot \left(1 + \dfrac{s}{\omega_z}\right)}{1 + s \cdot \dfrac{1}{\omega_z} + \dfrac{N}{K}(s^2 A_0 + s^3 A_1 + s^4 A_2)}, \quad (13.18)$$

where $K = K_{PD} \cdot K_{VCO}$, $A_0 = C_1 + C_2 + C_3$, $A_1 = R_2 C_2(C_1 + C_3) + R_3 C_3(C_1 + C_2)$, and $A_2 = R_2 R_3 C_1 C_2 C_3$.

13.2.2.2 PLL noise analysis

The linearized noise model of the synthesizer is shown in Fig. 13.8. The noise sources represent the overall noise in the corresponding building block in the synthesizer due to internal or external noise sources. The noise from reference, VCO and divider are represented by $\phi_{r,n}$, $\phi_{v,n}$, and $\phi_{fb,n}$, respectively. The overall feedback divider noise is denoted as $\phi_{fb,n}$. The current and voltage noise due to the charge pump and loop filter is represented as $I_{cp,n}$ and $V_{LF,n}$, respectively.

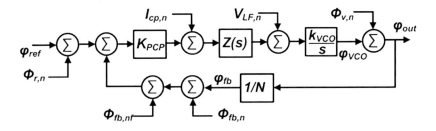

Figure 13.8 Linear noise model of frequency synthesizer.

The open-loop transfer function of the model in Fig. 13.8 is given by

$$G(s) = \frac{K_{PD} \cdot \dfrac{K_{VCO}}{s} \cdot Z(s)}{N}. \tag{13.19}$$

The noise transfer function of the various noise sources to the synthesizer output is given by

$$H_{ref}(s) = \frac{\varphi_{out(s)}}{\varphi_{r,n(s)}} = N \cdot \frac{G(s)}{1 + G(s)} = \frac{K_{PD} \cdot \dfrac{K_{VCO}}{s} \cdot Z(s)}{1 + \dfrac{K_{PD} \cdot K_{VCO} \cdot Z(s)}{sN}} \tag{13.20}$$

$$H_{PFD}(s) = \frac{\varphi_{out}(s)}{I_{cp,n}(s)} = \frac{N}{K_{PD}} \cdot \frac{G(s)}{1 + G(s)} = \frac{\dfrac{K_{VCO}}{s} \cdot Z(s)}{1 + \dfrac{K_{PD} \cdot K_{VCO} \cdot Z(s)}{sN}} \tag{13.21}$$

$$H_{LF}(s) = \frac{\varphi_{out}(s)}{V_{LF}(s)} = \frac{K_{VCO}}{s} \cdot \frac{1}{1 + G(s)} = \frac{\dfrac{K_{VCO}}{s}}{1 + \dfrac{K_{PD} \cdot K_{VCO} \cdot Z(s)}{sN}} \tag{13.22}$$

$$H_{VCO}(s) = \frac{\varphi_{out}(s)}{\varphi_{v,n}(s)} = \frac{1}{1 + G(s)} = \frac{1}{1 + \dfrac{K_{PD} \cdot K_{VCO} \cdot Z(s)}{sN}} \tag{13.23}$$

$$H_{fbd}(s) = \frac{\varphi_{out}(s)}{\varphi_{fbd}(s)} = -N.\frac{G(s)}{1+G(s)} = -\frac{K_{PD} \cdot \frac{K_{VCO}}{s} \cdot Z(s)}{1 + \frac{K_{PD} \cdot K_{VCO} \cdot Z(s)}{sN}}. \qquad (13.24)$$

Since the loop filter in the synthesizer has a low-pass filter characteristics, the noise sources from the reference, feedback divider and PFD/charge pump has a low-pass filter characteristics with a gain of N. The VCO and loop filter noise transfer function to the output noise exhibits a high pass and band pass characteristics, respectively. Therefore, the in-band phase noise of the synthesizer is dominated by the reference, PFD/charge pump and the divider. Since the gain of the in-band noise is multiplied by N, the in-band phase noise can be improved by increasing the reference frequency as large as possible to reduce N. At higher offset frequencies, the major noise source is the noise from the VCO. Therefore, the VCO gain K_{VCO} needs to be small to reduce the noise disturbance from the VCO control line.

13.2.3 Phase-Lock Loop Frequency Synthesizer Architectures

The classification of the frequency synthesizer architecture is based on the division ratio of the feedback divider. The popular frequency synthesizer architectures are the integer-N and fractional-N synthesizer as described briefly in this section.

13.2.3.1 Integer-N frequency synthesizer

The division ratio of the feedback divider in the integer-N frequency synthesizer is an integer and the relation between the output and input frequency is given by

$$f_{out} = N_p \times P \times f_{REF}. \qquad (13.25)$$

Therefore, the reference frequency for the integer–N synthesizer architecture is same as the frequency resolution. The channel selection in the integer-N synthesizer is realized using the programmable frequency divider typically implemented in pulse-swallow divider [5] architecture as shown in Fig. 13.9.

The overall division ratio of the integer-N synthesizer with a pulse swallow divider is

$$N_p = (N+1)S + (P-S)N = PN + S,$$ (13.26)

where N is the prescaler divider ratio and P and S are the values of the P and S counter in the frequency divider.

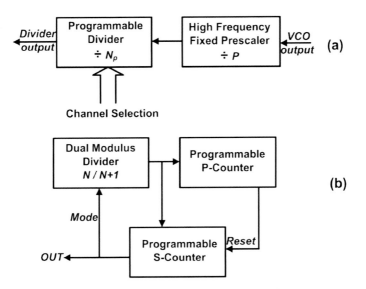

Figure 13.9 Frequency synthesizer divider chain (a) Integer-N divider, and (b) programmable frequency divider.

Due to its simple architecture and ease of implementation, the integer-N synthesizer is more popular frequency synthesizer architecture. However, the major limitation is the frequency resolution and settling time. When a small frequency resolution is required in the frequency synthesizer, the reference frequency is small and the division ratio of the feedback divider is large. Moreover, due to the small reference frequency, the loop bandwidth of the frequency synthesizer is small and the synthesizer takes a long time to settle. Third, the degradation of the phase noise of the synthesizer is increased due to the large division ratio. The amount of phase noise degradation within the loop bandwidth is equivalent to 20 log (N), where N is the overall division ratio.

13.2.3.2 Fractional-*N* frequency synthesizer

As mentioned previously, the main limitation in the integer-*N* synthesizer is requirement of large division ratio when a small frequency resolution is required. Therefore, fractional-*N* synthesizer is adopted to decouple the frequency resolution and division ratio. In the fractional-*N* synthesizer, the overall division ratio is a fraction and the reference frequency can be much higher independent of the frequency resolution. The block diagram of the divider in the fractional-*N* synthesizer is shown in Fig. 13.10. In the fractional-*N* synthesizer, the same prescaler as in integer-*N* can be used but it is controlled differently. The division ratio of *N/N* + 1 is changed constantly by the carry of the accumulator.

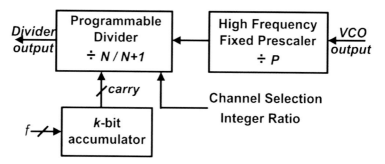

Figure 13.10 Fractional–*N* frequency divider.

Therefore, the relation between the input and output frequency in the fraction-*N* synthesizer is given by

$$f_{OUT} = \left[(N \times P) + \frac{f}{2^k} \right] \times f_{REF},$$

(13.27)

where *f* is the fractional control word and *k* is the length of the accumulator.

The major advantage of the fractional-*N* synthesizer is its ability to increase the reference frequency and have a reduced feedback divider ratio. However, one of the disadvantages of the fractional-*N* synthesizer is the increase in circuit complexity due to the increased accumulator bits. More importantly, the major limitation in the fractional-*N* synthesizer is the presence of fractional spurs in the synthesizer output due to the periodic changing of the division ratio by the carry bits of the accumulator.

13.3 Frequency Synthesizer Building Blocks

The frequency synthesizer by itself can be thought of as a black box with many individual building blocks connected in feedback configuration. The individual design blocks in the frequency synthesizer have a set of design specification which directly affects the performance of the frequency synthesizer. In this section, the discussion on the individual building blocks is presented.

13.3.1 Voltage-Controlled Oscillator

The VCO is one of the critical building blocks in the frequency synthesizer operating at the highest operational frequency. The most important VCO design parameters namely the frequency tuning range and phase noise directly determine the frequency synthesizer tuning range and phase noise performance. The most dominant types of VCO are ring and LC-based oscillators with each having their own advantages and disadvantages. In this section, the two types of VCO are described.

13.3.1.1 Ring oscillator

The ring oscillator is the simplest of oscillators formed by connecting chain of gain stages in the positive feedback configuration. A simple inverter can function as a ring oscillator as shown in Fig. 13.11. The main advantage of the ring oscillator is its small size due to the absence of any passive devices and it is easier to implement in standard CMOS technology. In addition, the ring oscillators can achieve a very large frequency tuning range. One of the major drawbacks in the ring oscillator is the poor phase noise in comparison to the LC-based oscillators. Also, the maximum frequency of oscillation of the ring oscillator is limited as it is inversely proportional on the RC delay in the feedback chain. Therefore, the ring oscillator is not quite often used in high-frequency high-performance applications and is limited to frequency applications less than few tens of GHz. Hence, the following discussions in this section will be based on the LC oscillators as they are typically used in high-frequency wireless communication systems.

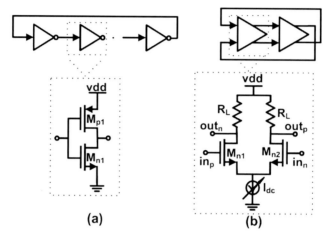

(a) **(b)**

Figure 13.11 Ring oscillator: (a) Single-ended and (b) differential.

13.3.1.2   LC oscillator

The LC oscillators are class of oscillators which have frequency selective elements, typically an inductor (L) and capacitor (C) in the tank circuit. Due to the frequency selective characteristics, the LC oscillators can achieve a very high operating frequency with low power consumption and better phase noise in comparison to their ring oscillator counterparts. However, the disadvantage of LC oscillator is large chip area due to the use of on-chip inductors in the LC tank. The more detailed circuit implementation of the LC oscillator was presented in Chapter 10. A brief description is presented here for completeness.

13.3.1.3   Phase noise in oscillators

The phase noise is one of the important design parameters in the VCO as it directly affects the spectral purity of the frequency synthesizer. More works have been reported in literature to reduce the phase noise in the oscillator [6–11]. The relation between the phase noise generators and LC oscillator design parameters is given by [7]

$$L(\Delta\omega) = 10\log\left[KTR_{\text{eff}}(1+F)\left(\frac{\omega_o}{\Delta\omega}\right)^2\frac{1}{V_{\text{rms}}^2}\right],\qquad(13.28)$$

where K is Boltzmann's constant, T is the absolute temperature, F is the excess noise factor, R_{eff} is the LC tank effective resistance, ω_o is the oscillation frequency, $\Delta\omega$ is the offset frequency and V_{rms} is the rms differential amplitude. Therefore, from Eq. (13.28), the phase noise of the LC oscillator can be improved by high quality factor in the tank circuit and increased output power from the VCO. However, the increase in output power to lower the phase noise is not trivial. For example, in the cross-coupled VCO as shown in Fig. 13.12a, the VCO is in current-limited mode until the output voltage is controlled by the bias current. As the bias current is increased, the cross-coupled transistors enter the triode region and the VCO enters the voltage-limited mode. Under this condition, one of the cross-coupled (–gm) transistors is cut-off. In this case, the –gm transistor acts as a switch and the transistor noise is up-converted to increase the phase noise. Therefore, in summary, following are the requirements to reduce the phase noise in the LC oscillators:

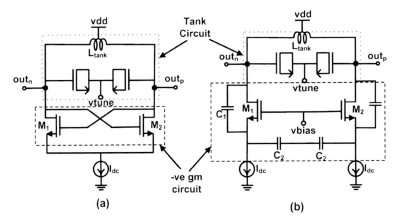

Figure 13.12 LC VCO (a) cross-coupled, and (b) Colpitts.

- high quality factor of the tank circuit
- increasing the output power of the oscillator and operating in the current limited mode
- reducing the noise from the active devices by choosing a proper bias point to achieve a low NF_{min};
- choosing a device with low flicker noise available in the process technology.

13.3.1.4   Circuit implementation of LC oscillators

The starting point for the design of high-performance LC VCO is the choice of resonator components. Ideally, the losses in the resonator should be small. However, in the current IC process technologies, the use of on-chip inductor introduces lot of resistive losses which dominate the losses in the resonator [7]. Therefore, for a high quality factor in the VCO resonator, the losses in the inductor need to be minimized. Moreover, for the VCO to start up, the losses in the resonator need to be compensated with an active device. This can be realized by connecting the active device either as a cross-coupled pair as shown in Fig. 13.12a or as in Colpitts structure as shown in Fig. 13.12b. The Cross-coupled and Colpitts VCO are most suitable for IC implementation of the VCO due to its simple structure and ease in implementation. Third, to sustain oscillations, the amount of negative resistance chosen to compensate the tank losses is chosen to be greater than 2.5 times the losses in the resonator. Based on the required transconductance in the active devices, the power consumption required for the VCO can be estimated. Typically, in the VCO, the power consumption can be reduced by maximizing the inductor to capacitance ratio.

13.3.2   High-Frequency Divider

In the frequency synthesizer, the frequency divider follows the VCO and is an important block in the synthesizer chain. Since the frequency dividers are used to divide the high-frequency VCO output down to reference frequency for comparison in the PFD, typically a chain of dividers operating at high to low frequencies are used in the frequency synthesizer. In this section, a brief description on the frequency divider is presented.

13.3.2.1 Static frequency divider

The source-coupled logic frequency divider topology as shown in Fig. 13.13 is the simplest and the most commonly adopted static frequency divider topology. This frequency divider is based on ring oscillator topology [12, 13] and formed by cascading two D-latches in positive feedback configuration by cross-coupling the output of the second stage to the input of the first stage realizing a divide-by-2 operation. One of the advantages of the static frequency divider is a wide locking range for low injected power levels. The major disadvantage is the limitation in the maximum frequency of operation dependent on the load capacitance and resistance given as

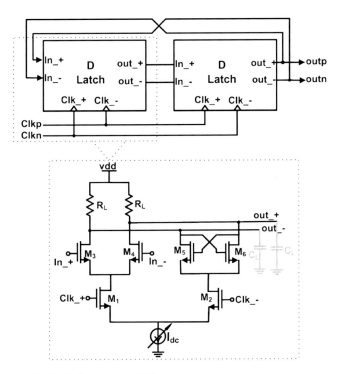

Figure 13.13 Static frequency divider.

$$f_{max} \le \frac{1}{2\pi R_L C_L}. \tag{13.29}$$

Therefore, to increase the frequency of operation with low power consumption, the size of the latch transistors M5 and M6 need to be carefully designed. If the size is too small, the gain condition $g_{mL} \cdot R_L > 1$ is not satisfied and the divider fails.

13.3.2.2 Injection locked frequency divider

The ILFD is the most attractive frequency divider for high-frequency operation. The ILFD is same as a LC VCO but with an injection transistor and the ILFD conceptual diagram is shown in Fig. 13.14. The ILFD works by injection locking the input signal to the free running VCO. With no signal injection, the ILFD is a free running oscillator. However, when the signal is injected, the free running oscillator frequency is shifted to the new frequency based on the frequency and amplitude of the injection signal. The range of frequencies the injection signals can be locked to the tank frequency is called the locking range. One of the main advantages of the ILFD is its ability to achieve a high-frequency operation with lower power consumption in comparison to static frequency dividers. Therefore, ILFD are more suitable for use at millimeter or microwave frequencies. However, one of the major downsides of the ILFD is its narrow locking range. The locking range of the ILFD is given as [14]

$$\frac{\Delta\omega}{\omega_o} = \frac{I_{inj}}{2Q \cdot I_{osc}}. \tag{13.30}$$

From Eq. (3.30), it is clear that wider locking range can be obtained with increased injected power levels. However, in millimeter wave frequencies, the injection power can be lower due to interconnect and buffer losses between the VCO and the divider. Therefore, increasing the locking range with lower injection power level is an important design specification in the ILFD. Also, the output power from the ILFD needs to be as high as possible to drive the subsequent stages. Therefore, the design challenge in the ILFD is to achieve a wider locking range with lower injection power level and providing high output power with low power consumption.

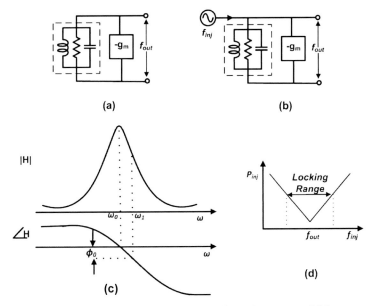

Figure 13.14 ILFD concept: (a) Free-running, (b) with injection, (c) frequency variation due to injection, and (d) locking range.

13.3.2.3 Circuit implementation of ILFD

The typical circuit schematic of the ILFD is shown in Fig. 13.15. The ILFD consists of cross-coupled transistors to generate the required negative resistance to overcome the tank losses and ensure ILFD start-up. The tank circuit in the ILFD is formed by the inductor and capacitance across the output terminals. The ILFD can either be tail injection or direct injection ILFD based on the location of the injection transistor as shown in Fig. 13.15. In comparison to the tail injection ILFD as shown in Fig. 13.15a, the locking range is improved in the direct injection ILFD due to reduced capacitance and higher injection efficiency [15]. The implementation of injection transistor in the ILFD can be either signal-ended or differential. However, since ILFD is placed following the VCO, the use of differential injection transistors can directly connect the ILFD to the VCO and the locking range can be improved.

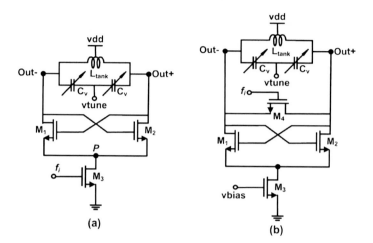

Figure 13.15 ILFD schematic: (a) Tail injection and (b) direct injection.

13.3.2.4 ILFD design example

Several ILFD focused on improving the transconductance of injection transistor to increase the ILFD locking range are reported in [16–21]. However, the locking range is narrow with low injected power levels. More advanced implementations of direct injection transformer-based ILFD design example achieving wide locking range with low injection power levels and compact size is presented in this section.

Example 1: *Increasing locking range with increased injection efficiency*

As discussed earlier, one of the ways to achieve a wide locking range in the ILFD is to increase the injection efficiency. The schematic of the ILFD with inter-coupled differential inductor to increase the injection efficiency is shown in Fig. 13.16 [22]. The ILFD is based on fully differential configuration with a single tank inductor operating at a center frequency of 54 GHz. For comparison of the proposed injection efficiency technique to the conventional method, the same ILFD is implemented with a single-ended injection inductor as shown in Fig 13.16a. The die micro-photograph and input sensitivity is shown in Figs. 13.17 and 13.18, respectively. Implemented in GLOBALFOUNDRIES 65 nm CMOS process, the ILFD's core occupies a chip area of only 200 μm × 100 μm excluding the injection efficiency enhancement inductors.

The single-ended injection enhancement inductor occupies an area of 245 μm × 105 μm, while the inter-coupled differential inductor occupies only 80 μm × 90 μm. With a supply voltage of 1.2 V, the ILFD core has a DC power consumption of 3.6 mW while the on-wafer probe measurement buffer consumes 2.6 mW. Therefore, the ILFD proposed inter-coupled differential inductor technique achieves two times the locking range in comparison to the single-ended inductor implementation with a compact size.

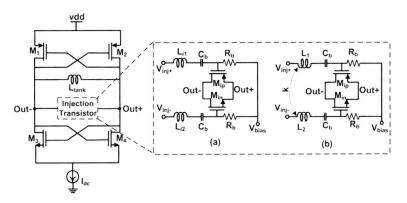

Figure 13.16 ILFD schematic: (a) Single-ended injection peaking and (b) transformer coupled differential injection peaking [22].

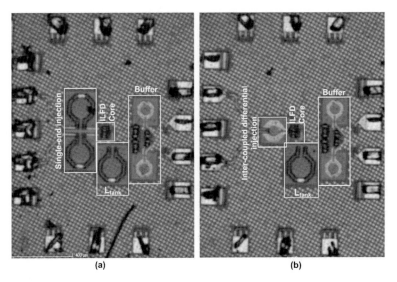

Figure 13.17 ILFD die microphotograph (a) single-ended injection peaking, and (b) transformer coupled differential injection peaking [22]. © IEEE.

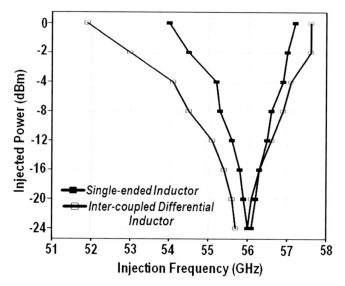

Figure 13.18 Measured ILFD input sensitivity [22]. © IEEE.

Example 2: *Increasing locking range with increased transconductance of injection transistor using multi-coupled inductors*

The schematic of the fully differential ILFD with multi-coupled inductor is shown in Fig. 13.19 [23]. The tank inductor in the ILFD consists of multi-coupled inductors L_1, L_2, and L_{inj}. Due to the coupling of the series peaking inductor L_{inj} to the primary inductor L_1, the transconductance of the injection transistor is increased [23] and the ILFD with wider locking range is realized. The die microphotograph of the proposed ILFD is implemented in GLOBALFOUNDRIES 65 nm CMOS process with a center frequency of 35 GHz is shown in Fig. 13.20. The ILFD occupies a core area of only 300 μm × 300 μm including the peaking inductors as in Fig. 13.20. With a supply voltage of 1.2 V, the ILFD core has a DC power consumption of 2.5 mW while the on-wafer probe measurement buffer consumes 2.3 mW. The input sensitivity of the ILFD is shown in Fig. 13.21. The ILFD achieves a locking range of 6.7 GHz (18.8%) for a low injection power of −8 dBm.

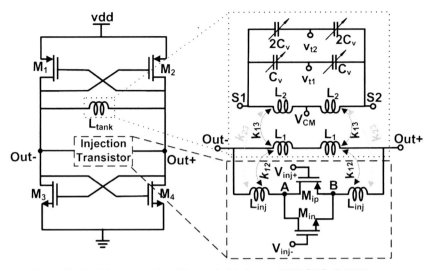

Figure 13.19 Schematic of multi-coupled inductor ILFD [23]. © IEEE.

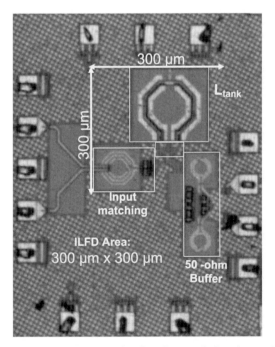

Figure 13.20 Die microphotograph of multi-coupled inductor ILFD [23]. © IEEE.

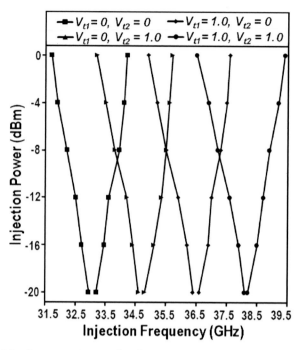

Figure 13.21 Input sensitivity of multi-coupled inductor ILFD [23]. © IEEE.

13.3.3 Low-Frequency Divider

In the frequency synthesizer, the VCO frequency is divided down to the reference frequency by chain of dividers. The low-frequency dividers are typically implemented in CMOS process and have very low power consumption. The typical operation range of the low-frequency dividers are few hundreds of MHz to GHz, though frequencies up to few GHz are reported in literature [24].

The most commonly used low-frequency divider is the true single phase clock (TSPC) divide-by-2 as shown in Fig. 13.22a. To perform as the divide-by-2, the output is connected to the input in feedback configuration similar to the static frequency divider. The operation principle of the TSPC divider is shown in Figs. 13.22b,c. When the clock input is low, node B is pre-charged to a "high" and output is maintained at the previous state. This mode is called the hold mode. However, when clock input is "high", the output is dependent on value at node A and this is the evaluation mode of the TSPC divider. When node A is "high", node B is "low" and output is "high". While node A is "low", node B is "high" and output is "low". Therefore, the divide-by-2 operation is realized when node A switches the state of node B for every 2 rising clock edges.

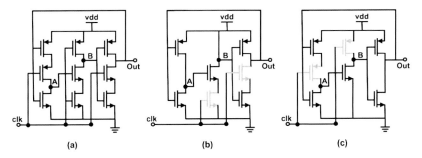

Figure 13.22 TSPC divider and operation: (a) Circuit schematic, (b) when clk = "low," and (c) when clk = "high."

13.3.4 Phase Frequency Detector

The phase detector (PD) block in the frequency synthesizer compares the phase of the VCO output to the reference input and generates an output signal equivalent to the phase difference. The phase detectors can be either analog or digital. The popular analog implementation is the multiplier-based PD [25, 26]. The drawback in the analog PD is it large power consumption and the dependence of the output phase difference on the amplitude of the input signal. The digital equivalent of the multiplier PD is the XOR PD [27]. In the XOR PD, the input voltage is rail to rail (0 to "vdd") and therefore, the PD gain is no longer dependent on the input amplitude. Though the XOR PD is simple and can achieve high operational speeds, it does not detect the frequency difference between the input signals.

The most popular digital PD used in the frequency synthesizer is the PFD. The PFD can detect both the phase and frequency difference and aid in the fast PLL locking. The circuit diagram of the PFD is shown in Fig. 13.23a. The D-flipflops in the PFD are designed as positive edge triggered and can be implemented as either TSPC D-flipflops or using RS-flipflops. The operation of the PFD is presented as follows.

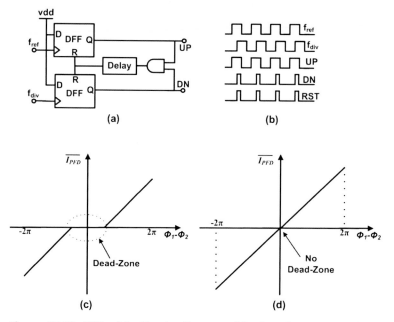

Figure 13.23 PFD: (a) Circuit diagram, (b) time-domain waveform, (c) transfer function characteristics with dead-zone and (d) no dead-zone transfer function characteristics.

During the initial phase acquisition process, the reference (REF) and feedback divider (DIV) signal are at different frequencies. Assuming the REF leads the DIV as shown in Fig. 13.23b, the DFF in the reference path is triggered and UP signal is switched while DN remains in "low" state. The UP signal maintains its value until it is reset by the rising edge of the feedback divider signal. When DIV leads REF, the DN signal is switched and UP is pulled to the "low" state. Again the DN is pulled to the "low" state with the next rising edge of the UP signal. Based on the UP or DN signal, the VCO frequency is steered in the corresponding direction either to increase or decrease the VCO frequency.

The advantage with the PFD is the large linear range or acquisition range of $\pm 2\pi$ in comparison to the range of multiplier and XOR PD. One of the major drawbacks in the PFD is the dead-zone. The dead-zone in the PFD occurs when the phase error between the reference and feedback divider signal is close to zero. When the PLL synthesizer is in the locked or close to locked state, the phase difference between the REF and DIV signal is zero. At this instant, the pulse width of UP and DN are at its lowest determined by the delay in the reset path as shown in Fig. 13.23a. In the frequency synthesizer, the charge pump following the PFD will not be able to react to the short pulse and no current is injected into loop filter to stabilize the VCO output. As a result, the gain of the PFD k_{PFD} is zero and the PLL synthesizer loop becomes non-functional. The typical transfer characteristic of PFD with and without dead-zone is shown in Figs. 13.23c,d, respectively. The simplest solution to avoid the dead-zone issue in PFD is to add more delays in the reset path. However, the downside is increase in the reference spur. Therefore, the reset path must be chosen with careful trade-off with reference spur.

The other downside of the PFD is the clock-skew between the complementary outputs UP and DN in the PFD. When the propagation delay in the two output paths is different, the output of PFD can be switched at different times causing unwanted glitches in the PFD output. These glitches interfere with the operation of charge pump and manifest itself as disturbances in the VCO control line generating spurious signals in the VCO output. The straightforward solution to reduce the clock-skew in the PFD is to add pass transistors in the UP or DN path to match the propagation the delay.

13.3.5   Charge Pump

The charge pump follows the PFD in the frequency synthesizer and it either sources or sinks current to the loop filter based on the PFD output. The schematic of the typical charge pump is shown in Fig. 13.24. The charge pump consists of two current sources which are switched by the UP and DN outputs from the PFD. The charge pumps can be either single-ended or differential and more details on circuit architectures can be found in [28]. In the locked state when UP and DN are same, the charge pump is in infinite impedance and there is no current output to the loop filter. Similar to the PFD, practical charge pump suffer from several non-idealities as presented briefly in the following section.

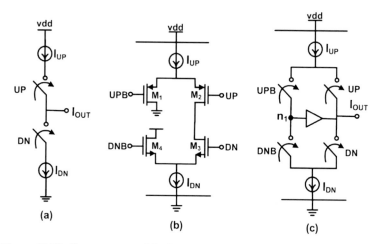

Figure 13.24 Charge pump: (a) Ideal schematic, (b) current–steering, and (c) with unity gain buffer.

13.3.5.1 Current mismatch

The most common non-ideality in the charge pump is the current mismatch due to the delay cells added in the PFD to eliminate the dead zone. In the locked state, the UP and DN outputs have a constant pulse width. Since, charge pump is typically based on CMOS, the UP and DN current paths are implemented by PMOS and NMOS transistors, respectively. In the ideal case, the net source and sink current is exactly the same and there is no current injection into the loop filter. However, under locked state, both the UP and DN current paths are turned ON for the period of the reset delay and some amount of charge is injected into the loop filter due to the current and switching time mismatch caused by the PMOS and NMOS transistors. This is shown in Fig. 13.24. Since the occurrence of current mismatch is over a reference period, it manifests as a spurious tone in the PLL synthesizer output. Therefore, to reduce the current mismatch in the charge pump, the reset delay in the PFD must be minimized.

13.3.5.2 Leakage current

Leakage current issue in the charge pump is caused if there is a small amount of current when both the UP and DN switches are OFF. In the submicron CMOS process, the leakage current can be in order of few nA [28] and the consequence is generation of reference spurs. Under locked condition, the average current over one reference period must be zero. However, in the presence of leakage current, there exists a constant phase error in the charge pump given by [28]

$$\varphi_e = 2\pi \frac{I_{leak}}{I_{cp}} \text{ (rad).} \tag{13.31}$$

13.3.5.3 Clock feedthrough

The issue of clock feedthrough in the charge pump is due to the coupling of high-frequency clock through the parasitic C_{gd} and C_{gs} of the UP and DN switching transistors in the charge pump. The error occurs when the switches in the charge pump are turned off due to periodic switching of UP and DN signals. When the current switches are turned off, the parasitic C_{gd} and C_{gs} forms a capacitive divider with the capacitance in the output node resulting in portion of clock signal appearing across the capacitance in the output node. Therefore, the clock feedthrough disturbs the output voltage in the charge pump. The issue of clock feedthrough can be reduced by using complementary switches or placing the current switches at the source and drain nodes farther away from the charge pump output node.

13.3.5.4 Charge sharing

The issue of charge sharing in the charge pump is due to the current switches being turned OFF after it was in the ON-state. As shown in Fig. 13.25a, when the UP and DN switches are turned OFF, node A is pulled to Vdd, node B is at GND and output node is floating. However, due to mismatches in the switching of UP and DN, the current switches are ON for a small instance. This results in the change of voltages at nodes A and B and consequently charge sharing between capacitors at node A, node B and the output capacitance due to the difference in voltages. Charge sharing in the charge pump causes glitches in the voltage at the loop filter output and thus degrades the PLL synthesizer spurious performance. The issue of charge sharing can be reduced by using unity gain amplifiers to maintain the voltages at nodes A and B to be same as the output voltage as shown in Fig. 13.24c.

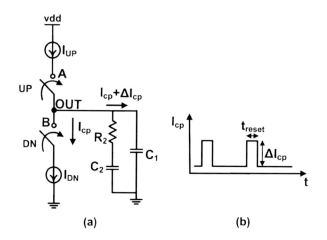

(a)   **(b)**

Figure 13.25 Charge pump non-ideality: (a) Conceptual schematic, and (b) current mismatch.

13.3.5.5 Charge injection

The issue of charge injection in the charge pump is due to the current switching transistors. When the current switches are ON, finite amount of charge is held under the gate (in the channel). Since the current switches are always operated in triode region, when the switches are turned OFF, some amount of charge is injected into the source and drain nodes of the switch transistor. As there exists a finite time for the switch control signal to make the low to high transition, this charge is injected into the charge pump output causing disturbance to the VCO control voltage. Therefore, to reduce the effect of charge injection, minimum transistor size is adopted for the switching transistors to increase the switching speed.

References

1. De Muer, B., and Steyaert, M. (2003). *CMOS Fractional-N Synthesizers: Design for High Spectral Purity and Monolithic Integration.* Springer Science & Business Media.

2. Roland E., Best, (2007). *Phase Locked Loops*. McGraw-Hill Professional.

3. Goldman, S. (2007). *Phase-Locked Loop Engineering Handbook for Integrated Circuits*: Artech House.

4. Brennan, P. V. (1996). *Phase-Locked Loops, Principles and Practice*: Macmillan.

5. Akazawa, Y., Kikuchi, H., Iwata, A., Matsuura, T., and Takahashi, T. (1983). Low power 1 GHz frequency synthesizer LSI's. *IEEE Journal of Solid-State Circuits*, 18(1), 115–121.

6. Leeson, D. B. (1966). A simple model of feedback oscillator noise spectrum. *Proc. of IEEE*, 329–330.

7. Craninckx, J., and Steyaert, M. (1995). Low-noise voltage-controlled oscillators using enhanced LC-tanks. *IEEE Trans. Circ. Syst. II: Analog Digit. Signal Proc.*, 42(12), 794–804.

8. Hegazi, E., Sjöland, H., and Abidi, A. (2001). A filtering technique to lower LC oscillator phase noise. *IEEE J. Solid-State Circ.*, 36(12), 1921–1930.

9. Rael, J. J., and Abidi, A. A. (2000). Physical processes of phase noise in differential LC oscillators. *Proc. IEEE Cus. Int. Cir. Conf.*, pp. 569–572.

10. Hajimiri, A., and Lee, T. H. (1998). A general theory of phase noise in electrical oscillators. *IEEE J. Solid-State Circ.*, 33(2), 179–194.

11. Lee, T. H., and Hajimiri, A. (2000). Oscillator phase noise: A tutorial. *IEEE J. Solid-State Circ.*, 35(3), 326–336.

12. Kim, J. (2006). Performance variations of a 66 GHz static CML divider in 90 nm CMOS. *IEEE Int. Solid State Circ. Conf.*, pp. 2142–2151.

13. Singh, U., and Green, M. M. (2005). High-frequency CML clock dividers in 0.13-μm CMOS operating up to 38 GHz. *IEEE J. Solid-State Circ.*, 40(8), 1658–1661.

14. Razavi, B. (2004). A study of injection locking and pulling in oscillators. *IEEE J. Solid-State Circ.*, 39(9), 1415–1424.

15. Tiebout, M. (2004). A CMOS direct injection-locked oscillator topology as high-frequency low-power frequency divider. *IEEE J. Solid-State Circ.*, 39(7), 1170–1174.

16. Wen, S. H., Huang, J. W., Wang, C. S., and Wang, C. K. (2006, November). A 60 GHz wide locking range CMOS frequency divider using power-matching technique. *IEEE Asian Solid-State Circ. Conf.*, 2006 pp. 187–190.

17. Takatsu, K., Tamura, H., Yamamoto, T., Doi, Y., Kanda, K., Shibasaki, T., and Kuroda, T. (2010, September). A 60-GHz 1.65 mW 25.9% locking range multi-order LC oscillator based injection locked frequency divider in 65 nm CMOS. *IEEE Cus. Int. Circ. Conf.* 2010.

18. Chien, J. C., and Lu, L. H. (2007). 40 GHz wide-locking-range regenerative frequency divider and low-phase-noise balanced VCO in 0.18 μm CMOS. *IEEE Int. Solid-State Cir. Conf.*, Dig. Tech. Papers (pp. 544–621).

19. Chen, C. C., Tsao, H. W., and Wang, H. (2009). Design and analysis of CMOS frequency dividers with wide input locking ranges. *IEEE Trans. Micro. Theory Tech.*, 57(12), 3060–3069.

20. Seo, H., Seo, S., Jeon, S., and Rieh, J. S. (2011). A-band injection-locked frequency divider with inductive feedback for a locking range enhancement. *IEEE Micro. Wire. Comp. Lett.*, 21(6), 317–319.

21. Yeh, Y. L., Chang, H. Y., Chen, K., and Wu, S. H. (2010, December). An innovative injection-locked frequency divider with transformer transconductance-boosted technique. *Proc. IEEE Asia Pac. Micro. Conf.* (pp. 778–781).

22. Nagarajan, M., Kaixue, M., Seng, Y. K., and Meng, L. W. (2014, August). Area efficient inter-coupled differential injection enhancement wide locking range injection locked frequency divider. *IEEE URSI Gen. Ass. and Sci. Sym. (URSI GASS)*, (pp. 1–4).

23. Mahalingam, N., Ma, K., Yeo, K. S., and Lim, W. M. (2015). Modified inductive peaking direct injection ILFD with multi-coupled coils. *IEEE Micro. and Wire. Comp. Lett.*, 25(6), 379–381.

24. Yuan, J., and Svensson, C. (1989). High-speed CMOS circuit technique. *IEEE J. Solid-State Circ.*, 24(1), 62–70.

25. Keliu, S., and Sánchez-Sinencio, E. (2006). *CMOS PLL Synthesizers: Analysis and Design: Analysis and Design*. vol. 783. Springer Science & Business Media.

26. Gray, P. R., et al. (2001). *Analysis and Design of Analog Integrated Circuits*. Wiley.

27. Lee, T. H., and Bulzacchelli, J. F. (1992). A 155-MHz clock recovery delay-and phase-locked loop. *IEEE J. Solid-State Circ.*, 27(12), 1736–1746.

28. Rhee, W. (1999, July). Design of high-performance CMOS charge pumps in phase-locked loops. *Proc. IEEE Int. Symp. on Cir. and Sys.*, (vol. 2, pp. 545–548).

Knowledge alone is inadequate in producing results. It needs to be intermingled with the ability to interact and network for one to think quickly and make good judgments.

—Kiat Seng Yeo and Kaixue Ma

Chapter 14

Digital IC Design for Transceiver SOC

Wang Yisheng,[a] Kaixue Ma,[b] and Kiat Seng Yeo[a]

[a]*Engineering Product Development, Singapore University of Technology and Design,*
8 Somapah Road, Singapore 487372
[b]*School of Physical Electronics,*
University of Electronic Science and Technology of China,
#4 Section II, Jianshe North Road, Chengdu, 610054, P. R. China

yisheng_wang@mymail.sutd.edu.sg, makaixue@uestc.edu.cn,
kiatseng_yeo@sutd.edu.sg

This chapter introduces the essential design steps needed in the digital hardware design flow for the low-power SOC design with detailed information about each step from the algorithm design to physical implementation. The goal of the chapter is to give the reader a basic understanding of digital design flow. The standard design methodology and background knowledge will be presented based on the tools from Synopsys.

Currently, the system-on-chip (SOC)-based design methodology is widely used in IC chip design flow as more and more reusable IP modules integrated in the standard design. The new design methodology has made it possible to deliver the SOC chips that

Low-Power Wireless Communication Circuits and Systems: 60 GHz and Beyond
Edited by Kaixue Ma and Kiat Seng Yeo
Copyright © 2018 Pan Stanford Publishing Pte. Ltd.
ISBN 978-981-4745-96-3 (Hardcover), 978-1-315-15653-8 (eBook)
www.panstanford.com

contain millions of logic gates in a short design period with higher level of integration and low power consumption. The mainstream of the digital fabrication technology is migrated from 130 nm to less than 65 nm in order to achieve that kind of requirements.

The chapter focuses on the hardware design portion of the SOC design only. It begins with a standard library introduction, following by the detailed explanation of design flow, from functional design to physical implementation. New technologies involved in low-power design methodology for deep sub-micron CMOS are also introduced.

The topic covered include

- digital IC flow introduction;
- standard library files introduction;
- frontend design flow;
- backend design flow;
- low-power methodology for deep-submicron node.

14.1   Digital Design Flow

Figure 14.1 shows the standard design flow for digital chip from design definition to layout. The design flow can be separated as frontend and backend design. The frontend functional design covers system algorithm, RTL coding and verification, gate-level netlist generation and providing system constraints. The backend design, also known as physical design, covers physical implementation which transfers logic gate-level netlist to physical layout and satisfies the design constraints.

Although the standard design flow as shown in Fig. 14.1 is quite common, the actual flow might change depending on the specific design requirements and the fabrication technology. The whole design flow or some steps in the flow may repeat several times in order to achieve better performances.

14.2   Standard Library Introduction

The cell library is the smallest design unit employed to build the digital IC. The library usually consists of timing models, power models, noise models, functional models, physical layout, abstract view, etc.

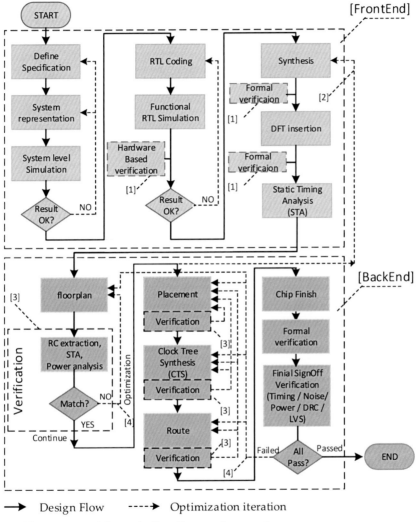

Figure 14.1 Standard digital design flow.

[1]. The step out of the main flow line can bypassed.
[2]. Floorplan database is used for improvement synthesis .
[3]. The verification used to verify the design every time when design updated,
[4]. No violation are allowed after finial signoff verification.

Process foundries typically provide the standard logic gate libraries which contain all standard logic gates for functional design and physical implementation. In addition to standard logic gate cells, the libraries also consist of random access memory (RAM), read only memory (ROM), and input-output pads user for digital IC chip design and IP implementation. For most of SOC chip, the additional design specific libraries are needed, either from third-party intellectual property (IP) vendor or created by the designer.

14.2.1 Technology File

The technology files usually with the extension .tf or .lef contain all of the physical information such as the number of metal layers for routing, design rules of each metal and vias, the routing grid, and resistances and capacitances of the routing layers for back-end digital implementation. Based on the physical information, the implementation and optimization are performed using the backend place and route tools. The additional delay time generated by the routing network is estimated based on the parasitic extraction rule defined in technology files.

For older process technologies, the routing delay can be simply calculated based on the resistance and capacitance (RC) values defined in the technology files. However, for newer technology (180 nm and below), the signal integrity (SI) noise becomes more important and the additional delay caused by the SI cannot be ignored. The new RC technology file with extension .captbl or .tluplus is used to extract the actual distributed parasitic parameter and intends to provide the actual additional delay timing caused by the SI noise.

The foundry may provide multiple versions of RC table files based on different process conditions.

14.2.2 Standard Cell

A standard cell (SC) is a completed gate design in digital design library. It is the smallest regular unit in the digital design and combinations of those cells are used to develop complex ASIC chips. There are hundred thousands or millions of those cells working together in a single chip. The quality of those cells is important to the stability and reliability of the final design. The foundry sometimes provides multiple versions of libraries in order to obtain the optimal of area, power, or operation speed.

The logic gate can be separated into several groups based on functionality as follows:

- **Combination and sequential logic**

  Cells used by synthesis tools to achieve the design functionality: e.g., NAND, NOR, XOR, DFF, Adder, etc.

- **Timing related logic**

  Cells used by physical implementation tools to fix electrical design rule violation and timing violations: e.g., BUF, DLY, CLKBUF, CLKINV, etc.

- **Special functionality logic**

  Cells used for special usage: e.g., Scan DFF, Clock Gated DFF, etc.

- **Physical related logic**

  Cells used to fix design rule violations: e.g., FILLER, ENDCAP, WELLTIE, etc.

14.2.3   RAM, ROM IP Compiler

The RAM is used to save temporary internal data. The storage density of the memory is much higher than the register array and it is widely used in digital design. In the memory IPs from the foundry, memory size, data width, memory depth, and the physical parameters, such as the aspect ratio, metal layer of the IO port, and the power ring, etc., can be specified. The ROM is used to save constant value in the chip and the value inside is retained when the chip is powered off. The ROM compiler is used to generate ROM IP.

The memory compiler automatically generates complete library files for the generated IP, from simulation, synthesis model to final GDS layout for final integration.

14.2.4   IP from Third-Party Vendor

In the past decade, technology progress in IC design and semiconductor manufacturing has resulted in circuits with more functionality at lower prices. In order to deliver much more complex IC in short design period, reused IP has become more important in digital design flow. The standard IPs can be integrated into user design easily either using standard SOC on chip bus or by a special user-defined interface.

The IP can be either hard-core IP or soft-core IP. The hard-core IPs provide the verification model and related physical design in which the users are not allowed to modify the core. Some examples of hard-core IPs are analog or mixed-circuit–related IP, such as analogue-to-digital converter (ADC), digital-to-analogue converter (DAC), phase lock loop (PLL), and IO pads. The soft-core IPs provide the gate-level netlist and design constraints. The encrypted RTL code is provided in most cases whose functionality cannot be modified by the user. However, the physical implementation can be done together with the user design. It can achieve better integration and area utility but needs more time for integration than the hard-core IP. Most of the pure digital design units are given by the soft-core IP, such as the microprocessor, on-chip-bus, and memory controller.

14.2.5   Power Management Kits

Almost all digital designs today need to consider power efficiency, and power management kits are used to further reduce power consumption. These kits provide some special logic gate for cross power domain operations.

The two major technologies in the low-power design methodology to save power are multiple-voltage and power gating technology. The detailed discussion on the two technologies will be covered in the low-power methodology section of this chapter (Section 14.5). For the power gating technology, the power switcher cell is used to turn on or turn off a specific module, and isolation cells are used to isolate the signal between the power-gated block and always on domain, and the state retain cells are used to keep the state when power is off. For multiple supply voltages, level shifters are needed to transfer the signal level between different voltage domains.

14.2.6   Library Files

Library files contain the cell macro module's detailed information needed in the design flow. Different library files contain different information and are used in different design steps. This section introduces some of most widely used library files and their importance in the design flow in brief.

14.2.6.1   Timing and power library (.lib, .db)

The timing libraries are usually given based on the process condition, supply voltage, and temperature (PVT), which is also known as the PVT corner. This method is used to define the timing tolerance for the cells caused by the variation of the fabrication process, supply voltage, and temperature. For older process technologies, only two or three corners, the best corner and the worst corner, as well as the typical corner, are provided. It is reasonable because the best condition always happens at higher supply and low temperature, and the worst condition happens in the reverse condition. However, in the deep sub-micron process technology (90 nm or below), more corners must be verified to confirm the design works under all PVT conditions due to temperature inversion effect [1] and on-chip-variation (OCV) [2].

The .lib file is used as the extension of the timing and power library. It is ASCII-based file which includes information such as the library name, PVT condition, wire load model, the timing delay, power consumption for every standard cell in the library. There is also another kind of library with .db extension, which contains the same information as the .lib and it is the compiled library for the Synopsys design flow.

14.2.6.2   Physical definition (LEF, GDS)

The two types of physical definition file given in the library are Library Exchange Format (LEF) and Graphic Database System (GDS). The LEF file contains the abstract information from the completed physical layout. It reduces the size of the design and discards unused information for place and route tools. The GDS file keeps the complete design layout file typically used for fabrication.

Figure 14.2 shows the same cell from the LEF and GDS views. The LEF view contains physical size, pin name and location, antenna information of input, and the routing obstruction layer. The layers below polysilicon are discarded as they are not used by place and route tools. The Synopsys Milkyway database provides completed physical library to replace the standalone the LEF and GDS files. It uses the similar solution as the LEF and GDS but with a different name. It creates a FRAM view to save the abstract information and use CEL view to keep the completed layout. The tools can load corresponding design view automatically from the library at different design steps.

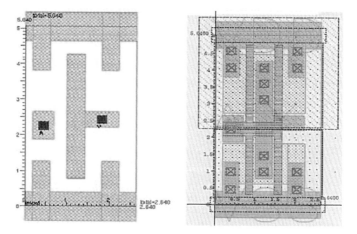

Figure 14.2 Inverter abstract view and GDS view in library.

14.2.6.3 Current source model

For the process node from 90 nm and below, the foundry provides current-based delay model for all standard cells to replace the non-linear delay model (NLDM) for static timing analysis (STA), such as the composite current source (CCS) model for Synopsys flow and the effective current source model (ECSM) model for Cadence flow. The files are given also based on the different PVT conditions.

The CCS library model can include the signal integrity noise and power model together with the timing model. It can do additional SI noise analysis based on the normal STA result. The power integrity analysis can sign off power under the same analysis environment with timing and noise analysis. The CCS model can achieve more accurate result and faster verification speed than using NLDM and non-linear power model (NLPM), but the downside is bigger size as it extracts much information [3].

The ECSM model is used for the timing and noise check in cadence design flow.

14.2.6.4 Verilog and spice module

RTL-based functional simulation can be run by the gate-level Verilog model. The Verilog model contains the internal timing delay for all gates. The Verilog module is usually used together with the Stand Delay Format (SDF) file, which contains the additional inter-connection delay to simulate functionality after physical implementation. However, the Post-layout simulation takes a longer time, and it is hard to cover all possible delay paths. Therefore, this method is only suitable for small designs. The formal check plus STA is usually used to replace the post-layout simulation in the standard design flow.

In some cases, the spice model may be available for the logic gates. The spice model is used for mixed circuit design and ultra-high speed digital design which cannot be verified using digital design tools. It can provide more accurate results for the specified working condition.

14.2.6.5 Layout vs. schematic (LVS) netlist

The .cdl file is used to do the layout vs. schematic (LVS) equivalent check after digital implementation. In most cases, digital libraries do not include schematic and symbol view for the logic gate cell. In such situation, the schematic-based netlist file is used instead of the schematic view.

The file can be imported into cadence virtuoso design environment and generates schematic and symbol view to do the schematic based on spice simulation.

14.3 Digital Frontend Design Flow

As shown in Fig. 14.1, the frontend steps are focused on the functional achievement and the design steps involved in the frontend from system specification, architecture design, behavior level RTL coding and simulation, and final deliver gate-level netlist. For the multi-million gate ASIC chip design, FPGA-based hardware verification may also be used to improve the speed of function verification. The different frontend design flow is discussed in this section.

14.3.1   System-Level Design

System design is the first step in the design flow. The design target and working condition are the important parameters for the system planning and architecture design. For the SOC design, the work also includes design partition, IP selection, cost, area and power estimation, etc. The design constraints need to be set at the same time to achieve the best trade-off for the entire system.

For example, Fig. 14.3 shows a two-chip communication system based on the 802.11ad standard. The BBIC chip is a SOC chip which contains PHY, MAC, PLL, and ADC/DAC.

For standard-based communication BBIC chip as shown in Fig. 14.3, frame package, symbol rate, and modulation and coding scheme (MCS) are all defined already in the specification based on both system-level simulation and onsite measurement result. From the designer's viewpoint, the design specifications such as supporting data rate (MCS), power consumption budget, chip size, detail block architecture, and specification for each block within the chip need to be defined. The RF transceiver's performance must take into account for the overall system simulation and the specification definition. Some of the important steps involved in the system design are as follows:

- Partition tasks to software and hardware

    The electronic system-level (ESL) design flow is used to partition the system task into the hardware and the software. The hardware creates the platform to contain the overall system, and the software runs on the given platform to control the system. The designer needs to consider the type of microprocessor and the number of microprocessors needed.

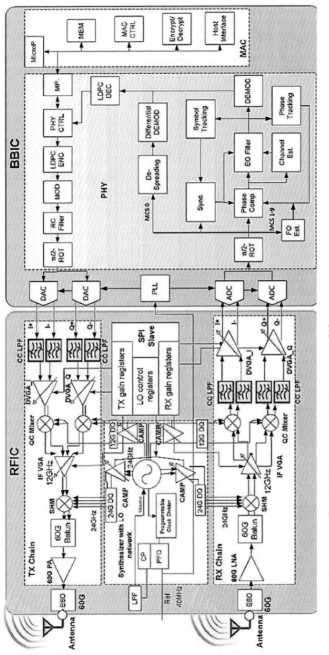

Figure 14.3 Block structure for 60 GHz communication system [3].

For the BBIC chip shown in Fig. 14.3, two microprocessors are implemented: one to handle MAC and the other to control the PHY. The sequential control program is more suitable to implement using software coding. Also, for the baseband processor, which needs high-density data processing in parallel, is more suitable to implement using hardware.

- ADC/DAC Sampling rate and resolution

  For the above system, the signal bandwidth and modulation method can be used to calculate the ADC/ADC's specification such as the sampling rate, resolution bits, etc. Higher sampling rate and better resolution can help achieve a better SNR but the power consumption increases.

- Clock rate

  System clock is an important parameter in the digital system. It is defined based on the application requirement and technology limitation. A higher clock rate achieves better processing capability. The newer fabrication technologies can support higher clock rate with lower power consumption but usually increasing the fabrication cost.

- Converting floating-point mathematic unit to fixed-point

  Converting the floating-point mathematics unit to fixed-point version involves the trade-off between speed, cost, and result accuracy. For hardware implementation, fixed-point mathematic processors are quicker, effective, and economical compared with floating-point unit.

Matlab and Simulink are most commonly and widely used tools for building the complex system and simulating the system performance. Designers can often create system-level model rapidly by integrating all the building models together. One of the main advantages is to estimate the system performance in advance, and the system performance should be checked under different working conditions by modifying the model parameters in simulation.

14.3.2 HDL Coding, Simulation, and Verification

The Hardware Description Language (HDL) is widely used to represent the digital design, such as Verilog and VHDL. The designer needs to convert C- or Matlab-based design to HDL. The HDL language is different from software programming languages as it includes the way to describe the timing and signal sensitivity and can execute in parallel. Sometimes the RTL code can be generated automatically from Matlab or Simulink code. For the SOC design, manual RTL coding is still common in the design flow to achieve the best coding performance.

RTL simulators such as Modelsim, VCS, and Incesive are used to verify the RTL code. The simulator verifies the code functionality by comparing the generated output with the expected output pattern. At the same time, the simulator reports the code coverage for the user to know the test coverage of the given input test pattern. A well-designed input test pattern is important for the verification.

There are more and more reusable IPs integrated in the SOC design, and the complexity of system increases rapidly. It is a challenge to design a test bench to verify a SOC system quickly and completely.

14.3.2.1 SystemVerilog-based verification

SystemVerilog is the extension to the existing Verilog-2001 and improves the productivity, readability, and reusability of the Verilog code [5]. It provides more concise hardware descriptions, while still providing an easy route with existing tools into the current hardware implementation flow.

The Universal Verification Methodology (UVM) is a standardized methodology for verifying IC design [6]. It is an open-source SystemVerilog library allowing the creation of flexible reusable verification components and assembling the test platform using directed and constrained random test bench generation, coverage-driven verification, and assertion-based verification methodologies. It is very important and widely used to improve test bench reuse and make verification code more portable in the SOC verification flow.

14.3.2.2 DesignWare IP

In the digital design flow, the designer can choose to use an existing IP block to speed up the design and verification process. Synopsys DesignWare IP provides some useful building block resources which can be easily integrated into the design. The IP can be separated into synthesizable IP and the verification IP.

DesignWare IP building block is highly integrated into the Synopsys design environment and it is a technology-independent IP library. The IP is optimized for the hardware and can be directly used in the RTL coding. The simulation module is also given at the same time to verify the model functionality.

A sample code is shown in Fig. 14.4. The code in Fig. 14.4 shows the coding example to create a 32-bit synthesizable floating-point adder using the DesignWare IP model.

```
module DW_Floating_Adder (A, B, rnd, Z, status);
        parameter   sig_width = 23;
        parameter   ext_width = 8;
        parameter   ieee_compliance = 0;
        input       [ sig_width + exp_width : 0]   A;
        input       [ sig_width + exp_width : 0]   B;
        input       [2:0]  rnd;
        output      [ sig_width + exp_width : 0]   Z;
        output      [7:0] status;
    // Instance of DW_fp_add
        DW_fp_add #(sig_width , exp_width , ieee_compliance)
            U1 (.a(A),.b(B),.rnd(rnd), .z(Z), .status(status));
endmodule
```

Figure 14.4 Example of DesignWare IP.

There are a number of synthesizable mathematics IPs available in the library, such as arithmetic components, floating-point unit, trigonometric, and more complex IP such as On-Chip-Bus, Microcontroller, and Digital Signal Processor (DSP) cores.

Synopsys also provides silicon-proven mixed-signal standard interface IPs such as PCIe, USB 2 PHY, and Ethernet. The corresponding verification IPs are provided to verify the functionality of those provided IPs.

14.3.2.3   Hardware-based verification

Most of the simulation platforms are created based on systems using common CPU and operating system. That is not an efficient way to verify a SOC design with special hardware and software. It will usually take a few days to simulate the full operation of a multi-million logic gate design. Hence, this method is difficult to meet the full coverage verification requirements of SOC designs. Therefore, hardware-based verification is introduced to solve the problem.

In the hardware-based verification, the FPGA-based ASIC prototype platform is used to verify the code functionality in real hardware. In most cases, the prototype boards are built using multiple high-performance FPGA chips with a large interconnection bandwidth and flexible extension capability. As shown in Fig. 14.3, the simulation cannot cover all possible input conditions and the hardware-based verification is the only way to find design bugs by using a large set of input patterns.

Also, the ASIC verification board should provide flexibility to extend the system capability by plugging a daughter card to an existing system, such as adding the ARM core, DDR memory, or hard-core communication interface.

There are some EDA tools available that can help the user to partition the existing design into multiple FPGAs and optimize the communication bandwidth between the chips. Synopsys provides the whole verification solution, including the hardware platform (HAPS) together with software tools (Ceritify, Synplify Premier).

14.3.3   Synthesis Based on Design Constraints

The synthesis tool is used to convert the behavior HDL to gate-level RTL by using a specified physical library. Design constraints are used to guide the synthesis tool to generate and optimize netlist.

The Design Compiler from Synopsys is the most widely used synthesis tool. The tool can generate gate-level netlist and then do optimization by using the embedded DesignWare library. Design constraint files are used to specify the working conditions, such as clock domain definition, IO signal delay referred to corresponding clocks signals, and the optimization target either timing or area. The Power compiler is the additional feature in the synthesis environment to optimize for power consumption.

The wire load model is used to estimate the additional delay by using a non-linear delay model (NLDM) defined in the timing library. The estimated delay time is used to optimize the generated netlist to match the timing requirement. For the deep sub-micron process technology, the timing accuracy based on wire load model is not enough [7]. Therefore, a physical location–based solution is introduced in the design flow to further optimize the synthesized netlist.

The Design Complier topography is intended to give more actual timing and power value by using the generated floorplan and to perform another round of optimization. It is shown in Fig. 14.1 as the backward iteration from floorplan back to synthesis.

14.3.4   Static Timing Analysis

Static Timing Analysis (STA) is one of many technologies used to verify the timing of a digital design. In this method, the design is static and does not depend on the data values being applied at input pins. The STA provides a fast way to perform the complete timing check for all possible paths and scenarios.

Given the gate-level netlist generated from synthesis alone with the design constraints, the purpose of the STA is to confirm if the design can operate at a specified clock speed without timing violations. The logic optimization must be done if there are timing violations, as the timing is typically worse in the backend design flow.

14.3.5   Formal Equivalence Checking

The behavior HDL model of the design is fully verified by the simulation tool or hardware. The gate-level netlist is generated by the synthesis tool, and ideally all the verification flow must run again to further confirm the design. It will spend more time than the behavior-level simulation because the gate-level design is much more complex than the behavior module. And the work is redundant as the functionality has already been verified.

Formal equivalence checking is used to formally prove that the two representations of a circuit exhibit exactly the same behavior. It is used to prove the designs are equal when the representation is updated. It gives faster verification method by checking all the checkpoints within the design and can cover all conditions without a test vector [8].

Formality is the formal check tool from Synopsys which performs the verification work in the flow when netlist is updated. It should be used to confirm the design every time if the design is updated, for example, after DFT insertion, after physical synthesis, after Clock tree insertion, and after physical implementation.

14.3.6 Design for Testability (DFT)

Design for Testability (DFT) is widely used in mass-production digital ICs. It makes it easier to develop and apply manufacturing tests for the hardware. The purpose of tests is to validate that the product contains no manufacturing defects that affect the product's functionality. Automatic Test Equipment (ATE) is used to test the chip automatically based on test patterns and response patterns.

Some of the DFT technologies are presented in this section:

- SC: Scan Chain

  Used to test the defects in the standard gate logic. The strategy is to make all gates controllable and testable through the scan chain [9]. A scan chain includes scan in pad, scan enable pad, scan out pad, and scan chain itself. The test pattern is shifted in from scan in and controlled by scan enable and checks shift out through scan out. More than one scan chain are used in design to achieve higher test coverage. Synopsys DFT Compiler can insert scan chain to a design automatically.

- BIST: Built-In Self-Test

  For the memory unit, BIST is used to make sure all memory addresses can be written and read correctly. The BIST modules are given using RTL code and are inserted into the design before the synthesis. IP vendors usually provide the corresponding BIST module together with the IP for DFT purpose.

- BSD: Boundary Scan

  Boundary scan is the method for testing interconnects in the chip. It is used to test the IO pad states inside the IC. Synopsys BSD Compiler can be used to generate boundary scan chain for boundary scan test.

- At-speed Scan Chain

  As the design size is increased to millions of gates and working frequency in the gigahertz range, at-speed test is crucial. The new deep sub-micron effects may finally decrease the absolute slack on the critical paths and that require testing the IC at application frequency. The at-speed scan testing must be considered before the RTL design in order to achieve the operation speed as well as the testability [10].

14.4   Digital Backend Design Flow

The digital backend design starts from gate-level netlist to final signoff of the design, including sending GDS to the process foundry. The target of the backend design is to translate the logic-based design into a physical layout and meet all design constraints.

The backend design is timing consuming and violations can happen at the any stage. In some cases, all the previous works may need to be repeated to meet the design constraints. High quality and well-prepared data are important to reduce the number of iterations and save design time.

14.4.1   Floorplanning

Floorplanning is the art of any physical design. It is important to achieve high performance and optimum area. This step decides the die size and aspect ratio of the ASIC chip and involves planning in the placement of I/O pads, macros as well as the power and ground structure. The clock network planning may also need to be considered at the same time.

Figure 14.5 shows an example of floorplan design with IO ring, hard-core IP placement, soft-core placement constraint for RTL module and power networks. The timing, power, and congestion analysis can be done based on the floorplan design above. Many EDA tools help the designer to analyze the design, know the issue as early as possible, and also provide the suggestion to fix them at early stages. The generated physical floorplan database can be used for the synthesis tools to further optimize the gate-level netlist.

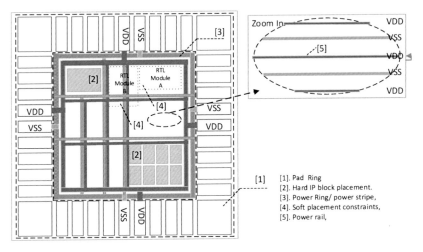

Figure 14.5 Example of IC floorplanning.

14.4.1.1   Pad ring

A pad ring is a group of pad cells around the chip core to provide IO capacity and supply the design core as shown in Fig. 14.5. The pad cells are groups of regular design and usually provided by the IP vendor as hard-core IPs. A completed pad ring includes functional pads and physical pads. The functional pads are assigned to provide signal and power interface of the design, while the physical pads are used to combine all pads together to form a pad ring. The pad ring provides ring connectivity and ESD protection.

The IO pad sequence is usually specified based on the board design. The power and ground pads need to be evenly inserted in the pad ring. Some design considerations for the pad ring design are presented as follows.

- Number of power pads for the core area

  The number of supply pads is roughly decided based on the current flow through the specified supply pads. Electromigration may damage power traces if the current flow through the power pad is larger than the affordable current density.

- Number of power pads for the pad ring

  Level shifter and buffers are implemented in the standard pad cell in order to provide flexibility to communicate with other chips. The pad ring power pad is used to supply the whole pad ring. The designer needs to estimate the maximum pad power consumption and consider simultaneous switching outputs (SOO) effect, and then decide the number of pads needed to supply the pad rings.

- Special cell insertion

  Other special functional pad cells need to be inserted into the pad ring. They are intended to make the pad ring complete, stable, and reliable, against the ESD, power on sequence, pad pitch, etc.

14.4.1.2   Macro IP placement

The macro IP cell placement can be either manual or automatic as specified by the designer. In most cases, the manual placement for macro IPs is more efficient than the automatic placement. For example, the mixed-signal IPs, such as ADC/DAC/PLL, are usually placed at a corner or edge of the die because of the standalone power network and the requirement of good isolation between the IP module and standard digital logics. Also, the memory units are usually placed close to the corresponding RTL logic module.

Soft placement constraint can be used to define the placement location of the specified RTL module, or the placement relationship between several modules. The information from the frontend designer is helpful for the backend designer to achieve optimized placement.

14.4.1.3   Power network

The power network synthesis here includes the power ring and power strips designed for both the core logics and macro IPs. The estimated static and dynamic power consumption is used for power analysis. IR drop analysis is used to confirm the power network. For the low-power design with multiple power domains, the power planning may need to consider the level shifter insertion and the needs of dual supply voltage for some of them.

14.4.2 Placement

The goal of the placement is to place the standard cells and the unplaced macro cells on the core area to a fixed location. The designer may also provide physical constraints to guide place tool and optimize the design. The few steps available in design flow to solve different issues are as follows:

- Global placement

  At this step, all standard cell will be assigned to a fixed location based on the timing-driven placement algorithm. The tools try to place all cells to the core area with as less interconnection length as possible. The global placement runs fast and can generate accurate cell location for the timing analysis. The physical synthesis technology is used here to optimize the netlist to achieve better timing, congestion, and power consumption.

- Detailed placement

  The detailed placement algorithm is executed to refine the placement result based on congestion, timing, and power requirements.

- Placement optimization

  For the design with the scan chains included, the scan chain should be reordered to achieve better timing and congestion for routing. The multi-threshold cells replacement can be done here to trade off the leakage power and operation speed.

14.4.3 Clock Tree Synthesis

The concept of clock tree synthesis (CTS) is the insertion of buffers/inverters along the clock paths of the ASIC design to balance the clock delay to all clock inputs. The clock buffers and inverters used for the clock paths must have equal rise and fall delay time.

Although the clock tree specification can be generated from design constraints file directly, user-specified clock tree specification typically yields the optimized result. For the clock tree synthesis, less skew means more buffering levels, and it will increase the overall clock propagation delay. CTS flow needs to run multiple iterations to get better results by fine-tuning the parameters in the specification files.

After the clock tree synthesis, the timing violations such as setup and hold time need to be resolved. The clock network is the most important and special network in the design and the Non-Default Routing (NDR) rule is usually used for the network routing to reduce the crosstalk noise. The clock network can be routed directly after the clock tree synthesis. The clock tree routing rule usually uses wider metal and prefers higher metal layer to reduce parasitic RC.

The clock distribution network consumes 50% or more of the dynamic power of a typical ASIC design. The main reason is it has large capacitive loading and operates at the highest switching speed [11]. The power consumption of the clock tree is very important for power optimization.

14.4.4   Routing

Routing is the final step to complete the chip by connecting all unconnected signals. The routing tools are timing driven and do routing based on the estimated timing delay. The routing is performed in three stages as follows:

- Special Routing

  Special routing is used to connect the power and ground net of standard cells and macro blocks to main power and group net.

- Global Routing

  Global routing is used to estimate the routing resource and final routing delay without generating the actual layout. The global routing engine decomposes the routing requirements of a placed design and tries to assign those requirements into available routing resources [12]. It estimates the final routing congestion by comparing the required routing resource with the available resource. In addition, it provides optimization guide for increased placement if needed. It is useful to check the congestion report and know whether the routing can be done without design rule violations. The global routing also includes wire estimation methods to calculate routing wire length and roughly extract corresponding parasitic RC value for timing optimization.

- Detail Routing

  Detail routing performs the actual physical interconnect for all unconnected signals based on the global route result. The antenna violation generated on the routing phase should be resolved here.

- Chip finish

  Chip finish performs the filler insertion and metal fill insertion to finish the chip design. Incremental timing optimization may be needed to resolve the small violations caused by the metal fill insertions.

14.4.5   RC Extraction

A parasitic extraction tool is used to calculate all routed net resistances, capacitance, and inductance based on the final layout and RC generation technology file. It is performed by analyzing each net in the design and taking into account the effects of the net's own topology and proximity to other nets. The three-dimensional (3D) model is used for most physical extraction tools [13]. The generated file can be used for final static timing analysis, signal integrity, and power analysis.

The distributed RC model is appropriate for timing analysis and signal integrity analysis, where the effects are due to resistance and capacitance values. The Standard Parasitic Extended Format (SPEF) is the most widely used distributed RC parasitic from the IEEE standard.

The library may provide multiple RC extraction technology files for different corner conditions and the analysis and optimization must be done under corresponding conditions.

14.4.6 Multi-Mode, Multi-Corner (MMMC) Analysis and Optimization

The ASIC chip needs to work under some different conditions and it may need to support multiple working modes. It is not easy to make the design work properly under all modes and all corners [14]. In the traditional backend flow, the designer needs to switch the working mode by loading different constraint files and then performing optimization independently. The standard STA must run at all working corners after the optimization. The problem is optimized based on the specified mode and the corner may affect the result at other modes and corners. The iterations for optimization may increase a lot to fulfill all modes and corners. The STA should run again each time after optimization iteration.

Multi-mode, multi-corner analysis provides a solution to verify specified modes and corners in parallel instead of serial in the original solution. The MMMC analysis is intended to provide high confidence result for timing without the simulation of all possible conditions [15]. The user can define several scenarios and specify the corresponding best and worst condition for each scenario. The MMMC engine can do timing optimization for all the loading scenarios concurrently.

The MMMC-based optimization is the common design methodology for timing closure in the SOC design flow. It can achieve the design target with less iteration and save design time.

14.4.7 Signoff Static Timing Analysis

STA timing verification can be inserted anywhere in the design flow. It reports the critical timing path for the user to optimize. The STA works together with RC extraction tool and physical optimization tool to make sure the timing target.

The STA used to sign off the final timing before delivering to foundry. On-Chip Variation (OCV)-based STA analysis is used in the signoff flow for the deep-submicron design. It intends to resolve the timing variations at different portions of the chip caused by process, voltage, or temperature. A derating value is introduced in the STA verification flow to cover the OCV condition. The OCV technology checks the timing path from signal source to destination using the most pessimism estimation. It considers signal start point using the slowest timing model and, at the same time, signal destination point using the fastest model. This is too pessimism for STA analysis as there is shared clock tree for both in most of the paths. The Clock Re-Convergence Pessimism Removal (CRPC) technology is the method introduced to reduce the pessimism by removing the estimation error on the shared clock path [16].

The final STA must cover all possible working modes and corner conditions introduced above [17]. The STA needs to calculate the actual delay caused not only by routing trace but also by crosstalk noise [18]. The current-based standard cell library models (CCS) and extracted distribute RC model (SPEF) are used for the STA signoff flow.

The power consumption signoff can be included in the STA flow too. Both dynamic power and static power can be estimated by using those STA inputs with user-defined signal toggle rate. It is used to make sure the IR drop and electromigration rules are not violated.

14.4.8 Formal Verification

The final netlist generated from the place and route is different from the one before the place and route. Formal verification needs to be run again here to confirm that their functionalities are equal.

For DFT design, scan chain is inserted, and usually the scan chain reorder is executed during the implementation. As the mentioned works change the functionality, it causes verification failure. In this situation, designers have to set formal verification mode manually to make the scan shift signal inactive. Usually, the mode selection is achieved by connecting the control signal to a constant dc voltage. The formal verification can be quite complex for recent multi-mode or multi-voltage designs. Hence, it has to be planned early and carefully.

14.4.9 DRC/LVS

This is the final step to complete the design. Design Rule Check (DRC) used to confirm the design can be fabricated successfully. And Layout Versus Schematic (LVS) used to confirm the layout represents the corresponding schematic. For the digital design, netlist is used as a schematic in LVS.

14.5   Low-Power IC Design Methodology

The low-power methodology is involved in most of the ASIC designs in the past decade to achieve higher energy efficiency, better stability, and longer battery time for a portable device. For most of SOC designers, the power budget is one of most design goals of a project together with the cost, area and timing today. The low-power design methodology intends to reduce power consumption without any performance drop.

This section starts with an introduction to some background knowledge of power consumption in a CMOS circuit and then introduces some technologies to reduce power. The low-power chip design is a complex work and involves many designers, such as system engineer, RTL engineer, IP engineer, and physical implementation engineer. The low-power design methodology is intended to provide a method for all the designers can work together to achieve the design goal.

14.5.1   Power Consumption Source

The power consumption can be separated into dynamic power and static power. Dynamic power is the power consumed when the device is in operation, and the static power is consumed when the device is just powered up in the quiescent mode.

14.5.1.1   Static power

In CMOS devices, static power consumption is due to the leakage current. Figure 14.6 shows the leakage current in a CMOS device.

- Sub-threshold leakage current (I_{sub})

  The current which flows from the drain to the source when a transistor is operating in the weak inversion region.

- Gate leakage (I_G)

  The current which flows directly from the gate through the oxide to substrate due to oxide tunneling and hot carrier injection.

- Gate-Induced Drain Leakage (I_{GIDL})

  The current which flows from the drain to the substrate induced by a high field effect in the MOSFET drain caused by a high (V_{DG})

- Reverse Bias junction leakage (I_D)

  The current caused by minority carrier drift in the PN junction.

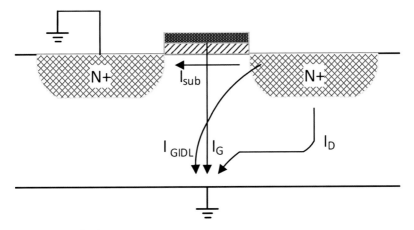

Figure 14.6 Leakage current.

The total static power consumption in CMOS circuit is determined by the contribution of leakage current in each transistor, which has two main sources: subthreshold leakage (I_{sub}) and gate leakage (I_G) [19–20]. Starting from the 90 nm process to the 65 nm process node, the gate leakage current can be nearly the same as the sub-threshold leakage in some cases. High-k dielectric materials are required to keep the gate leakage in check for the future nodes [8] and that depends on the innovation of the process technology.

Subthreshold leakage occurs when a CMOS gate is not turned off completely. For a good approximation, the leakage current value is given by Eq. (14.1) [21]:

$$I_{sub} = \mu_0 C_{ox} \frac{W}{L}(m-1)(V_T)^2 e^{\left(\frac{V_{GS}-V_{th}}{mV_T}\right)}\left(1-e^{\frac{-V_{DS}}{V_T}}\right), \qquad (14.1)$$

where W and L are the dimensions of the transistor, $V_T = KT/q$ is the thermal voltage, and parameter m is a function of device fabrication process. In the case here, V_{DS} is much higher than V_T and the last term in Eq. (14.1) approaches unity. And it is clearly shown that the leakage current can be reduced when using high V_{th} devices.

At the same time, the peak current for the CMOS device can be expressed as [22]

$$I_{D,max} = \mu_0 C_{ox} \frac{W}{L}(V_{GS} - V_{th})^2 \tag{14.2}$$

and the discharge time of CMOS can be written as

$$T_{discharge} = \frac{Q}{I_{D,max}} = \frac{V_{DD} C_{Load}}{\frac{1}{2}\mu_0 C_{ox} \frac{W}{L}(V_{DD} - V_{th})^2}. \tag{14.3}$$

From Eq. (14.3), the charge and discharge time will be increased when using a higher V_{th} device. That means the operation speed of the circuit is exchanged for the lower leakage power. In order to achieve a better trade-off between the leakage power and the operation speed, multiple V_{th} devices are used.

14.5.1.2 Dynamic power

There are two kinds of dynamic power consumption as shown in Fig. 14.7. Figure 14.7a shows the switching power required to charge and discharge the output capacitance on a signal net and gate of transistors. Figure 14.7b shows the switching short circuit current flowing through the PMOS and NMOS transistors. The dynamic power consumption of one active network can be expressed as follows:

$$P_{dyn} = (\alpha_i C_i)V_{DD}^2 f_{ck} + t_{sc}V_{DD}I_{peak}f_{ck}, \tag{14.4}$$

where the first item is the switching power and the second item is the short circuit power, α_i is the activity ratio of the specified net, and C_i is the related capacitor value of that point; t_{sc} is the short circuit time and I_{peak} is the short circuit current during the short circuit period. The first item shows the domination of the dynamic power [11].

For the dynamic power reduction, all the given factors in the first item of Eq. (14.4) are introduced into the low-power design methodology to reduce power consumption, such as reduced capacitance, reduced activity ratio, or reduced V_{DD}, etc.

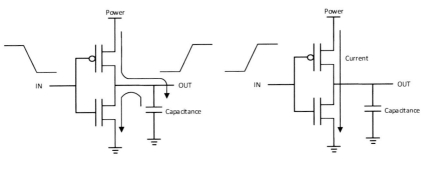

(a). Switching power   (b). Crowbar current

Figure 14.7 Dynamic power consumption.

14.5.2   Low-Power Technologies

The following section describes in brief some of the approaches to low-power design which is already used in the design flow.

14.5.2.1   Clock gating

The clock network consum es a high percentage of the dynamic power on the system as the clock tree has the highest toggle rate of the system; there are lots of them, and they often have high drive strength to minimize clock delay. In addition, the flip-flops receiving the clock dissipate some dynamic power even if the input and output remain the same.

Clock gating is a method to turn the clock off when they are not required. It can result in considerable power savings for the design using wide width registers to save the internal generated data and that data activity ratio is low. Figure 14.8 shows the method for the clock gating insertion without change functionality. Today, the synthesis tool can automatically insert the clock gating to the existing RTL design to reduce dynamic power.

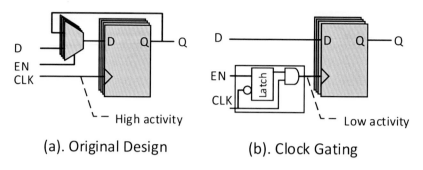

(a). Original Design   (b). Clock Gating

Figure 14.8 Clock gating.

14.5.2.2   Logic-level power reduction

A number of logic level–based optimizations can be performed to minimize dynamic power by reducing α_i or C_i in Eq. (14.4).

All the signal changes on the circuit consume dynamic power and the changes can be separated into expected change and glitch noise. The logic-level power optimization intends to reduce C_i for expected change and reduce α_i for unexpected change caused by glitch noise.

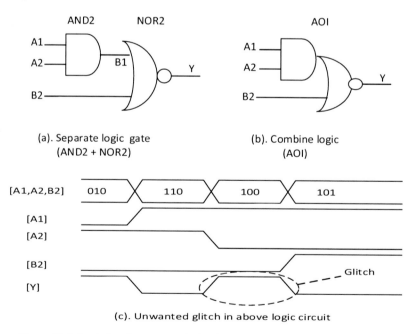

(a). Separate logic gate   (b). Combine logic
(AND2 + NOR2)   (AOI)

(c). Unwanted glitch in above logic circuit

Figure 14.9 Logic-level power optimization.

Figure 14.9 shows an example of logic optimization by using AOI instead of the separated AND + ANOR2. The net load capacitor of B1 in Fig. 14.9a is reduced in Fig. 14.9b by moving into the gate. Figure 14.9c shows the unwanted glitch noise generated at the AOI output pin due to the unbalance of the three input signals. The optimization target is minimizing the total activity ratio by refining the gate-level netlist.

The EDA tools can optimize the netlist to reduce power consumption by remapping the logic gate, swap the pin order, and resize gate size. Also, the glitch can be optimized by balanced delay timing. In most cases, there is a trade-off between timing and the power, and the logic-based power optimization should not violate the timing constraint.

14.5.2.3 Multiple-V_T design

The multiple thresholds have become a common way to reduce the leakage power when the geometries have shrunk to 90 nm and below. Many libraries today offer two or three versions of cells: low V_T, standard V_T and high V_T. As discussed before, the low-V_T library has higher operation speed and high leakage current and high-V_T library has reversed performance compared with low-V_T library.

The multiple-V_T flow is supported by EDA tools to take advantage of all those libraries and optimize timing and power simultaneously.

For the performance-centric design, high performance and high leakage library are used for synthesizing first and then relaxing back any cells not on the critical path by swapping them for their lower performing, low leakage equivalents. The design can be done the other way around for the power-centric design.

14.5.2.4 Multiple-voltage design

The dynamic switching power is proportional to V_{DD}^2, lowering VDD on selected blocks helps reduce power significantly. Unfortunately, lowering the voltage also increases the delay of the logic gates in the design.

The multiple-voltage design divides the design into several power domains and assigns different supply voltage to different domains. The approach can provide significant power savings without performance drop. However, there are some design challenges in the multi-voltage design, such as level shifters insertion, floorplan and power plan, power-up and power-down sequence, multiple-voltage STA analysis, cross-power domain DFT insertion, and formal checking.

14.5.2.5   Power gating technology

Power gating is another way of further reducing static power by switching off the unused module. Unlike a block that is always powered on, the power-gated block receives its power through a power-switching network. This network switches either VDD or VSS to the power-gated block.

In order to implement the power-gated module, the power gating controller and power-switching fabric are needed. The power gating controller is used to control the CMOS switches to provide power to the gated block and specify the condition to power on or power off. And the power switch fabric module is used to support the power-gated model such as isolation block and retention registers. The isolation block is needed between the output pin of power-gated block and input of always on block. Retention register is used to keep the internal states of power-gated block and can restore to the original working condition when powered on again.

14.5.2.6   Unified power format

Unified Power Format (UPF) is the new industry standard for low-power integrated circuit design and verification. The UPF provides the ability for an electronic system to be designed with power as a key consideration easily in the process.

As no existing HDL adequately supports the specification of power distribution and management such as the power on, power off, assign supply voltage, etc. [23], the UPF addresses the need for a common standard to describe the low-power design throughout the whole design flow, including logic design, verification, synthesis, physical implementation, and signoff. The UPF flow extends the design without changing the design logic and does no re-verification of the existing design.

The UPF-based low-power design flow has been provided by Synopsys. The designer can run the Multi-Voltage Simulator (MVSIM) with VCS by using RTL+UPF to verify a variety of dynamic issues. Most of the power management sequence- and control-related issues can be caught with dynamic verification. The Multi-Voltage Rule Checker (MVRC) helps critique the low-power intent and overall power architecture.

Although the UPF-based power intent description file can be read into the design flow at either the frontend or backend stage, different tools may just take part of it and perform corresponding operation. The design tools usually generate UPF files for further design and verification purposes, such as formal equivalence check and the timing and power integrity check and so on.

References

1. A. Dasdan and I. Hom (2006). Handling Inverted Temperature Dependence in Static Timing Analysis, *ACM Transactions on Design Automation of Electronic Systems,* vol. 11, no. 2, pp. 306–324.

2. PrimeTime Advanced OCV Technology (2009). White paper by Sunil walia, April 2009.

3. Synopsys Liberty NCX User Guide (2013). *Version H-2013.03.*

4. K. Ma and more authors (2014). An integrated 60 GHz low power two chip wireless system based on IEEE802.11ad standard, *Microwave Symposium (IMS), 2014 IEEE MTT-S International.*

5. SystemVerilog 3.1a Language Reference Manual. Accellera's Extensions to Verilog.

6. https://verificationacademy.com/verification-methodology-reference/uvm/docs_1.2/html/index.html.

7. CCS Timing Technical White Paper, version 2.0. (Synopsys, Inc. Mountain View, CA, USA).

8. Synopsys Formality User Guide (2015). *Version K-2015.06.*

9. Synopsys DFT Compiler, DFTMAX, DFTMAX ultra User Guide (2015). *Version K-2015.06-sp4, December 2015.*

10. X. Lin, R. Press, and more author (2003). High-Frequency, At-Speed Scan Testing, *IEEE Design & Test of Computers,* pp. 17–25.

11. M. Keating, D. Flynn, and more authors (2008). *Low Power Methodology Manual For System-on-Chip Design,* Chapter 2, pp. 13–20.

12. K. Golshan (2007). *Physical Design Essentials, An ASIC Implementation Perspective,* Chapter 4 "routing" (Conexant System Inc, Newport Beach,CA).

13. Synopsys StarRC User Guide and Command Reference (2015). *Version K-2015.12, December 2015.*

14. A. Tetelbaum (2014), Corner-base timing Signoff and What Is Next (Abelite Design Automation, Inc. Walnut Creek, USA).

15. B. M. Riess (2011). Multi-Corner Multi-Mode Synthesis in Design Compiler–A Must or just Nice to Have? (Infineon Technologies AG).

16. L. Bo Graversen, J. Salling, and more authors (2002). Crosstalk Analysis, Prevention and Repair Using PrimeTime-SI and Mars-Xtalk (MIPS technologies, Inc.).

17. T. McConaghy and more authors (2013). *Variation-Aware Design of Custom Integrated Circuit: A Hands-on Field Guide,* Chapter 2, pp. 13–39.

18. J. Bhasker, R. Chadha (2009). Static Timing Analysis for Nanometer Designs, A practical Approach (eSilicon Corporation, USA).

19. A. Agarwal, and more authors (2005). Leakage Power Analysis and Reduction: Models, Estimation and Tools, *Proc. IEE,* vol. 152, no. 3, pp. 353–368.

20. S. Mukhopadhyay and more authors (2005). Accurate Estimation of Total Leakage in Nonometer-Scale Bulk CMOS Circuit Based on Device Geometry and Doping Profile, *IEEE Transactions on Computer-Aided Design of Integrated Circuits,* vol. 24, no. 3, pp. 363–381.

21. K. Roy and more authors (2003). Leakage Current Mechanism and Leakage Reduction Techniques in Deep-Submicrometer CMOS circuit, *Proceeding of the IEEE,* vol. 91, no. 2, pp. 305–327.

22. B. Razavi (2000). Design of Analog CMOS Integrated Circuit, Chapter 2.2. (University of California, Los Angeles, USA).

23. Synopsys Low Power Verification Tools Suit User Guide (2015). *Version K-2015.09-sp1, December 2015.*

The path to success is never going to be easy. You need the guts and gumption to make unconventional decisions and the determination to succeed.

—Kiat Seng Yeo and Kaixue Ma

Chapter 15

60 GHz Transceiver SOC

Kaixue Ma[a] and Kiat Seng Yeo[b]

[a]*School of Physical Electronics,*
University of Electronic Science and Technology of China,
#4 Section II, Jianshe North Road, Chengdu, 610054, P. R. China
[b]*Engineering Product Development, Singapore University of Technology and Design,*
8 Somapah Road, Singapore 487372

makaixue@uestc.edu.cn, kiatseng_yeo@sutd.edu.sg

Recently, 60 GHz millimeter wave short-range communication has gained much attention [1–5] for next-generation WiFi applications supported by the IEEE802.11ad standard. The major driving factor for the 60 GHz band is the recent progress of silicon-based IC technologies such as SiGe BiCMOS [1–3] or CMOS [4, 5], which dramatically brings down the cost of 60 GHz ICs for the application scenarios of the consumer electronics. The other driving factor is that the huge unlicensed frequency bandwidth of 9 GHz worldwide in millimeter wave brings lots of low-cost applications for low-cost commercial uses. According to the applications and the system classification of standards, the 60 GHz communication system can be classified into two major parts: 60 GHz RF transceiver and 60 GHz baseband. The challenges for the design of these two parts are to support high-date-rate communication with data rate up to multiple Gb/s. So for the

Low-Power Wireless Communication Circuits and Systems: 60 GHz and Beyond
Edited by Kaixue Ma and Kiat Seng Yeo
Copyright © 2018 Pan Stanford Publishing Pte. Ltd.
ISBN 978-981-4745-96-3 (Hardcover), 978-1-315-15653-8 (eBook)
www.panstanford.com

60 GHz RF transceiver, it needs to handle both high data rate and millimeter-wave frequency operation, which bring lots of challenges from the building blocks introduced in the previous chapters as well as system architecture for low power and cost and system integration with full consideration of the data rate, EMC and EMI to SOC for the dedicated high speed reliable applications.

To form or design a 60 GHz transceiver system-on-chip (SOC), first we need have a deep understanding of applications, which becomes the fundamental design constraints for the SOC specifications. For example, if we designed for mobile or portable applications, we may need to design the circuits and systems with low power consumption as low as possible to save the battery life. Another example is that for the portable applications, the communication link is not fixed, so we have to design the system with dynamic link budget, which need to be automatically adjusted according to the different communication distance. This means the SOC must have re-configurable capability, which is preferred to be automatically rather than manually. These two simple examples are introduced to demonstrate the importance of the proper application scenarios. Of course, all of these application requirements or constraints need to be defined in the specifications of the SOC, which are also required to be implemented in the building-block circuits introduced in the previous chapters. Moreover, the well-functioning standalone circuits may have operation issues when we integrate them into the SOC due to the EMI/EMC issues and interconnects issue. Also, for the practical use, the SOC itself need to be well protected for the harsh application scenarios based on industry standards.

This chapter focuses on the hardware design portion of the 60 GHz transceiver SOC, which is controlled by SPI interfaces as introduced in the previous chapter. The basic development is based on the fundamental building blocks introduced in the previous chapters under the constraints of the system specifications and the architecture. A 60 GHz re-configurable full transceiver SOC with serial peripheral interface (SPI) in a commercial 0.18 μm BiCMOS technology is developed as the demonstration case. This reconfigurable chip is composed of a synthesizer and LO feed network, transmitter and receiver with AGC, ESD protection, etc. The 60 GHz transceiver SOC has the re-configurable capabilities for both gain and operation frequency bands covering 9 GHz bandwidth in total. For the SOC DC power consumption of less than 270 mW, the measured link up to 3 m shows EVM of 10.9% and 9.8% at 2 Gbps@QPSK and 4 Gbps@16QAM, respectively. More information about the system level design and consideration are to be given in this chapter.

The topics covered include the following:

- 60 GHz RF Transceiver SOC architecture
- synthesizer and the feeding network design
- interface and spurious control
- I/O ESD protection
- interconnects and overall layout consideration

15.1   60 GHz RF Transceiver SOC Architecture

The transceiver architecture, including the transmitter and the receiver is important for the targeted SOC performance. The selection of the architecture is determined mainly by the applications, bandwidth, power consumption as well as the IC process capability, etc. The 60 GHz transceiver SOC is better to cover all of the 60 GHz applications worldwide; thus, the 9 GHz bandwidth with four frequency channels is targeted to cover the frequency band of the USA, Europe, Japan, China, etc.

Figure 15.1 shows the proposed system block diagram of the re-configurable 60 GHz full transceiver SOC, composed of the transmitter (Tx) chain, receiver (Rx) chain as well as the synthesizer and its LO feed network. The transceiver, operated in time division duplex (TDD) mode, is based on sub-harmonic sliding IF scheme with two-time conversions. For the Rx chain, the 60 GHz signal in each 2.16 GHz channel of the four channels. The system is designed to be symmetrical in terms of the frequency plan for sharing of the LO based on TDD operation.

For the Rx chain side, the single-ended RF signal in the frequency range of 57.24 GHz~65.88 GHz is amplified by a LNA with ~15 dB gain and converted to a differential signal by 60 GHz compensation balun, and then the output differential signals from balun is down-converted to ~12 GHz IF with the K-band, i.e., ~24 GHz LO through the 60 GHz sub-harmonic mixer (SHM). The output ~12 GHz IF is amplified by 12 GHz differential IF gain controllable amplifier and then fed into the quadrature direct conversion mixer through direction down-conversion scheme with 12 GHz LO drive, which is half frequency of K-band LO. The four output analogy signals, IFI+, IFI-, IFQ+, and IFQ-, cover DC to 1.2 GHz, pass through four cross-coupled (CC) LPFs then fed to two sets of differentially DC offset canceling (DCOC) digitally variable gain amplifier (DVGA) operating in the 2 MHz~1.2 GHz for baseband processing in IFI+_O, IFI-_Q, IFQ+_O and IFQ-_O with gain of 0~30 dB.

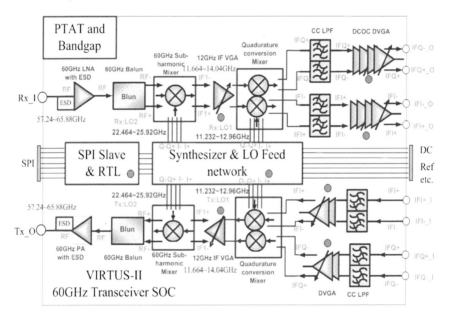

Figure 15.1 The 60 GHz re-configurable transceiver.

The Tx chain is symmetrical to the Rx chain in frequency conversion scheme. In the Tx chain, the baseband differential quadrature signals are filtered by four set of CC LPFs and then amplified by two sets of differential drive DVGAs, each with a variable gain of –12~8 dB. The differential output of the ~12 GHz quadrature up-conversion mixer is amplified by 12 GHz differential IF gain controllable amplifier and then fed into the

60 GHz up-conversion SHM, which is connected to differential ports of the 60 GHz balun. The single-ended 60 GHz PA connected to single-ended port of the balun has a gain of 20 dB, P1 dB of 5.6 dBm and dedicated ESD protection in the output port. The SOC can be re-configured in gain, operating channels and LO reference frequency, etc., by the SPI slave through the register transformer layer (RTL). The SPI can also turn on or off the key building blocks such as DVGA, IFVGA, and DCOC DVGA in Tx or Rx when the transceiver is operating in the Tx or Rx mode, respectively, for power-saving consideration. The full ESD protection for all 64 I/O pads include analogy, IF, digital and 60 GHz RF protection for commercial use environment consideration. The proportional to the absolute temperature (PTAT) and the bandgap reference are adopted in the DC supply to compensate for the temperature changes. The SOC is designed and fabricated in Tower Jazz Semiconductor using 0.18 μm SiGe bipolar process SBCH2, where HBT transistors have fT/fMAX of 180 GHz/200 GHz.

15.2 Synthesizer and the LO Feed Network

Figure 15.2 shows the proposed architecture for the K-band synthesizer with the LO feed network, which is shared as LO by either Tx or Rx by using the LO feed network for two-time up-/down-conversion. Together with the LO feed network, the K-band synthesizer provides two differential quadrature output LO drive signals, i.e., LO1 and LO2 for transceiver use. The operation frequency of LO1 is exactly the half of that of the LO2. The synthesizer is composed by a K-band VCO based on our proposed triple coupled LC tanks; transformer-based divide-by-2 injection locked frequency divider (ILFD) and a composite PLL. The composite PLL includes an emitter-coupled logic (ECL) frequency divide-by-4, a dual modulus divide-by-3/4 prescaler, a MASH 1-1-1 sigma delta sigma modulator; a CMOS phase frequency detector (PFD); a CMOS variable current charge-pump (CP); CMOS reference divider and selector to choose between multiple reference frequencies; and an off-chip loop filter. The synthesizer itself dissipates 42 mW from a 1.8 V supply with external loop filter and exhibits a locking range of 23.07 GHz to 26.48 GHz with a phase noise of –97 dBc/Hz@1 MHz. The proposed composite PLL, which can operate in either fractional or integer mode to compatible with multiple standards like IEEE 802.11ad, IEEE 802.15.3C, gives flexibility for the reference frequency selection of 40 MHz, 108 MHz, 120 MHz, 240 MHz, 216 MHz, etc.

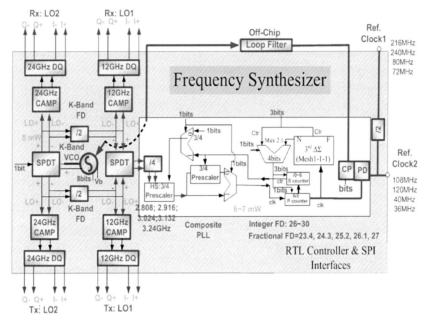

Figure 15.2 Proposed synthesizer and LO feed network.

For the LO feed network, there are architectural or topological design trade-offs due to chip area, chip cost, power consumption and phase noise performance. The LO feed network includes DC~30 GHz low loss single-pole double-throw (SPDT) switches and our proposed broadband passive differential quadrature (DQ) converter, which converts differential signals into differential I and Q signals in frequency ranges of 11 GHz~30 GHz. The differential power splitters at ~24 GHz in the output of 24 GHz SPDT are also designed for the sharing the differential LO signal to DQ converter and the frequency dividers, while the ~12 GHz differential power splitters are designed to share the ~12 GHz LO to ~12 GHz DQ and SPDT for PLL operation. The gain controllable compensation amplifiers, i.e., 12 GHz CAMP and 24 GHz CAMP with gain of about 7~9 dB and P1 dB of ~7 dBm at ~12 GHz and ~24 GHz for the optimum drive power level of –5~0 dBm at LO port of the mixers. The CAMPs have power on/off control set by the RTL for the power saving under TDD operation. The total power consumption of the synthesizer including LO feed network is only 73 mW.

15.3 Interface and Spurious Control

Here, we show several building blocks used in the transceiver. A passive low-pass filter by adopting the new cross-coupling topology by fully utilizing the conventional drawback of the parasitic effects as an advantage for the stopband extension is adopted with embedded active devices for good control. The designed cross coupled LPF has achieved a 1 dB cutoff frequency f_C of 1.8 GHz, a return loss of less than 2 dB and a stopband rejection of 40 dB up to 61 times of f_C, i.e., 110 GHz, as given in Fig. 15.3.

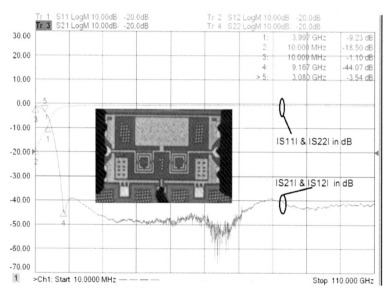

Figure 15.3 Results and die photograph of the proposed SEMCP LPF.

A compact digitally controlled variable gain amplifier (DVGA) with capabilities of both temperature-compensated dB-Linear gain control and DCOC inside of DVGA is used. The DVGA design has three-stage inductorless cascaded amplifiers that are integrated with a temperature-compensated dB-Linear gain control,

DCOC, an output common mode feedback (CMFB), a 6-bit digital gain control (with 64-step resolution), a power-off circuit, and a linearizer for improving the 1 dB gain compression point. The DCOC DVGA measures a gain range of 18.4 dB with an average step size of 0.3 dB, a 3 dB bandwidth from 2 MHz to 1.9 GHz with a ±0.75 dB gain flatness from 2.75 MHz to 1.2 GHz, an input 1 dB gain compression point better than –12.5 dBm, input matching better than –16 dB, output matching better than –30 dB, and a DC power consumption of 12.2 mW from a 1.8 V supply. Detailed information about DVGA, VCO, etc., used in this transceiver can be found in the previous chapters.

Figure 15.4 shows die photograph of 60 GHz transceiver SOC. The die has a size of 5 mm by 3.9 mm and 64 ESD protected I/O pads. The Tx and Rx are located symmetrically on the die top and bottom, while the synthesizer and its LO feed network are in the center. The amplitude and phase balance of the differential or differential quadrature signals are considered with electric matching during the integration of the 18-key building blocks listed in Fig. 15.4 (some blocks are used multiple times). The measured transmitter output P1 dB is 5.6 dBm with gain of more than 25 dB in three 60 GHz channels as shown in Fig. 15.5 and DC power consumption of less than 160 mW while the receiver input P1dB is –24.8 dBm with noise figure about –5.5~7 dB, maximum receiver gain of 46 dB and DC power consumption of 120 mW.

Figure 15.6 shows the setup of the 60 GHz wireless link test. The ball-bumped SOC is assembled to the RF board in flip-chip type assembling on the RF board with periodically slot loaded Vavadi antennas with gain about 12~14.5 dBi. The measured distance is 3.0 meter with maximum output power 100 mVp-p for each of the differential quadrature I/O ports. Under this test platform, the phase noise measurement is carried for the investigation of the phase noise and overall wireless link performance is evaluated based on the communication performance under high-date-rate transmission conditions. The measured wireless link system phase noise of 92 dBc@1 MHz from transmitter IF to receiver IF is shown in Fig. 15.6.

Figure 15.6 shows the measured high-data-rate constellation of BPSK and 16QAM for high modulation operation. As shown in Fig. 15.7, the constellation is stable with link EVM of 10.9% and 9.8% at 2 Gbps@QPSK and 4 Gbps@16QAM, respectively.

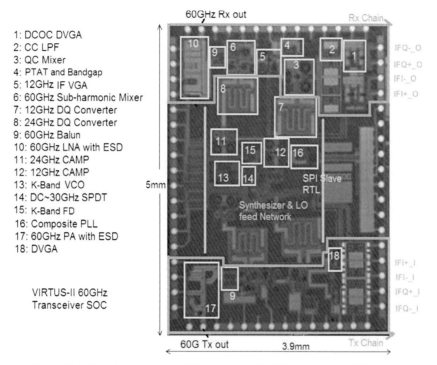

1: DCOC DVGA
2: CC LPF
3: QC Mixer
4: PTAT and Bandgap
5: 12GHz IF VGA
6: 60GHz Sub-harmonic Mixer
7: 12GHz DQ Converter
8: 24GHz DQ Converter
9: 60GHz Balun
10: 60GHz LNA with ESD
11: 24GHz CAMP
12: 12GHz CAMP
13: K-Band VCO
14: DC~30GHz SPDT
15: K-Band FD
16: Composite PLL
17: 60GHz PA with ESD
18: DVGA

VIRTUS-II 60GHz
Transceiver SOC

Figure 15.4 Die photograph and blocks of the 60 GHz transceiver SOC.

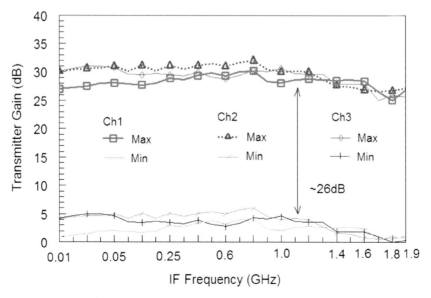

Figure 15.5 The transmitter gain ranges for different channels.

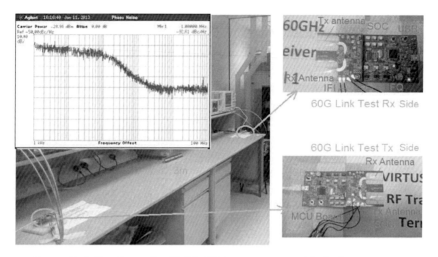

Figure 15.6 Test Setup for 60 GHz RF demo system and link phase noise.

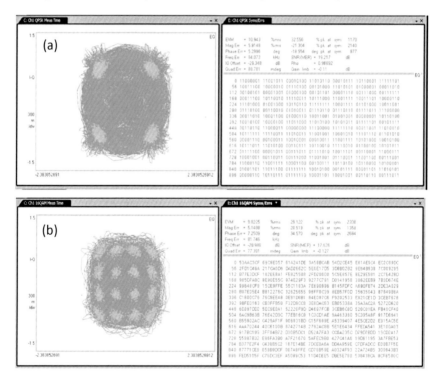

Figure 15.7 Tested 60 GHz Wireless Link performance based on QPSK, 16QAM. (a) 60 GHz Link with QPSK modulation. (b) 60 GHz Link with 16QAM modulation.

Table 15.1 List of the specifications of the designed transceiver as contrast to the state of the arts

		This work	[1]	[2]	[3]	[4]
Tx + Rx + LO, SOC	Process	SiGe 0.18 um	SiGe 0.18 um	SiGe 0.13 um	SiGe 0.18 um	65 nm CMOS
	Power	<325 mW	—	—	—	<257 mW
	Die Size	5 × 3.9 mm^2	—	—	—	4.2 × 4.2 mm^2
	Control I/O	SPI Slave	—	—	—	N.A.
	PIN No.	64	—	—	—	>100
	ESD	Yes (all I/O)	—	—	—	Yes
	DC	1.8 V	—	—	—	1.2 V
Rx	Gain (dB)	42	16	38~40	—	23
	NF	5.5~7dB	14.8	5~6.7	—	5~6 dB
	P$_{1dB}$ (dBm)	−24.8 dB	−17	−36	—	N.A.
	DCOC	Yes	—	No	—	NO
	IF BW	2 MHz~1.9 GHz	N.A.	—	—	14
	AGC	40 dB	No	No	—	N.A.
	RF BW	57~66 GHz	—	59~64 GHz	—	57~66 GHz
	ESD	All I/O	No	N.A.	—	Yes
	Input	Single end	Single	Single	—	Single
	P$_{DC}$	58.3 mA, 1.8 V	112 mA, 2.7 V	195 mA, 2.7 V	—	126 mA, 1.2 V
Tx	Gain (dB)	34	—	34–37	20.2	15
	P$_{1dB}$ (dBm)	4.7~5.6	—	10–12	15.8	5.6 (ch3)
	IF BW	2 MHz ~ 1.9 GHz	—	—	DC~2 GHz	DC~1 GHz
	RF BW	57~66 GHz	—	59~64 GHz	58~62 GHz	57~66 GHz
	AGC	25 dB	—	59~64 GHz	58~62 GHz	57~66 GHz
	ESD	All I/O	—	N.A.	No	N.A. (in BB)
	Ouput	Single end	—	Single end	Single	Single
	P$_{DC}$	80.6 mA, 1.8 V	—	190 mA, 2.7 V	281 mW	214 mA, 1.2 V

(Continued)

Table 15.1 *(Continued)*

		This work	[1]	[2]	[3]	[4]
LO	Frequency (GHz)	23.07~26.48 Synthesizer	External LO	16.6~19.5 Synthesizer	28.4~305 VCO	19.44–21.6
	Phase noise @ 1 MHz	–85~92 dBc	—	–85~90 dBc	–82.2 dBc	<–95 dBc
	DC power	23 mA, 1.8 V	—	—	N.A.	50 mA, 1.2 V

Table 15.1 lists the specifications of the designed transceiver. Based on the 0.18 um SiGe BiCMOS process from Tower Jazz, we achieved a total power consumption of 261 mW, which is less than our design target of 325 mW, and the die size is 5 mm by 3.9 mm. The control interface for the re-configuration of the transceiver status like operation frequency channel, gain of AGC, blocking on/off control for power saving and synthesizer setup, etc., is set by using the SPI interface–based slave mode. The details for the digital control can be found in Chapter 14. For all of the I/O pads, the ESD protection pads are designed for operation in harsh environment. The DC supply voltage of 1.8 V is chosen for normal operation. For the receiver portion, the overall maximum gain for the Rx operation is 42 dB with a noise figure of 5.5~7 dB and the DC offset canceling circuit is embedded for good linearity.

References

1. S. Reynolds, et al., 60 GHz transceiver circuits in SiGe bipolar technology, *ISSCC Dig. Tech. Papers*, pp. 442–443, 2004.

2. B. Floyd, et al., A silicon 60 GHz receiver and transmitter chipset for broadband communications, *ISSCC Dig. Tech. Papers*, pp. 218–219, 2006.

3. C.-H. Wang, et al. A 60 GHz transmitter with integrated antenna in 0.18 μm SiGe BiCMOS Technology, *ISSCC Dig. Tech. Papers*, pp. 659–668, 2006.

4. K. Okada et al., A Full 4-Channel 6.3 Gb/s 60 GHz direct-conversion transceiver with low-power analog and digital baseband circuitry, *ISSCC Dig. Tech. Papers*, pp. 218–219, 2012.

5. K. Ma, et al., An integrated 60 GHz low power two chip wireless system based on IEEE802.11ad standard, *International Microwave Symposium (IMS), 2014 IEEE MTT-S International*, 2014.

Index

ABCD parameters 25, 26
amplifier design 43
  high-linearity low-noise 121
  parameters 65
  post 69
  stacked transistor 86
amplifiers
  controllable 322
  first-stage 87, 88
  post 69–71, 73
  second-stage 87, 88
anti-parallel diode pair,
      balanced 163, 164
anti-parallel diode pair (APDP)
      160–164
APDP, see anti-parallel diode pair
APDP cores 162, 163
APDP SHM designs 164
artificial resonator, switchable 15,
      208, 213
ASIC designs 11, 303, 304, 308
auxiliary coupled lines 218, 219

backend design 284, 300
  digital 300
baseband 14, 63, 123, 124, 137,
      322
  digital 64, 65, 88, 227
baseband chipset 11, 13, 63, 105
BDA, see bi-directional amplifiers
BDA designs 125–127
beam-forming technique 226

bi-directional amplifiers (BDA) 14,
      121, 123, 124, 126, 128
bi-directional low-noise amplifier
      121, 122, 124, 126, 128, 130,
      132
  examples 127
bipolar junction transistor (BJT)
      41, 44, 45, 67, 85, 125, 126,
      148, 200
bipolar transistors 45, 140
BIST, see built-in self-test
BIST modules 299
BJT, see bipolar junction transistor
BJT transistors 170, 171, 200
breakdown voltage 84, 85
built-in self-test (BIST) 299

capacitance 52, 55, 150, 190, 193,
      194, 209, 250, 267, 277, 286,
      305, 309, 311
  equivalent shunt 210, 211
  parasitic bottom plate 52, 53
  variable 193
capacitors 13, 49, 50, 52, 53, 88,
      154, 160, 186, 189, 192, 193,
      199, 234, 235, 262, 277
  linear 193
  lump 214, 215
CCS, see composite current source
cell–based double-balanced mixers
      169, 177
chip design 286, 305

low-power 308
multi-million gate ASIC 292
chip-scale-packaging (CSP) 12
circuit design 4, 215, 227
circuit networks 21, 23
  fundamentals of 22, 24, 26, 28,
    30, 32, 34
circuits
  active 185, 186
  current-bleeding 175
  interconnect 109, 110
  large-signal nonlinear operating
    43
  parallel LC 32, 33
  series LC 29, 32, 33
clock feedthrough 277
clock gating 311, 312
clock inputs 272, 303
clock-skew 275
clock tree synthesis (CTS) 285,
    303, 304
CMOS, *see* complementary metal
    oxide semiconductor
CMOS-based VGA design 66
CMOS circuit 308, 309
CMOS design reference 233
CMOS designs 233
CMOS devices 308, 310
CMOS FET transistor 15, 208, 209,
    211
CMOS transistors 42
CMOS variable gain amplifier
    design 73
Colpitts oscillator 198, 199
Colpitts VCO 198, 200, 264
common source amplification 143
complementary metal oxide
    semiconductor (CMOS) 4,
    8, 41, 45, 66, 73, 74, 76, 106,
    108, 112, 127, 130, 165, 220,
    228, 238, 276, 310, 319, 329
composite current source (CCS)
    290, 307

composite III–V semiconductors
    84
control, bi-directional 125, 126
control signal 139, 140, 307
control voltage 193, 212, 213
conversion gain 152, 155–158,
    169, 176
conversion loss 123, 150, 151,
    165
coplanar waveguides 58, 113,
    126, 130
coupled differential injection
    peaking 269
couplers, hybrid 168, 170, 171,
    173
CPWG-based interconnect
    networks 127, 131
cross-coupled LC 195, 197, 198,
    200
cross-coupled transistor 152, 165
cross-coupled transistors 152,
    186, 195, 263, 267
CSP, *see* chip-scale-packaging
CTS, *see* clock tree synthesis
current-reuse topology 86, 156
cut-off frequency 4, 8, 67, 73, 148,
    157, 160
cutoff-frequency 160, 161

DCOC, *see* DC offset cancellation
DC offset cancellation (DCOC) 67,
    68, 77, 322, 325, 326, 329
design
  algorithm 16, 283
  antenna 122
  dB-linear gain control 67
  deep-submicron 306
  feeding network 321
  gate-level 298
  high-frequency amplifier 44

inductor 55
iteration 12
line–based coplanar waveguide
    106
logic 314
logic-based 300
low-phase-noise 197
low-power 302, 311, 314
millimeter-wave 8, 13
millimeter-wave circuit 50
mixed circuit 291
multi-million logic gate 297
multiple-voltage 313
multi-voltage 307, 314
passive mixer 123, 124
performance-centric 313
power-centric 313
programmable PLL 11
semiconductor circuit 39
state-of-the-art millimeter-wave
    178
design compiler 297
design complexity 174
design complier 298
design constraint files 297
design constraints 8, 9, 124, 284,
    288, 292, 297, 298, 300
  fundamental 320
design constraints files 304
design flow 11, 16, 284, 289, 292,
    295, 298, 303, 306, 311, 314,
    315
  backend 284, 298
  cadence 291
  digital 16, 283, 284, 288, 295
  digital hardware 283
  frontend 284, 292
  standard 284, 291
design for testability (DFT) 285,
    299, 307
design for transceiver SOC 283,
    284, 286, 288, 290, 292, 294,

296, 298, 300, 302, 304, 306,
    308, 310, 312, 314
design phase shifters 230
design rule check (DRC) 285, 307
DesignWare IP 295, 296
DFT, *see* design for testability
differential inductors 55
differential power splitters 324
differential quadrature 173,
    322–324, 326
differential signals 55, 321, 324
digital backend design flow 300,
    301, 303, 305, 307
digital design 15, 16, 286–288,
    294, 298, 307
  ultra-high speed 291
digital design library 286
digital design units 288
digital frontend design flow 291,
    293, 295, 297, 299
digitally variable gain amplifier
    (DVGA) 65, 66, 322, 323,
    325, 326
digital signal processor (DSP) 296
diodes 13, 40, 41, 50, 138, 139,
    148, 151, 159–161, 165, 176
diplexer 122, 123
down-conversion mixer 151, 157
DRC, *see* design rule check
DSP, *see* digital signal processor
DVGA, *see* digitally variable gain
    amplifier

ECL, *see* emitter-coupled logic
ECSM, *see* effective current source
    model
effective current source model
    (ECSM) 290
electronic system-level (ESL) 292
emitter-coupled logic (ECL) 323

ESL, *see* electronic system-level

exponential current converter 69

FCC, *see* Federal Communications
Commission

Federal Communications
Commission (FCC) 84, 102

feedback
linear 185
transformer-based 197, 198

feedback divider 247, 258, 259,
274

feed-forward DCOC 68, 69

FET resistance 148

FET resistive mixers 148–150,
177

FET resistive mixer topology 149

FET transistors 149, 165

figure of merit (FoM) 15, 190, 210,
238

filtering network 149, 162

floorplan 285, 298, 314

floorplan design 300

floorplanning 300, 301

FoM, *see* figure of merit

frequency
microwave 266
mm-wave 225, 231, 234

frequency divider 15, 253, 259,
260, 264–266, 324
locked 323
programmable 258, 259
static 265, 266, 272

frequency synthesizer 15, 160,
227, 245–252, 254, 256–262,
264–266, 268, 270, 272–276,
278
design of high-performance 15,
245
direct 246

linear noise model of 257

frequency synthesizer
architectures, popular 246,
258, 259

frequency synthesizer building
blocks 248, 261, 263, 265,
267, 269, 271, 273, 275, 277

frequency synthesizer loop filter
250

frequency synthesizer
performance 249, 250

frequency synthesizer tuning
range 261

frequency-tunable load 87, 91

frequency-tunable load design 91

frequency-tunable load tank
circuit 87

gain boosting 108

gain contours 104

gain control 64–66, 73, 75, 88, 105
temperature-compensated
dB-linear 325

gate leakage 308, 309

gate-level netlist 288, 292, 297,
298, 300, 301, 313

gate resistances 150, 151, 209

GDS, *see* Graphic Database
System

Gilbert cell–based topology 151,
154

Graphic Database System (GDS)
289, 290

Hardware Description Language
(HDL) 294

HDL, *see* Hardware Description
Language

HDMI, *see* high-definition media interface
high-definition media interface (HDMI) 7
high-performance frequency synthesizers 15, 245
high spectral purity and monolithic integration 278

ILFD, *see* injection locked frequency divider
impedance matching 64, 124, 126
impedance transformation 126, 232, 233
industry-science-medical (ISM) band 84, 102
injection locked frequency divider (ILFD) 266–270, 323
injection transistor 266–268, 270
in-phase loop signals 125
integrated circuit design 39
  low-power 314
integrated circuits 49, 50, 83, 199
interconnect network, three-port 125, 126
interconnect network design 126
interconnects, three-port CPWG 131
interdigital capacitors 52, 53
ISM, *see* industry-science-medical

K-band synthesizer 323

LC-based oscillators 261
LC oscillator design parameters 263

LC oscillators 184, 262–264
LC tank 15, 183, 184, 190–193, 198, 201, 262, 263
LC VCO 263, 266
LC-VCO 15, 183, 195, 197, 201
  cross-coupled 195–198
LC-VCO topologies for millimeter-wave frequency 195, 197, 199
LEF, *see* Library Exchange Format
Library Exchange Format (LEF) 286, 289, 290
LLPS, *see* loaded-line phase shifter
LNA, *see* low-noise amplifier
LNA design analysis 103, 105
LNA designs 14, 101, 104–106, 128, 144, 156
  trade-offs 106
  variable gain 105
loaded-line phase shifter (LLPS) 231, 237–239
low-noise amplifier (LNA) 14, 86, 101–104, 106, 108, 110, 112, 114, 116, 124–128, 131, 144, 158, 208, 227, 321
  examples 106, 107, 109, 111, 113, 115, 129, 131
low-pass filter characteristics 258
low-power design methodology 16, 284, 288, 308, 311

Matlab 294, 295
metal-insulator-metal (MIM) 52, 193, 234
microprocessors 288, 292, 294
micro-strip lines (MSL) 86, 126, 127
millimeter wave 4, 5, 8, 9, 11–13, 49, 163, 164, 193, 207, 225, 319

millimeter-wave beam forming
225, 226, 228, 230, 232, 234, 236, 238
millimeter-wave frequencies 10, 15, 84, 145, 148, 150, 160, 162, 164, 165, 174, 177, 183–185, 190, 192, 195, 197, 199, 201
millimeter-wave frequency bands 4
millimeter-wave frequency range 9, 11, 13, 84
millimeter-wave mixer 138, 140, 142, 144, 146, 148, 150, 152, 154, 156, 158, 160, 162, 164, 166, 168, 170, 172, 174, 176–178
millimeter-wave SOC 9, 10
millimeter-wave sub-harmonic mixer 174, 175
millimeter-wave switch designs 209
millimeter-wave VCO design 185
MIM, *see* metal-insulator-metal
MIM capacitor 52, 53, 193
mixer designs 144, 150, 154, 156, 158, 173, 177
mixer fundamentals 139, 141, 143, 145, 147, 177
mixers
  cell–based 148, 153, 154, 156
  double-balanced 147, 148
  fundamental-mode 138, 160
  single-balanced 142, 145, 146
MMIC, *see* monolithic microwave integrated circuit
MMMC, *see* multi-mode, multi-corner
MOM capacitor 193, 194
monolithic microwave integrated circuit (MMIC) 50, 58

monolithic transformers 56, 57
MOS devices 45
MOSFET 125, 126
MOS transistors 45, 66, 147
MOS varactors 91, 193
MSL, *see* micro-strip lines
multi-coupled inductor ILFD 271, 272
multi-coupled inductors 270
multi-mode, multi-corner (MMMC) 306
multiple-VT design 313
multi-voltage rule checker (MVRC) 315
multi-voltage simulator (MVSIM) 314
MVRC, *see* multi-voltage rule checker
MVSIM, *see* multi-voltage simulator

NDR, *see* non-default routing
NLDM, *see* non-linear delay model
NLPM, *see* non-linear power model
non-default routing (NDR) 304
non-linear delay model (NLDM) 290, 298
non-linear power model (NLPM) 291
NPMT, *see* N-poles M-throws
NPMT designs 208, 212
N-poles M-throws (NPMT) 207

OCV, *see* on-chip variation
on-chip inductors 262, 264
on-chip variation (OCV) 289, 306
oscillators 160, 177, 184–186, 191, 197, 201, 261–264
  resonator-less 184

out-of-phase loop signals 125
out-phased signals 141

PAE, *see* power added efficiency
PCB, *see* printed circuit board
PFD, *see* phase frequency detector
PGA, *see* programmable gain
  amplifier
phase change 252
phase detector 69, 74, 75, 93, 257,
  273
phase frequency detector (PFD)
  15, 247, 249, 253, 257, 264,
  273–276, 323
phase-locked loops, composite
  323, 324
phase-locked loops (PLL) 189,
  195, 246, 247, 251, 252, 256,
  288, 292
phase noise
  close-in 197, 199
  in-band 258
phase shift 185, 186, 191, 233,
  234, 236, 237
phase shifter designs 229, 230
  capacitor-based 234
phase shifters 15, 228–231, 234
  loaded-line 231, 237, 238
  reflective-type 231, 238
  switched-type 231, 233–235,
  238
  variable 227–229
  vector-modulation 236–238
PLL, *see* phase-locked loops
PLL-based frequency synthesizer
  246, 252, 253
  linear model of 253
PLL-based indirect frequency
  synthesizer in RF
  communication system 247

PLL-based indirect frequency
  synthesizers 246
PLL loop 251, 252, 254
PLL loop bandwidth 251, 254
PMOS 195–197
PMOS transistors 175, 195, 197
port-to-port isolation 151, 155,
  178
power added efficiency (PAE) 85,
  86, 94
power amplifier 14, 83–96, 163,
  170, 227
  examples 87, 89, 91, 93, 95
power consumption 8, 9, 44, 64,
  74, 103, 105, 167, 173, 189,
  190, 197, 227, 228, 251, 252,
  264, 288, 289, 294, 298,
  302–304, 308, 310, 311,
  313, 321, 324, 325, 330
power gain 85, 103, 105
power gating controller 314
power optimization, logic-level
  312
printed circuit board (PCB) 41
process downscaling 8, 9
programmable gain amplifier
  (PGA) 65, 68–72
PVT-sensitive design 103

radio frequency (RF) 5, 13, 14,
  39, 42, 49, 50, 63, 83, 101,
  123, 124, 137, 138, 140,
  144, 145, 148–150, 157,
  160–162, 168, 175, 187,
  227, 245
radio frequency integrated circuit
  (RFIC) 44, 49, 50, 63, 238
RAM, *see* random access memory
random access memory (RAM)
  286, 287

read only memory (ROM) 286, 287

received signal strength indicator (RSSI) 105

re-configurable capabilities 320, 321

reflective-type phase shifter (RTPS) 231, 238, 239

register transformer layer (RTL) 11, 285, 301, 323, 325

resonance frequency 32, 33, 216

RF, *see* radio frequency

RF designs 42

RF front-end 15, 123–125

RFIC, *see* radio frequency integrated circuit

RF signals 14, 85, 137, 140, 142, 149, 154, 158, 163, 165, 177, 210

RF-to-IF port isolations 154, 167

RF VGA design constraints 230

ring oscillator 184, 185, 261, 262

ROM, *see* read only memory

RSSI, *see* received signal strength indicator

RTL, *see* register transformer layer

RTL code 295

RTL design 11, 300, 311

RTPS, *see* reflective-type phase shifter

Schottky diodes 162

SDF, *see* stand delay format

self-inductance 56, 92

self-mixing paths 158, 159

serial peripheral interface (SPI) 16, 320, 323, 330

SHM, *see* sub-harmonic mixer

SHM topology/designs 162, 168, 170, 174, 177

SiGe 41, 42, 78, 84, 200, 329

SiGe BiCMOS 4, 13, 14, 42, 44, 94, 319, 330

SiGe HBT transistors 94, 113

signal flow direction switch control 125

signal input transistors 155

signal integrity 286, 305

signal leakage 150, 159, 171

silicon 4, 9, 319

silicon substrates 40–42, 84, 150

single-ended injection peaking 269

single-pole double-throw (SPDT) 208, 214, 324

small-signal circuit model 208

small-signal equivalent circuit model 215, 216

SPDT, *see* single-pole double-throw

SPEF, *see* Standard Parasitic Extended Format

SPI, *see* serial peripheral interface

spiral inductors 54, 55, 194

STA, *see* static timing analysis

Standard Parasitic Extended Format (SPEF) 305, 307

stand delay format (SDF) 291

static timing analysis (STA) 285, 290, 291, 298, 305–307

STPS, *see* switched-type phase shifter

sub-harmonic mixer (SHM) 138, 139, 159–167, 169, 171, 173–178, 322

  Gilbert cell–based 169, 174

  transistor-based 14

switched-type phase shifter (STPS) 231, 233–235, 237–239

switching transistors 144, 147, 153, 158, 165, 166, 175

Synopsys DesignWare IP 295

system-level design 292

TDD, *see* time division duplex
temperature coefficient 51
time division duplex (TDD) 321
TLT, *see* transmission line
    transformer
transconductance 45, 65, 66, 87,
    88, 107, 108, 139–143, 153,
    155, 268, 270
transconductance-controlled
    mixer 140
transconductance stage 175, 177
transconductance stage design
    177
transconductor 142
transistor cut-off frequency 239
transistors
  amplifier 125, 126
  amplifying 65, 85, 86
  cascode 107, 108
  stacked 153, 166, 167
transmission line transformer
    (TLT) 86
true single phase clock (TSPC) 272
TSPC, *see* true single phase clock
two-port networks
  asymmetrical 33
  elementary 25

Unified Power Format (UPF) 314
universal verification methodology
    (UVM) 295
UPF, *see* Unified Power Format
UVM, *see* universal verification
    methodology

varactor 46, 87, 160, 190,
    193–196, 232

variable gain amplifier (VGA) 13,
    63–66, 68, 70, 72–76, 78, 87,
    102, 230, 237, 322
  examples 68, 69, 71, 73, 75, 77
variable gain control 105
VCD, *see* video compact disc
VCO, *see* voltage-controlled
    oscillator
vector-summation phase shifter
    (VSPS) 231
VGA, *see* variable gain amplifier
VGA design 67
  analysis 64
  examples 68
video compact disc (VCD) 7
voltage-controlled oscillator (VCO)
    14, 15, 43, 86, 183–198, 200,
    246–248, 251–253, 256–258,
    261–264, 266, 267, 326, 330
  basics 14, 183–185, 187, 189
  design parameters 261
  designs 155, 167, 169, 177
  high-frequency 193
  high-frequency output 264
  low frequency 196
  phase noise 186, 191, 248, 251
  tuning voltage 253, 254
VSPS, *see* vector-summation phase
    shifter

wireless communication 3, 4, 7–9,
    122
  fifth-generation 3, 4
wireless communication systems,
    high-frequency 262
wireless docking stations 5, 7
wireless personal area network
    (WPAN) 5, 7, 102
WPAN, *see* wireless personal area
    network